Multi-faith Activity Assemblies

Packed with ideas for the primary school teacher, this book includes stories, songs and dramatic activities from six major world religions: Christianity, Buddhism, Hinduism, Islam, Judaism and Sikhism. The book is helpfully split into topic areas which include:

- New beginnings
- Places of worship
- Friends
- Festivals
- Rites of passage
- Water themes
- Animals and birds
- Inspirational leaders.

There is also a useful section on background information for teachers with pronunciation guides for the different world religions featured.

Multi-faith Activity Assemblies brings together Elizabeth Peirce's previous books, *Activity Assemblies for Christian Collective Worship 5–11* and *Activity Assemblies for Multi-racial Schools 5–11*. Taking the best ideas from both and adding some new material, it will be invaluable to head teachers, deputy head teachers, and primary school teachers or any trainee teacher who is looking for a collection of assembly ideas that promote tolerance and understanding of the multi-faith society in which we live.

Elizabeth Peirce has extensive teaching experience and was formerly General Primary Schools' Adviser (Early Years) for East Sussex Education Authority.

Peace is like gossamer –
vulnerable, yet indestructible:
tear it and it will be rewoven.
Peace does not despair.
Begin to weave a web of peace:
start in the centre
and make peace with yourself
and your God.
Take the thread outwards
and build peace within your family, your community
– and in the circle of those you find it hard to like.
Then stretch your concern
into all the world.
Weave a web of peace
and do not despair.
Love is the warp in the fabric of life:
truth is the weft:
care and integrity together –
vulnerable,
but ultimately
indestructible.
Together,
they spell
peace . . .

Kate Compston

Multi-faith Activity Assemblies

90 + Ideas for Primary Schools

Elizabeth Peirce

RoutledgeFalmer
Taylor & Francis Group

LONDON AND NEW YORK

First published 2003
by RoutledgeFalmer
11 New Fetter Lane, London EC4P 4EE

Simultaneously published in the USA and Canada
by RoutledgeFalmer
29 West 35th Street, New York NY 10001

RoutledgeFalmer is an imprint of the Taylor & Francis Group

© 2003 Elizabeth Peirce
Typeset in Sabon by
Keystroke, Jacaranda Lodge, Wolverhampton
Printed and bound in Great Britain by
TJ International Ltd

British Library Cataloguing in Publication Data
A catalogue record for this book is available from the British Library

Library of Congress Cataloging in Publication Data
A catalog record for this book has been applied for

ISBN 0–415–30359–1

Contents

With Thanks

The author wishes to record her gratitude and indebtedness to the following experts who kindly read and corrected the original draft manuscript: Riadh el Droubie for reading the sections on Islam; Eleanor Nesbitt for reading the sections on Hinduism; Piara Singh Sambhi for reading the sections on Sikhism; Dr Paul Williams for reading the sections on Buddhism; Angela Wood for reading the sections on Judaism and for suggesting the Jewish songs; Veronica Clark and Marjory Heasman for help with the music notation. The staff of the East Sussex Schools' Library Service (Eastbourne) for all their help with book research; Fiona Shore, BBC Schools' Radio Producer and Editor of *Hands Together* (Scholastic) who first commissioned some of the original work in a series of magazine articles and School Radio Programmes.

Acknowledgements

The author and publishers would like to thank the following for permission to reproduce material in this book:

Frontispiece 'Peace is like Gossamer' is reproduced with the kind permission of Kate Compston, from *Leaves from the Tree of Peace*, published by the United Reform Church.

1 New Beginnings

page 4   'Sleepy Baby' from *Fingers, Feet and Fun* by Delphine Evans published by Century Hutchinson is reproduced with permission from The Random House Group Limited.

page 5   'Moving House' is an adaptation by E. C. Peirce from 'Love is a Runner Bean' by D. Moss in *Today's Talks for Today's Children*, Chester House Publications, 1967.

page 10   Psalm 150 and other Bible quotations in the text, where indicated, are quoted from the *Good News Bible* published by Bible Societies/HarperCollins Publishers Ltd., UK © American Bible Society 1966, 1971, 1976, 1992, 1994. Used with permission.

page 10   'Be-Rosh Hashana'/'On New Year' by Naomi Shemer from *The Second Book* published by Lulav Israel Press Ltd., is reproduced by kind permission of Naomi Shemer.

page 21   'Yom Ze M'chubad', music and words are from *Z'mirot Anthology, Traditional Sabbath Songs for the Home*, compiled and edited by N. Levin published by Tara Publications, Cedarhurst, N. Y. It is reproduced with the kind permission of the publishers.

page 23   Illustration of 'The Cycle of the Chinese Years' is taken from *Chinese New Year* in the Living Festival Series by Anne Bancroft, published by RMEP, Exeter 1984, page 21. It is reproduced by kind permission of SCM-Canterbury Press Ltd. (RMEP is a division of SCM-Canterbury Press Ltd.)

2 Places of Worship

page 31   Illustration 'Inside a Synagogue' and Colour transparency 'Rabbi and Bar Mitzvah Boy' is from *My Belief: I am a Jew* by C. Lawton published by Franklin Watts 1984. Artwork by T. Payne and Photograph by

C. Fairclough, is reproduced with kind permission of The Watts Publishing Group Ltd.

page 42 Illustration 'Outline of a Mosque' is from *Islam in Words and Pictures* by S. Thorley published by RMEP 1982, page 9. It is reproduced with the kind permission of SCM-Canterbury Press Ltd. (RMEP is a division of SCM-Canterbury Press Ltd.).

3 Friends

page 48 Contemporary story from Matthew 6: 19–21 is based on an idea in *Activity Talks with Boys and Girls*, by the Revd R. Wood, NCEC 1972.

page 50 Poem 'Loneliness' by Tracy Stevens, aged 10 years is from *Awareness 2* by R. Deadman and A. Razzell (1977) published by Macmillan Education.

page 55 'The Unforgiving Servant' by P. Burbridge and M. Watts (1979) is from *Time to Act* published by Hodder and Stoughton.

page 57 'Giving and Sharing' by E. C. Peirce was first broadcast on the BBC Radio Programme *Discovery*, 3 December 1987.

page 62 'True Love' is an adaptation by E. C. Peirce of 'The Gift of the Magi' (1906) by O. Henry.

page 64 'The Chess Game' is an adaptation by E. C. Peirce of 'The Chess Match' by R. Brandling (1977) in *Assembly Poems and Prose* published by Macmillan Education. E. C. Peirce's adaptation was first broadcast on the BBC Schools' Radio Programme, *Discovery*, 1987. It is reproduced by kind permission of R. Brandling.

4 Festivals

page 75 'Harvest: A Loaf of Bread' is based on an idea given to E. C. Peirce by the Revd D. Jennings. Used with the kind permission of his widow, Mrs G. Jennings.

page 76 Psalm 117 is quoted from the *Good News Bible* published by the Bible Societies/HarperCollins Publishers Ltd., UK © American Bible Society 1966, 1971, 1976, 1992, 1994. Used with permission.

page 77 'Hodu L'Adonai Ki Tov'/'Thank the Lord for He is Good' (Psalm 118) is from *Sephardic Songs of Praise* by Abraham Lopes Cardozo published by Tara Publications. The music was arranged by Veronica Clark. The words were sung and taped by Angela Wood.

page 85 'Sharing our Harvest Gifts: A Bowl of rice' is an adaptation by E. C. Peirce from a lesson in *RE Handbook: A Resource for Primary School Teachers*, edited by M. Ashby, published by Scripture Union, 1983. It is reproduced with the kind permission of Scripture Union.

page 88 'Easter: The Ugly Man' is an adaptation by E. C. Peirce from 'He Died for Us' by D. Moss in *Today's Talks for Today's Children*, Chester House Publications, 1967. The adaptation by E. C. Peirce was first broadcast on the BBC Radio Programme, *Discovery* in 1987. It is reproduced with kind permission of D. Moss.

page 95 'Pentecost or Whitsunday Assembly' is based on an idea given to E. C. Peirce by the Revd R Mann, and is reproduced with his kind permission.

page 101 'How Many Candles' (Origin Unknown). Song was translated, sung and taped by Angela Wood. Music was arranged by Veronica Clark.

page 108 'Ani Purim' lyrics: Kipnis, Levin; music: Nardi, Nachum in *Sefer Hamoadin Vol 6*, Yom-Tov Levinski Ed. (1955) published by Tel–Aviv Agudat Oneg Shabbat. Lyrics are reproduced with permission of the author and ACUM Ltd. Music is reproduced with kind permission of Tarbut-Vechinuch Educational Publishing House and ACUM Ltd., Israel.

page 109 'Der Rebbe' is a Traditional Yiddish East European Folk Song. The song was translated, sung and taped by Angela Wood. The Music was arranged by Veronica Clark.

5 Rites of Passage

page 122 'Hava Nagila', lyrics by M. Nathanson is from '*Israel in Song*' compiled, edited and arranged by Velvel Pasternak published by Tara Publications, Cedarhurst, N.Y. Tara Publications kindly gave permission to use the music notation.

6 Water Projects

page 137 'The Rain' by S. Holroyd, 1966 and 'The Song of the Waves' by Bernard W. Martin, 1966 from E.J.M. Woodland (Ed) *Poems for Movement*, Evans, 1966 are reproduced with kind permission of HarperCollins Publishers Ltd.

page 146 'Ose Shalom', a traditional Jewish refrain; music by Hirsch Nurit, arranged by R. Neumann in *Israel in Song*, compiled edited and arranged by Velvel Pasternak, published by Tara Publications, Cedarhurst, N.Y. is reproduced by kind permission of the author and ACUM Ltd., Israel.

page 148 'The Money Tree' is an adaptation by E. C. Peirce, from 'Beating the Tree' by Ken Ma in *That'd Be Telling* by M. Rosen and J. Griffiths, Cambridge University Press, 1985. It is reproduced with the kind permission of Ken Ma.

page 150 'How the Kingfisher Got its Name' is an adaptation by E. C. Peirce from 'How a Bird Got its Lovely Colour' by S.G. Pottam in *Indian Folk Tales* published by Sabbash Publishers, Bombay, India.

7 Animals and Birds

page 159 'The Lost Sheep' is adapted from an idea in *Show Me, Creative Resources Two* by Judy Gattis Smith published by Bible Society, 1985. It is reproduced with the kind permission of the publishers.

page 160 Psalm 23 and other quotations from the Bible are from the *Good News Bible* published by Bible Societies/HarperCollins Publishers Ltd., U.K. © American Bible Society 1966, 1971 1976, 1992, 1994 and is used with kind permission.

page 171 'The Thirsty Dog' is a liberal adaptation by E. C. Peirce of the story 'A Thirsty Dog' in *Love all Creatures* by M.S. Kayani published by The Islamic Foundation, Leicester, UK. and is reproduced with their permission.

8 *Inspirational Leaders*

page 176   'Jesus: Friend of the Friendless' is based on an idea about Zacchaeus in *Show Me, Creative Resources Two* by Judy Gattis Smith published by Bible Society, 1985. It is reproduced with kind permission of the publishers. This adaptation was first published by E. C. Peirce in *Assembly File 1*, Folens 1996.

page 180   'Oz V' Shalom', music notation was arranged by Veronica Clark. The Song was sung, taped and translated by Angela Wood.

page 181   'Adon Olam' in *Sephardic Songs of Praise* by Abraham Lopes Cardozo, published by Tara Publications, Cedarhurst NY. The song was sung, taped and translated by Angela Wood.

page 185   Mahatma Gandhi was first published by E. C. Peirce in *Assembly File 1*, Folens, 1996.

page 194   'Sybil Phoenix Tackles Racism' is based on an account by John Newbury in *Living in Harmony*, RMEP (Chansitor) Canterbury Press, 1985. RMEP is a division of SCM-Canterbury Press Ltd., and is reproduced with their kind permission.

page 203   'The Unknown Boy Hero' is an adaptation by E. C. Peirce from 'People Aren't Always What They Seem' by Revd. R. H. Lloyd in *Assemblies for School and Children's Church*, published by RMEP (Chansitor) 1974. This adaptation was first broadcast by E. C. Peirce in the BBC Schools' Radio Programme, *Discovery*, 1987. It is reproduced with the kind permission of the Revd Canon R. H. Lloyd.

9 *Background Information For Teachers*

page 227   Illustration of 'The Seder Table' is from *Judaism in Words and Pictures* by S. Thorley published by RMEP (Chansitor) Canterbury Press, 1986. It is reproduced with the kind permission of SCM-Canterbury Press Ltd. (RMEP is a division of SCM-Canterbury Press).

page 234   Illustration of Hebrew Script is from *My Belief: I Am a Jew* by C. Lawton published by Franklin Watts, 1984. Artwork is by Tony Payne. Reproduced with the kind permission of the publishers The Watts Publishing Group Ltd.

page 240   Illustration of Hindi Script is from *My Belief: I Am a Hindu* by M. Aggarwal published by Franklin Watts, 1984. Artwork is by Tony Payne. Reproduced with the kind permission of the publishers The Watts Publishing Group Ltd.

Every effort has been made to trace the owners of all copyright material. In one or two cases this has proved impossible. The Author will be pleased to correct any omissions in future editions and give full acknowledgements.

Introduction

In these times of great racial and religious tension, it is very important for all children to have some understanding of and insight into other people's religions. This is not a book that sets out to 'convert' children in primary schools to other faiths, but rather an assembly book that attempts to 'inform' children about other people's beliefs.

Hence, children are introduced to the major places of worship; they are enabled to feel their way into other people's faiths, through the assemblies on Festivals; they are encouraged to see what it is like to stand in other people's shoes by looking at famous leaders; to learn some of the universal truths, through the teaching of the founders of faiths, such as the Buddha's teaching about suffering and death, etc. Kindness, wisdom, integrity, honesty, truth, obedience, etc., can be taught in a number of different ways. Children need to learn how to treat one another in this multi-racial society, to empathize and not condemn one another, because they do not happen to believe what someone else believes. This, therefore, is my chief concern for all primary school children. If we learn about each other's beliefs, we do not necessarily have to be disciples of them to understand them. Gandhi's achievements through non-violence have lessons for us all. Leading children into a particular faith is the task of the home.

It is the well-rounded personality that is important; the need for children to learn love, mercy, justice, tolerance and truth in a variety of ways. Jesus said, 'Love your neighbour as yourself' – perhaps this is the hardest concept for all mankind to learn. The school should create an atmosphere where belief in God can grow. It is part of our spiritual development that makes us into complete people. There is a need to help children to develop a sense of awe and wonder, a positive attitude to life and learning, to be aware of the needs and gifts of others. I hope that nothing offends any particular group, but rather creates a better understanding of each other's beliefs. After all, parents still have the final sanction, to withdraw their child from school assembly. But if this happens, then much of the community feeling, the ethos of the school, will be lost forever, and children will grow up holding on to many of the deep prejudices that divide our world today.

To assist the teacher, I have indicated the origin of the particular faith at the top of each assembly. However, as already stated, I have tried to choose those stories that have fundamental truths and interest for *all* children. An attempt has also been made to indicate the appropriate age ranges for the assemblies and activities, but it must be understood that these are only guidelines. The children's ability to understand and participate will vary enormously, according to many factors, including their intellectual and emotional readiness to grasp some of the ideas presented. It may be necessary to adapt teaching styles and techniques to suit older or younger children.

In addition, the needs of the small rural primary school will vary enormously from the needs of the large inner city school, and teachers will have to use their professional judgement to assess appropriateness in selecting material. Projects are not inter-dependent and so can be selected at random to reinforce topic work being followed in school.

Hall space too, will be a major consideration. It may be that for some, much of the activity will have to take place in the confines of the classroom, where hall space is limited or non-existent. It is intended that assemblies or collective worship will form an integral part of the whole of school life. Therefore themes and projects have been provided that cover a great deal of curricular activity, culminating in the assembly or collective worship. Children learn best from concrete experience, from which abstract ideas will gradually be understood. Therefore, much of the material presented is intended to be experiential, starting from where the child is, and moving on to widen horizons and to extend experiences, by taking children out on visits, or inviting visitors into school.

Finally, in the text, I have tried to draw the teacher's attention to specific, important beliefs and practices in the introductory paragraphs of each assembly and also in the teachers' reference notes at the back of the book. (These are deliberately brief for easy/quick reference.) However, it is perhaps worth reiterating some important points here. It should be noted that Muslims pay respect to Muhammad's ﷺ name by saying the words 'Peace be upon him' each time his name is spoken, or writing the sign for this ﷺ after his name. Also, there is no music in Islamic services, therefore, I have not included hymns in the suggestions for Islamic assemblies; and although prayers have been suggested sometimes, the teacher must decide whether *a time of quiet reflection* is more appropriate for a particular assembly. The inclusion of hymns is to save time for busy teachers who need to find music quickly on a particular theme.

Jews, Christians and Muslims all see Abraham from different perspectives. These should be noted by the teacher, and where there is a conflict of beliefs, these should be very carefully handled, with a clear explanation of the differences in belief. An example of this is in telling the story of Abraham and his willingness to sacrifice his son. Jews and Christians believe that it was Isaac who was prepared for sacrifice; Muslims believe that it was Ishma'ail.

Another area of difficulty between cultures may be the way each culture interprets the events of history. This will be as true for Hindus and Sikhs as for Christians and Muslims. I have tried to be as fair as possible in my interpretation of events in the stories I have told.

If we are to draw all children together in an assembly, then some of these great tales from different world faiths must be retold, so that all children feel a sense of belonging, a sense of community, a sense of being part of a caring, sharing group with the common title of 'Our School'.

One final point about the books in the bibliographies: every book that has been recommended has been checked for availability at the time of going to press. However, in one or two cases, some books dating from the 1980s or earlier were occasionally out of print, but often they could still be found in children's libraries. They have been included where it was considered that the books were classics on a particular topic and that it was worth trying to obtain a copy.

1 NEW BEGINNINGS

Who Am I?

At the beginning of the new school year or a new term, it is most important to remind the children about the sort of qualities that are needed in any community. With this in mind, think of the various qualities that you would like to encourage in school. Write down some words on large strips of card that can be, threaded with string and then worn around the neck of some children.

With careful preparation, the whole 5–11 age range can be involved in this assembly. The very youngest children can demonstrate, or explain, or paint their phrase e.g. 'I am helpful', whereas, an 11-year-old could explain the meaning of 'I am a Peace-Maker', either by performing a short mime with one or two of his friends who are quarrelling, or by explaining other examples of peace-making activities.

This assembly has endless possibilities. Phrases such as the following could be included:

> I am kind, I am helpful,
> I am tolerant, I am polite,
> I am caring, I am unselfish,
> I have patience, I can let others go before me,
> I can be generous, I can let others have the best toy,
> I can share, I can tell the truth,
> I can comfort those in distress, etc.

At the end of the assembly, the class or group who has prepared the work can say together, 'I know who I am, who are you?'

Let the children meditate on this penetrating question, by having a time for quiet reflection.

Prayer

Father God, make each one of us the sort of people you want us to be. Kind and helpful, caring and tolerant, ready to put others first. Amen.

Song

No 35, 'Take care of a friend' in *Every Colour Under the Sun*, published by Ward Lock Educational.

Babies

5–7
Assembly
All

Invite a mother and her baby into school. Explain to the children that this assembly is going to be a celebration of new life. Many young children will have had to come to terms with a new baby at home and may need help in coping with feelings of jealousy and rejection. We need to transmit something of the joy, fun and great interest that a new baby can bring.

Preparation for the Mother

If the mother is willing, explain that one of your aims is to make siblings feel loved and wanted, and so ask the mother if she will tell the children this, while chatting about the new baby at home. Perhaps she could bring in some baby clothes, or bath the baby for the children in the assembly and talk about all the equipment that is needed for bathing, dressing, feeding, etc.

Preparation for the Children in School

Perhaps the Year 2 children could prepare a list of questions to ask the mother from the floor:

1 What is the baby's name?
2 How old is the baby?
3 How much did the baby weigh at birth?
4 How much does the baby weigh now?
5 How many times a day is the baby fed?
6 What do you feed the baby?
7 What sort of noise does the baby make when happy? sad? angry?
8 What time does the baby go to bed?
9 What time does the baby get up?
10 How many times a day do you change his nappy?

11 What happens when the baby goes to the clinic?
12 How many times do you bath the baby a week?
13 How do you get the water to the right temperature?
14 What sort of games do you play with the baby?
15 What sort of toys does the baby have?

Allow sufficient time for questions and answers. Then thank the mother and baby for coming into school. Explain that the children will say a special prayer of thanks for this wonderful new life and for the well-being of mum, and then the children can sing a quiet hymn.

Prayer

Heavenly Father, we do thank you that Mrs . . . [name] was able to visit us today and bring in baby . . . [name]. We have so enjoyed their visit and have learned so much about new babies. We know that you love each one of us just as much as you love this new baby. Thank you for the gift of new life and we ask you to bless . . . [name] and all the family. Amen.

Hymn

No 36, 'we will take care of you' in *Every Colour Under the Sun* (Ward Lock Educational); or No 3, 'Morning has broken' in *Someone's Singing Lord* A. and C. Black.

Poem

Suitable for 5-year-olds:

Sleepy Baby

I am a baby fast asleep.
  Eyes closed, head resting on hands.
I open my eyes to take a peep.
  Open eyes.
I lift up my head to look around.
  Lift head and look around.
I open my mouth – make a yawning sound.
  Yawn.
I lift up my arms and stretch up high.
  Stretch.
I think I might be going to cry.
  Arms down sad face.
Oh no, I won't, I'll go back to sleep.
  Head resting on hands again.
I'll close my eyes and not even peep!
  Close eyes and be very still.

Delphine Evans

Moving House	Assembly 5–9 All

(Adapted from the story 'Love is a runner bean' in D. Moss (1967) *Today's Talks for Today's Children* (Chester House Publications.)

This story could be mimed while it is being told.

Two friends, John and Mary, lived next door to each other in a tall block of flats in a huge city. Soon they were going to move to a new housing estate and each would have a small garden. They were both delighted because they had never had a garden before. Everything had to be packed up and put into big boxes and there was a lot of rubbish that had to be thrown away.

Soon the great day for removal arrived and the children couldn't contain their excitement. They were looking forward to moving into their new homes and to going to their new school and to making new friends. They were especially looking forward to having a garden of their own. The men loaded all the furniture onto the van and helped the two families move into their new houses on the same estate. The children were not next door to each other this time, but they were only a few doors away from each other.

Although it was a bit strange at first, as soon as the children's own special things were unpacked, the houses began to feel more like homes and the children's parents told the children that they could each have a very small patch in their new gardens to grow their very own vegetables or flowers.

After a great deal of thought, the children decided to grow runner beans. They worked very hard in their own gardens, first digging the soil [mime the action], then planting the beans and finally planting firm canes into the ground to support the beans as they grew. Each day the children watered the seeds and kept their garden patch free from weeds and soon the bean plants began to grow and twist around the poles and produce little tiny beans.

As soon as John's beans were as big as his little finger, he picked them and gave them to his Mum to cook for the family's Sunday lunch. It was a very special occasion and there were just enough beans to give each person in John's family a tiny portion to taste. They were delicious.

Mary, on the other hand, decided not to pick her beans or to share them with anyone. She told her Mum that she wanted to let them grow until they were the biggest and fattest in the whole neighbourhood and then eat them all by herself as she had grown them.

In the meantime a very strange thing happened. Every time John picked his small green beans, more and more appeared. So he gave some to his new neighbours and to an old lady who lived on her own down the street, and he took some to his new teacher and to the lollipop lady at school and still more beans grew and grew.

Mary's beans, however, continued to grow very long and fat. No *new* beans appeared on her plants. The original beans just grew longer and fatter. Indeed, they were the biggest beans in the whole neighbourhood.

The great day came when Mary decided to pick her beans and have them for Sunday lunch. But they were so tough and stringy that no one in her family could eat them. So they were left politely on the side of the plate. Mary burst into tears. Why were her beans so tough and inedible, when she knew that lots of people had greatly enjoyed eating John's beans?

Her mother explained. The more you pick runner beans, the more you get. They just keep on growing. But if you leave them, they grow very long and tough. She told Mary that this was a bit like being friendly. The more you give friendship to others, the more you get back. John lovingly gave all his beans away to feed his new neighbours and his plants produced many beans. But Mary kept all her beans to herself and as a result the beans became old and tough and stringy.

John made lots of new friends and settled very quickly and happily into his new home and school. But Mary felt lonely and unhappy and wanted to return to the big city.

A time for quiet reflection is kept.

Hymn

No 42, 'Seeds of kindness', in *Every Colour under the Sun* (Ward Lock Educational); or No 51, 'I've just moved into a new house', in *Tinder-box 66 Songs for Children* A. and C. Black.

First Day at School

5–9
Assembly
All

Ask the older children to write about all that they remember of their first day at school. Allow the children to read their work to the rest of the school. The teacher could comment as necessary. The work could be accompanied by children's paintings depicting some of the most important aspects of school life – their new friends, their new teachers, what they do at school, etc.

These children should then be encouraged to help all the new children to settle in as quickly and as happily as possible. Perhaps the older children could each befriend a new child and help him/her throughout the week, especially at play times and at dinner times and show him/her the daily routine.

This could be followed by the older children dramatizing an incident about including and rejecting friends in movement and mime. To do this, a group of children should mime playing happily together – 'Ring a Ring o' Roses', or 'In and out the Dusky Bluebells'. One child is left out – an outsider, a new child. She makes several attempts to join the group, to link hands with the other children. As she does this, every child in the group stops playing and puts both hands up in a threatening and forbidding gesture and simultaneously the group turn their heads away from the outsider. The children freeze in this position for one or two seconds, and then the child tries to join the group once more, only to be rebuffed in a similar way.

Eventually the lonely child turns away from the group and goes and sits on her own with her head in her hands and quietly weeps. At this point the teacher should explain that she does not want anyone in her school to feel as lonely and as left out as this child and that all the children in the school must make a real effort to make new children feel welcome, especially on their first day.

The mime is then performed again and this time the new child is made to feel welcome and loved.

Prayer

Heavenly Father, help us to make our schools warm and welcoming places where all feel that they belong and everyone has a friend.

Hymn

No 31, 'Thank you for my friends' in *Tinder-box 66 Songs for Children*, A. and C. Black.

Resources

A very poignant story to read to the school that makes the point about what it means to feel lonely, sad, afraid, isolated and unable to speak the language of others is:

Hoffman, M. (2002) *The Colour of Home*, (Frances Lincoln).

Retold with the aid of beautiful pictures, it recounts the story of a new boy from Somalia who joins the school, unable to speak any English. He is very traumatized by the tragic events that he encountered back home through war and genocide. He saw things that most young children should not see. Through an interpreter, he is gradually able to describe the beautiful colours of his homeland before the war. But on coming to England, he finds that everything is dark and grey; the sky, the buildings and even the furniture in his new home. As he retells his story, the teacher has tears in her eyes, but somehow in the telling, he is able to begin to come to terms with it all and through painting the happier colours of his old home, he is able to brighten up his new one.

This book will certainly help children gain valuable insights into the plight of refugees or displaced children and to feel something of their pain in a strange, new place.

New Year Celebrations

Assembly
5–11
All

Begin with a child dressed up as an old man walking slowly across the front of the hall. In one hand he carries a stick; in the other hand he lifts a lantern to light his way.

A little boy stops him and says, 'Old man, give me your lantern, so that I can see clearly into the New Year.'

The old man replies, 'No. Go out into the darkness and put your hand into the hand of God. That will be much better than my light and much safer than any other way' (M. Louise Haskins).

The theme of New Year celebrations could be spread over the first few weeks of the new term.

Diwali, the Hindu festival of lights, does not coincide with our own New Year but provides a marvellous starting point for New Year celebrations. Diva (special lights) could be placed all around the hall. The story of Rama and Sita could be retold in dramatic form. (See p. 102).

The Chinese New Year (p. 23) can also provide a stimulating and colourful starting point for further investigation. This falls on a day between the middle of January and the middle of February. Parcels of sweets and money are wrapped in red paper; everyone puts on their best clothes and visits friends and relations; there are games and fireworks. It is the time when the popular Lion Dance is performed. Perhaps a group of children could make a Chinese lion mask and dance their version of this traditional activity. Read the Chinese New Year story in the Tinder-box Assembly book.

Other New Year celebrations could include a traditional English or Scottish Hogmanay celebration. The whole school could be asked to think out their personal and corporate New Year resolutions. These could be written on a large piece of card and reviewed at intervals to see whether promises can be kept.

Each celebration could end with a simple prayer of thanks for the old year and a request for God's blessing on the New Year.

Hymn

No 25, 'A New Year has started', by M. Martin and V. Stumbles (Holt, Rinehart and Winston); or No 58, 'New things to do' and No 62, 'Diwali' in *Tinder-box 66 Songs for Children*, (A. and C. Black) or No 122, 'Shalom Chaverim' in *New Life* (Galliard).

Rosh Hashana and Yom Kippur

5–11
Assembly
Judaism

Rosh Hashana, the Jewish New Year, takes place in the Hebrew month of Tishri, that is September or October.

Try to find a picture of a Shofar or ram's horn to show the children, or visit the Jewish Museum in London and see a real one (see address on p. 29). A shofar is blown in the synagogue at this time. Jews send each other New Year cards and eat apples or hallah (bread) which has been dipped in honey. This symbolizes the Jewish wish for a happy and sweet New Year.

It is also a time to make a fresh start and to ask God's forgiveness for sins. The Day of Atonement, that follows ten days after Rosh Hashana, is called Yom Kippur. During these ten days, Jews say sorry to their friends and neighbours for anything they may have done to hurt each other. They try to make amends for all wrong doings and ask God's forgiveness too. Of course, they do this at other times of the year, but this is the special festival for new beginnings.

At Rosh Hashana families go to the synagogue for a special service. Someone is chosen to read from the Sacred Scrolls, Psalms are sung and a sermon is preached, prayers are said. The distinctive part of the service is the blowing of the ram's horn. Sometimes, Jews go to the seaside or to rivers, and empty their pockets and throw away any crumbs on to the water. This is called Tashlich or throwing away. It is a symbol of throwing away old sins, bad thoughts and deeds.

Families enjoy special Rosh Hashana meals together. Bread is baked in different shapes, i.e. Ladders 'as a symbol of prayers rising to God', or Crowns 'because God, the Creator, is King of the world' (From: *A Jewish Family in Britain* by Vida Barnett, Published by Religious and Moral Education Press, division of SCM-Canterbury Press Ltd.) After the fast of Yom Kippur, Jews believe God will forgive their sins and seal their names in the 'Book of Life' (Barnett).

Why not teach your class one of the shorter Psalms, like Psalm 150. This could be done as a choral speaking exercise. The words could be softly spoken in the beginning and then built up to a crescendo. See Psalm 150 p. 10, taken from the *Good News Bible*, 1994.

During the assembly, ask the children to think of any bad things in their minds that they could metaphorically throw away, something bad that they have done or thought and will try not to do again.

Make a display of the instruments mentioned in Psalm 150, such as drums, flutes, cymbals, etc. These could be played at the appropriate times either before the choral speaking or during the piece, or afterwards.

PSALM 150

1 Praise the Lord!
   Praise God in his Temple!
   Praise his strength in heaven!
2 Praise him for the mighty things he has done.
   Praise his supreme greatness.
3 Praise him with trumpets.
   Praise him with harps and lyres.
4 Praise him with drums and dancing.
   Praise him with harps and flutes.
5 Praise him with cymbals.
   Praise him with loud cymbals.
6 Praise the LORD, all living creatures!
   Praise the LORD!

(*Good News Bible*)

End with a simple prayer asking God's forgiveness for all wrong deeds.

Prayer

O Father God, we ask your forgiveness for all the wrong thoughts and words and deeds that we have committed. Help us to make a fresh start today and to live our lives in love and peace and harmony with each other. Amen.

Song

'On New Year'/'Be-Rosh Hashana' is a modern song written by a popular Israeli vocalist and composer called Naomi Shemer. It is about the Jewish New Year but fits any time of fresh starts and new beginnings.' Angela Wood. (see pp. 229–233 for pronunciation guide).

'On New Year'/'Be-Rosh Hashana'

Be-rosh hashana, be-rosh hashana
Parcha shoshana etzli ba gina
Be-rosh hashana sira levana
Agena la bachof pitom

Be-rosh hashana, be-rosh hashana
Libbenu ana bitfilla noshana
Sheyafa veshona tehe hashana
Asher matchila ha yom.

La la la la la la
Yafa veshona tehe hashana
Asher matchila ha yom.

Be-rosh hashana be-rosh hashana
Parcha anana birkia ha setav
Be-rosh hashana kener neshama
Ala ba sade hatzav

Be-rosh hashana be-rosh hashana
Libbenu ana bitfilla noshana
Sheyafa veshona tehe hashana
Asher matchila la akhshav.

La la la la la la
Yafa veshona tehe hashana
Asher matchila la akhshav

Be-rosh hashana, be-rosh hashana
Parcha mangina she'ish lo hikkir
Vetokh yemama ha zemer hama
Mikkol hallonot ha ir.

Be-rosh hashana be-rosh hashana
Libbenu ana bitfilla noshana
Sheyafa veshona tehe hashana
Asher matchila la akhshav.

La la la la la la
Yafa veshona tehe hashana
Asher matchila la akhshav.

On new year's eve
A rose bloomed in my garden,
A white boat
Anchored suddenly in my shore.

On new year's eve,
Our heart answered with an old prayer,
For a better or different year
Starting today.

La la la la la la
For a better and different year
Starting today.

On new year's eve
Rode a cloud in the autumn skies,
In the field, like a candle
Grew the squill.

On new year's eve
Our heart answered with an old prayer,
For a better and different year
That's starting now.

La la la la la la
For a better and different year
Starting today.

On new year's eve
A melody was born, which no one knew,
And within a day a song was heard
Throughout the town.

On new year's eve
Our hearts answered with an old prayer
For a better and different year
Starting now.

La la la la la la
For a better and different year
Starting today.

Naomi Shemer

Vesākha or the Buddhist New Year

This is the most important full moon festival for Theravāda Buddhists. (See p. 206 for note about Theravāda Buddhism.) It is usually held in April or May. It is the celebration of the Buddha's birth, his Enlightenment and his death.

As a New Year celebration, it could be a time when children could remember some of the teachings of the Buddha, i.e. not to harm animals, not to steal, not to tell lies, etc. (See p. 206–11 for further information.)

Perhaps one of the Jātaka stories could be retold (see *Twenty Jaātaka Tales* by H.I. Khan published by H. Campbell Books, London, 1998).

It is also known as the Festival of Lights, because candles are lit standing for Enlightment, and incense is burnt. Buddhists visit the temple on this day and give money to the poor. Since the Buddha taught his followers that they should hurt no living thing, perhaps the school could use this occasion to support a charity for the Protection of Animals (i.e. RSPCA, RSPB see addresses below). Generous giving is part of the Buddhist tradition at Vesākha.

In addition, because the lotus flower has become a symbol of the Buddha's Enlightenment, perhaps the children could make a large frieze of lotus flowers for this New Year assembly, and make individual lotus badges as a sign that they will try to be kind to animals and to one another.

'The lotus is a symbol of enlightenment since it grows in muddy water (samsara) but raises its flower on a long stem to the sun (enlightenment).' (*World Religions in Education Festivals*, 1987. The Shap Working Party on World Religions in Education, published by Commission for Racial Equality, London, p. 20.) Lotus flowers can be made out of crêpe paper using the pear shapes on p. 14.

A candle can be lit while a time for quiet reflection is kept to think about being kind to animals and to each other.

Hymn

No 80, 'All the animals that I have ever seen', in *Come and Praise 2*, (BBC).

Useful Addresses

Royal Society for the Prevention of Cruelty to Animals
Wilberforce Way
Southwater
Horsham
West Sussex RH13 9RS
Tel: 08700 101 181
Fax: 08707 530 048
Website: www.rspca.org.uk (Details of resources for Teachers, some are downloadable)
Videos are available for different Key Stages at reasonable rates

Royal Society for the Protection of Birds
UK Headquarters
The Lodge
Sandy
Bedfordshire SG19 2DL
Tel: 01767 680 551
Fax: 01767 692 365
Website: www.rspb.org.uk (Details of classroom materials)
Video Guides and CD-ROM Guides available for bird identification; cassettes of
bird sounds available

Commission for Racial Equality
Elliot House
10/12 Allington Street
London SW1E 5EH
Tel: 02078 287 022
Fax: 02076 307 605
Email: info@cre.gov.uk
Website: www.cre.gov.uk

Baisakhi: Sikh New Year

For Sikhs, this is the most important festival. It commemorates the formation of the Khalsa or first Sikh brotherhood of arms in 1699, by the tenth and last human Guru, Guru Gobind Singh. (See p. 253 for futher information.)

It also commemorates the beginning of the Sikh New Year and is accompanied by an elaborate celebration and a continuous reading of the Guru Granth Sahib, the Sikh's Holy book. It was originally a Hindu Festival, but the third Sikh Guru, Guru Amar Das, in the middle of the 16th century commanded his followers to meet on this day for their own festival to show Sikh solidarity and unity.

Today, the festival takes place on the 13th or 14th of April and if this falls on a week-day, the Guru Granth Sahib will be read continuously, for forty-eight hours before the main celebration, which is usually held on the nearest Sunday. The reading is completed on the morning of the celebration. This continuous reading from the holy book is known as Akhand Path, (p. 108, *Celebrations: Festivals in a Multi-faith Community* by C. Collinson and C. Miller, published by Edward Arnold, London, 1985).

Prayers are said, and Karah Prasad, the Sikh's holy food, is distributed to each person in the Gurdwara. An important part of the festival is the renewal of the Sikh flag, called the Nishan Sahib. There is always a flag and a flagpole outside a Sikh Gurdwara to denote that it is a place of worship.

Once the ceremony is in progress, the flagpole is lowered and the old flag and flagpole coverings are removed. The flagpole is then carefully washed and many of the worshippers will bow before the pole as a mark of respect. It is recovered with fabric and a new flag is inserted. Five men, representing the five men who were prepared to die for their Guru, will bless the flag and lead the worshippers back into the Gurdwara for the festival meal. The meal is prepared by the women and usually consists of a vegetable curry and rice, and chapatis, a special kind of bread.

Often during the Baisakhi Festival, the Amrit Sanskar ceremony will take place (see p. 254). This is the ceremony where Sikh men and women commit themselves to the Sikh faith and to the Khalsa (brotherhood).

Before the communal meal, hymns from the Guru Granth Sahib are sung and a lecture is given to the people, reminding them of the important aspects of being a Sikh. The ceremony ends with everyone wishing each other a happy new year.

The emblem on the flag is a picture of the double-edged sword or Khanda. 'One edge symbolizes God's power and justice, the other freedom and authority given to the man who obeys God. On the outside of the Khanda, in the emblem, are two curved swords symbolizing religious and political freedom; it was for this cause that Guru Gobind Singh founded the Khalsa. Surrounding the Khanda is the Chackra, a circle symbolic of the unity of the Sikhs and their belief in one God "whose name is truth"' (C. Collinson and C. Miller, p. 109).

For this assembly talk about the symbolism portrayed on the flag and ask the children to design their own flags that could embody the ideals of the school community or a friendship club. The children could work in groups of three to produce

Source: Collinson, C. and Miller, C. (1985) *Celebrations: Festivals in a Multi-faith Community*, London: Edward Arnold, p. 106.

their own flag. The teacher may need to suggest topics for symbolism, for example, honesty, but the children will have many ideas of their own including the symbols for clubs that they may have already joined.

End the assembly with a parade of flags and a brief explanation of the word/s that are being depicted.

Prayer

Father God, today we have been reminded of truth, justice, freedom, unity and peace. May these qualities abound in our school. Amen.

Hymn

No 37, 'Working together', in *Every Colour Under the Sun* (Ward Lock Educational).

Sunrise

5–7
Assembly
All

Read Psalm 113:3 (*RSV*), 'From the rising of the sun to its setting the name of the Lord is to be praised.'

The following idea could be the basis of a class tableau that gradually builds up and includes every child.

One child wears a simple 'sandwich board' structure. One side is pitch black; the other side is a golden sun. The tableau begins by the child standing in the centre of the stage, black side towards the rest of the children and gradually, as the words of the psalm are read aloud, the child turns around so that the full sun faces the children. A few children, with yellow/gold crêpe paper attached to their arms, join the child in the centre and extend their arms at different angles to represent the radiating rays of the sun. Simple masks are needed for the rest of the children as they build up the picture of sunrise.

An owl flits across the stage with a gentle hoot and goes to sleep at one side, signifying the end of night. Cockerels with fine combs and tails strut and crow to mark the beginning of a new day and then they stand still. Other tiny birds with different masks dance in the dawn chorus, before taking their positions around the sun. Rabbits scamper across the stage and begin feeding and washing (simple ears and powder puffs can be worn). Other animals could be added. Man wakes up. The city bursts into life; the song 'Who will buy this beautiful morning?' could be played as children re-enact selling their wares.

The teacher should explain that the rising of the sun heralds God's gift of a new day – a new beginning – a new chance to do something worthwhile.

End with a simple prayer about making the most of the opportunities that are presented to us today. The children could be encouraged to think of helpful or thoughtful acts that they might pursue.

Hymn

No 6, 'I have seen the golden sunshine', in *Someone's Singing Lord* A. and C. Black or No 13, 'We praise you for the sun', in *Someone's Singing Lord* A. and C. Black.

Myself

The aim of this assembly is to introduce ourselves to one another. It could be spread over several days, beginning with the school staff, i.e. the teachers, the headteacher, the caretaker and cleaners, cooks, dinner helpers, school crossing patrol person, First-Aid person, secretary, etc.

Just a brief word from each person saying who they are and what they do is needed, and a simple prayer of thanks for their contribution to school life at the end of the assembly will help the children to appreciate the different roles.

A class of children could develop this theme by doing a project on Myself: Who am I? Include the following points: hair colour, weight, eye colour, height, my mother or father or family; I am a boy or girl; I can shout, laugh, cry, smile; I can jump, skip, swim; food I like, the time I go to bed, etc.; I am unique.

At the beginning of the school year it is fun to weigh each child in each class and then add all the weights together for the whole school. Then do the same thing at the end of the school year and compare the weights. It is great fun to compare the additional weight gained by the children (and staff) at the end of the year with the weight, say, of an elephant at London Zoo!

Prayer

Thank you God, for making me, me. Thank you for my special gifts and talents, for my ability to laugh and sing and shout and play. Help me to make my own proper contribution to school life. Amen.

Hymn

No 19, 'He gave me eyes so I could see' in *Someone's Singing Lord* A. and C. Black or No 73, 'Glad that I live am I', in *New Life* (Galliard) or No 94, 'If I were a butterfly', in *Junior Praise*, (Marshall Pickering) (with the refrain: 'But I just thank you Father, for making me, 'me'.).

The Creation Story

A movement mime to involve the whole class or whole school. *You will need the following characters*:

(Depending on the numbers of children you wish to involve, you can add more children to each group).

> Children representing Darkness
> Children representing Light
> Children representing Earth
> Children representing Sea
> Children representing all kinds of Plants and Trees
> Child representing Sun
> Child representing Moon
> Children representing Stars
> Children representing all kinds of Creatures
> Children representing all kinds of Birds
> Children representing all kinds of Domestic Animals
> Children representing all kinds of Wild Animals
> Child representing first Man
> Child representing first Woman
> A Narrator

Simple costumes, headdresses and masks can be worn to enhance the characterization.
  The story unfolds in the following way:

Narrator: This is the story about how God created the world. In the beginning there was nothing but darkness.

> (*Children dressed in black from head to foot, move about the hall spreading darkness. They come to rest in the front of the hall and build themselves in a black semicircular structure, just touching at different points to represent night. See p. 22 for music to which to dance.*)

Narrator: And God said, 'Let there be light' and light appeared (Good News Bible).

> (*Children dressed completely in white move about the hall, spreading light. They also come to rest opposite the children dressed in black at the front. Once again these children build themselves into a light semicircular structure, just touching at different points to represent day.*)

Narrator: (*Pointing first to the white group of children, and then to the black group.*) 'God called the light Day, and the darkness He called Night. There was morning and evening on this first day.'

(*The groups revolve around each other; the white group miming a lively 'waking-up' dance, and the black group miming a 'sleepy' dance. Both groups come together to form a morning and evening structure, before going back to sit in their places in the hall.*)

Narrator: On the second day, God created the sky.

(*Children dressed in blue, dotted all around the hall, stand up exactly where they are, and do a stretching, spreading dance, trying to reach their partners across the hall and then sit down.*)

Narrator: And God said 'Let the waters under the heavens be gathered together into one place, and let the dry land appear.' And it was so. God called the dry land Earth, and the waters that were gathered together he called Seas (Revised Standard Version).

(*Two groups – one dressed in brown representing the earth and the other group dressed in different shades of green representing the seas – dance together. The whole scene can be made to look more effective if the 'sea' group dance with long strips of fabric which they pretend are the waves, and move in a wave-like dance across the 'earth' group.*)

Narrator: And God created all kinds of plants and trees on this third day.

(*Children wearing flower masks or twig headdress can do their dance.*)

Narrator: And on the fourth day God created the Sun, and the Moon and the Stars.

(*A child dressed in a shift with a brilliant sun radiating outwards on both sides, can dance first. Similarly, a child with a crescent-shaped headdress, and a crescent-shaped moon collage attached to a shift, can do his or her dance. Finally, a number of children, representing the stars, with stars on their heads and silver cut-out stars, stitched onto simple shifts, can do their dance and then return to their places.*)

Narrator: And on the fifth day, God created all the creatures that live in the sea and all the birds that fly in the air.

(Children dressed as all kinds of sea creatures have their turn to dance. Include an octopus and a whale as well as different types of fish. Children with bird masks can make flying movements around hall.)

Narrator: And then God created all the creatures that live on the earth, creepy creatures, crawly creatures, wild animals and pets.

(A pageant of children march around the hall, showing off their different costumes to the rest of the children.)

Narrator: And God created the first man and woman and He blessed them and said they could rule over the animals and birds and fish and eat the fruits and plants. And this was the sixth day and God was very pleased with his work.

(Two children representing the first man and woman, can move across the hall looking at all the flowers and plants and animals.)

Narrator: On the seventh day, God looked at all His handiwork and saw that it was finished so he rested. God blessed this seventh day and set it apart as a special day of rest.

End the assembly with a simple prayer of thanks to God for all his creatures and the beauty of the earth, the sea and the skies.

Hymn

No 1 'Morning has broken', in *Come and Praise* (BBC), or 'Yom ze M'chubad', in *Z'mirot Anthology* (see p. 229–233) for pronunciation guide).

Yom ze M'chubad

Yom ze m'chubad mikol yamin, ki vo shabat tzur olamim.

Sheshet yamim taaseh m'lahteha, v'yom hashvii l'eloheha
Shabat lo taaseh vo m'laha, ki hol asa sheshet yamim.

Yom ze . . .

More than all other days the Sabbath is blessed;
for the Rock of all time made it His day of rest.

For completing your work He has given six days;
but the seventh belongs to your God.
On that day no work should be done,
for in six days He completed the work of creation.

More than all other days the Sabbath is blessed;
for the Rock of all time made it His day of rest.

Some Suggestions for Dance Music for The Creation Story

Darkness	Massenet, 'Thais' – Meditation.
Light	Richard Strauss, 'Also sprach Zarathustra' – Sunrise
Sky	Rachmaninov, Rhapsody on a theme of Paganini – Variation 18
Sea	Tchaikovsky, 'The Nutcracker' – 'Waltz of the Flowers'
Earth	Falla, 'El Amor brujo' – Ritual Fire Dance
Plants, Trees and Flowers	Mascagni, 'Cavalleria Rusticana' – Intermezzo
Sun, Moon and Stars	Offenbach, 'The Tales of Hoffman' – Barcarolle
Sea Creatures and Birds	Grieg, 'Peer Gynt' – Morning
Creepy Crawlies	Wagner, 'Ride of the Valkyries'
Man and Woman	Pachelbel, 'Canon' and 'Gigue'

Chinese New Year: The Dance of the Years

5–11
Assembly
All

Source: The diagram is taken from 'Chinese New Year', the Living Festival Series, by Anne Bancroft, published by Religious and Moral Education Press, Exeter 1984, page 21. Reproduced by kind permission of SCM-Canterbury Press Ltd. (RMEP is a division of SCM-Canterbury Press Ltd.)

The Chinese New Year follows the lunar calendar. It usually takes place in January or February, depending when the second new moon occurs after the winter solstice. The actual celebrations for the New Year can last for fifteen nights, with each night having a special significance and festival. For instance, the eighth night is called 'The Night of the Stars'. Little oil lights are lit and hung around the house to keep away evil spirits. The thirteenth night is part of the Lantern Festival, when everyone carries beautiful, different shaped and coloured lanterns in the street. Perhaps the most famous night of all is the last night, the night of the Dragon Dance.

Any of these festivals provide suitable material for activity assemblies to perform for the rest of the school in music, movement and dance. For this assembly, it will be assumed that a Dance for the Years has been chosen for younger children. Simple masks and costumes will be needed, for the following named years:

The year of the Tiger
The year of the Rabbit
The year of the Dragon
The year of the Snake
The year of the Horse
The year of the Sheep
The year of the Monkey
The year of the Cockerel
The year of the Dog
The year of the Pig
The year of the Rat
The year of the Buffalo
Narrator

For the second part of the assembly, older children could choose a significant *event* that happened during each one of the above cycles, i.e. the outbreak of World War 2 in 1939, the Year of the Rabbit, or the Olympic Games in 1988, the Year of the Dragon. Then each of the years will have a partner, who will mime the special event.

Suggestions for the events could be as follows (although teachers may prefer to think of their own):

The Tiger	1914 Outbreak of the First World War
The Rabbit	1987 The Great Storm in Britain
The Dragon	1988 the Seoul Olympic Games
The Snake	1989 the demolition of the Berlin Wall
The Horse	1966 the 900th Anniversary of the Norman Conquest of England
The Sheep	1919 First direct flight across the Atlantic by Alcock and Brown
The Monkey	1992 Single European Market
The Cockerel	1945 End of the Second World War
The Dog	1922 Treasure found in Tutankhamun's tomb
The Pig	1947 School leaving age raised to 15 years in Great Britain
The Rat	1936 Accession and Abdication of King Edward VIII
The Buffalo	1961 Gagarin made the first space flight

The dance takes place in the round. All the main characters sit in a circle, with the rest of the assembled children and parents (if it is to be a parents' assembly) sitting around and behind the main dancers.

The Narrator needs to explain that the children will dance the different *animal* signs for each Chinese year and that the legend behind the naming of the years is supposed to come from the fact that twelve creatures came to say farewell to the Buddha, when he was leaving this planet, therefore he named each year after each of the following dancing animals.

Some explanation also needs to be given about the fact that it is a *twelve-year* cycle, and that the cycle keeps repeating itself, so that the Tiger always follows the Buffalo, etc.

If it is decided that more than one class is to be involved in the dance, then the Narrator can introduce each section in the following way: 'These are the tiger years, 1914, 1926, 1938, 1950, 1974, 1986, 1998, 2010. The tigers will now dance for you.' Suitable taped music is played as the tigers dance their dance. Labels can be pinned to the costumes, to denote the year that the child is representing. (See below for suggestions for dance music).

In addition to the simple costumes, masks, leotards and tights, the rabbits could also wear powder puffs, the cockerels could wear plumes or combs, the rats could wear tails, the horses could wear manes or ride on simple hobby horses made out of a dowling stick and a horse's head, consisting of some tights or large socks stuffed with newspaper ears, eyes and mane attached.

For the dragon dance, percussion instruments such as symbols, could be played along with the taped music. Percussion instruments could also enhance the music of the other dances, such as the rats or monkeys.

A ribbon attached to a dowling rod makes a very pretty alternative to the character dancing. For instance the snakes could simply stand in the centre of the circle and wave their rods and ribbons to snake-like music.

For the second part of the assembly, the Narrator needs to introduce the pairs of significant *dates* with their partner, i.e. 'This is 1914 in the year of the Tiger, the outbreak of World War I'; 'This is 1987 in the year of the Rabbit, the year of the Great Storm in Britain', etc. The pairs of children can then process and mime their parts around the circle, wearing their simple costumes and labels denoting the event, before returning to their seats.

End the assembly with the actual year, and a forceful message for the New Year, i.e. 'This is _____ the year when we must feed the starving people in the world.'

Prayer

Heavenly Father, make us conscious, this New Year, of the needs of others. Help us to give generously, of our time, and talents and money to help others. Amen.

Hymn

No 141, 'Tomorrow is a highway broad and fair,' in *New Life* (Galliard); or No 106, 'It's a new day, there's hope,' in *Come and Praise 2* (BBC).

Some Suggestions for Dance Music for the Dance of the Years

(Taken from various classical CDs. It should be noted that modern popular music can be used just as effectively as classical music.)

Tigers	Strauss, 'Roses' from the 'South Waltz'
Rabbits	Strauss, 'Pizzicato Polka'
Dragon	Gounod, Ballet Music from 'Faust' no. 2 Extract
Snake	Schubert, 'Impromptu no. 4 in A Flat'
Horses	Tchaikovsky, Waltz from 'Sleeping Beauty'
Sheep	Mozart, Andante from Piano Concerto no. 21
Monkey	Tchaikovsky, 'Dance of the Sugar Plum Fairy' from the 'Nutcracker Suite'

Cockerel   Mozart, 'Romanze' from 'Eine Kleine Nachtmusik'
Dog   Mendelssohn, 'Spring Song' 'Song without Words Op 62' no. 6
Pig   Schubert, 'Andantino' from 'Rosamunde'
Rat   Haydn, 'Minuet' and 'Trio' from 'Symphony no. 83' 'La Poule'
Buffalo   Gounod, Ballet Music from 'Faust' no. 1 Extract

2 PLACES OF WORSHIP

Exploring a Synagogue

5–11
Activity/Assembly
Judaism
(Preparation Needed)

In Britain today, there are many synagogues. Before involving the children in a class project, the teacher will need to make a preparatory visit, in order to establish whether the local synagogue is an Orthodox one, or whether it is one of the Reform or Progressive synagogues. There will be some differences in styles of worship, etc.

It is also important to know something about the layout of the synagogue, the architecture, furniture, history, etc. and the provision of toilets.

Perhaps the local Rabbi could be invited into a school assembly prior to the visit, to talk about special features that can be seen inside and outside the synagogue, or slides could be shown. It is important that the teacher briefs the Rabbi beforehand. For instance, he will need to know the age range of the children, the sort of language levels, something about the child-centred approach, permission to tell funny stories.

It is important to decide how the project work is to be tackled – individual work, small groups or the whole class. Very young children may find it simpler to work in small groups with a parent helper, concentrating on one particular aspect of the synagogue. Then the whole class could come together at the end of the project to share their findings. Older children may like to have a prepared worksheet of items to look out for and then to concentrate on and to research one particular aspect of the synagogue that interests them – or make their own project book about the artefacts.

Approximately half an hour should be allowed for the visit for the younger children. Older children may need a little longer. Prepare the children by asking them to stand quite still inside the synagogue and listen to the sounds in the building. Remind the children not to shout or run about, but to treat the place with respect.

Art/Craft

1   Make a large fabric collage of the Aron Hakodesh, the Holy Ark, with the 'dressed' Torah Scrolls inside.

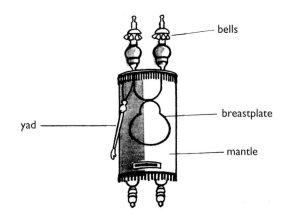

Art/Craft

Try to draw or paint a picture of the inside/outside of the synagogue; include the bimah (raised platform), seats, women's gallery (Orthodox Jews), decor – motifs, roof, floor, foyer, kitchen, rabbi's study, garden, gates, etc. Make a collage/painting of the Aron Hakodesh, the Holy Ark or the lamp which is kept alight to show God's Presence.
Make some Torah Scrolls (see p. 30)
Make a Menorah or seven-branched candle stick. Make some 6-sided star mobiles, the Magen David.
Make Rosh Hashana cards (New Year)
Make Tablets of the Ten Commandments.

Religious Education

Re-enact a typical synagogue service. (Orthodox or Progressive).
Find out about Abraham, Moses, David, Elijah, etc. Find out about some famous Jewish people throughout history, i.e. Albert Einstein, Yehudi Menuhin, etc. Find out about the Holocaust.

Story/Poetry

Queen Esther Saves Her People by P. Frank (1986) Lion Publishing.
Sam's Passover by L. Hannigan (1994) A & C Black.
Rose Blanche by R. Innocenti (1996) Harcourt Brace International
Anne Frank by C. Senker (2000) Wayland.
Jewish Tales, The Eight Lights of the Hanukkiya by L. Parlat (1986) Beehive.

Writing/Language/Discussion

Describe the visit. Make two lists: what did you expect to see? What did you actually see? Make a people book. Make an artefacts book. Discuss the differences between Orthodox and Progressive Services.
Why is there no graveyard/tombstones? (Answer: because of the need for ritual purity). Where are people buried?
Make a concertina book showing the sequence of Shabbat.
Find out about special festivals, services. Write out the Hebrew Alphabet (see p. 234)

Artefacts

The Jewish Museum
Raymond Burton House,
129–131 Albert Street
London NW1 7NB
Tel: 0208 349 1143
Web: www.jewishmuseum.org.uk

Articles of Faith
Kay Street, Bury BL9 6BU
Tel: 0161 763 6232
Web: www.articlesoffaith.co.uk

Exploring a Synagogue

Maths

Look out for different shapes inside/outside – circles, triangles, squares, etc.
Count doors, windows, etc. Time: What time is sunset in the winter/summer? Try and obtain a timetable.
Money: How much does each person pay to belong to the synagogue?
If there is a shop – how much does each item cost?

People who go to Synagogue

Rabbi
Cantor (Reader)
Congregation
School
Choir
Ladies Guild

Science

Kosher Food – preparation, specialities, what can **not** be eaten i.e. pig, rabbit, shell-fish, etc. (See Leviticus, Chapter 11 for full list).

Displays in the Classroom

Display tallits (prayer shawls)
Display yamulkahs (skull caps)
Display tefillins (*prayer boxes containing Torah verses. NB should **not** be touched.*)
Display a shofar (ram's horn)
Display a yad (silver pointer used to follow the words in the Torah)

2   Let the children make individual replicas of the Torah Scrolls using a roll of paper and two dowling rods.

3   Make some six-pointed star mobiles. These can be made by joining two triangles together to make a star shape. Make large and small stars for effect, and suspend them from hoops hanging from the ceiling. Stars could be decorated with silver paper, silver paint or crayon.

4   Make some Rosh Hashana (New Year) cards.
    Pictures of Israel (obtainable from Travel brochures) could be cut out and stuck onto cards, or children could design their own card by using the star motif or special shofar motif or other artefacts found in synagogues today. If the latter method is chosen, perhaps the children could print their own cards using potato/lino prints.

Inside a Synagogue

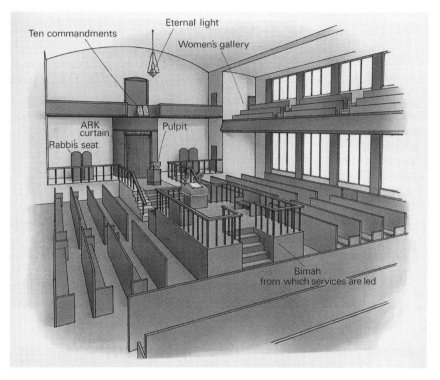

Source: *My Belief: I am a Jew*, C. Lawton, Franklin Watts, 1984 Artwork by Tony Payne. Reproduced by kind permission of Franklin Watts.

Rabbi and Bar Mitzvah Boy

Source: *My Belief: I am a Jew*, by C. Lawton published by Franklin Watts, 1984 (photograph by Chris Fairclough).

RE/Assembly

This could take the form of re-enacting a typical Sabbath Service. It must be decided whether the service is to be strictly Orthodox in character, or like one of the Reform services. For this purpose, an Orthodox service will be described.

The Sabbath evening service begins fifteen minutes before sunset (see time-table). The Sabbath morning service will commence around nine o'clock the next day and will last for approximately two or three hours.

Men and women are segregated. The men sit in the main part of the synagogue and the women sit in the women's gallery. Men and married women must cover their heads, and men put on their special prayer shawls to pray.

The service is in Hebrew and the most important part of the service is when the Torah is read. A Torah scroll is taken out of the Ark, and after some prayers have been said, it is taken around the synagogue. Some people bow before the scroll as a mark of respect. Seven men usually have the honour of being called up to the bimah or platform to read from the Torah. Then it is held up for everyone to see the words. A yad, or pointer is used for reading the scroll, as the words are Holy and must not be touched. After the reading, the scroll is dressed before it is returned to the ark. It is dressed with a special mantle, breastplate, yad and bells.

There are also readings from the Haftara or Prophets which are also in Hebrew. Then prayers are said before the sermon. The Rabbi preaches the sermon and will display his great learning by explaining the scriptures.

After the service, the congregation often joins together for the blessing or kiddush. This is said over wine and challot, the special twisted loaves of bread. Everyone can have a piece of bread and drink some of the wine, although children usually drink orange juice.

The rest of the day, of course, is spent at rest, as God commanded. No work is done, the meals have been prepared and cooked the day before and so the family spend the day relaxing together.

End the assembly by lighting a candle as a sign of God's presence and allow a time for quiet reflection or a short prayer of thanks to God for his Holy words and the day of rest can be said.

Hymn

'*Hine Ma Tov*', Psalm 133, 'Look how good and how lovely it is when people live together in unity'. In *An Easy To Play Third Collection of Hebrew Melodies* by Elisheva Myers (The Pelican Press) 1990.

Exploring a typical English Church

5–11
Activity/Assembly
Christianity
(Preparation Needed)

Following the ideas outlined overleaf the children can present an assembly using the detailed studies of their findings. Each child or group can be given a different aspect of the church to study, draw or paint. Perhaps models could be made. At the assembly each child can be given an opportunity to hold up his or her painting and read a short descriptive piece about what he or she has discovered.

Preparation

1   The teacher needs to visit the local church first alone, making sure that the layout is known, that something is known about the church architecture, furniture, history, etc., and the provision of toilets.
2   Talk to the minister, perhaps invite him to a school assembly to talk about some interesting features of the church prior to the children's visit. Perhaps he or she could bring his or her special robes and talk about them.
3   Show slides of the local church, pointing out interesting features.
4   Decide how the project work is to be tackled – by individuals, small groups or the whole class. Very young children may find it simpler to work in small groups with a parent helper, concentrating on one particular aspect of the church. Older students may like to have a prepared worksheet of items to look for and then research one particular aspect of the church that interests them, or make their own project book about the artefacts.
5   Allow approximately half an hour for the visit by younger children. Older children may need a little longer.
6   Prepare the children by asking them to stand quite still inside the church and listen to the quietness. Remind them not to shout or run about, but to treat the place with respect.
7   Find out about other places of worship in the area. Perhaps a follow-up study could be made next term.

Figure 1 Shows how the *Theme can be developed* across the curriculum.

Figure 2 Shows how the *Theme can be explored using all the senses.*

Figure 3 Summarizes the *Skills, attitudes and concepts that can be developed* using this topic.

TYPICAL ENGLISH CHURCH

Art and Craft

Brass rubbings: you will need a roll of paper, wax crayons or cobblers' wax; adhesive tape, small brush to brush away any dirt. *Permission needs to be obtained from the Vicar.* Try rubbing walls, floors, doors, locks. Printing shapes: try white paint on black paper

Make 3-D models of church out of a shoe box and waste materials.
Nativity scene out of weighted plastic salt containers with plasticine heads.
Large fabric collage of Holy Family
Stained glass windows out of tissue paper
Potato wreaths using large potatoes, holly, tinsel, ribbon
Doily angels, mobiles, stars
A frieze of church mice

Religious Education

Belonging: People: Interview the Vicar.
Who was Jesus – His life, stories, friends, parables.
Festivals: Christmas, Easter, Harvest, Whit Sunday, etc.
Celebrations: weddings, baptisms, birthdays, food, death, funerals, saints
Artefacts, furniture, signs and symbols, the Bible.
Compare church buildings: ancient and modern
Light – a topic worth studying in greater depth.

Reference Books

Bennett, O. (1994) *Exploring Religion: Buildings*. Bell and Hyman.
Bradley, C. (2002) *Churches*, Let's Discover Series, Franklin Watts.
Brown, A. and Seaman, A. (2000) *Christian Church*. A & C Black.
Fewins, C. (1993) *Be a Church Detective*, Church House Publishing.
Group Diagram (1987) *Great British Churches*, Franklin Watts.
Rock, L. (1995) *Discovering Churches*, Lion Publishing.
Ross, M. (1999) *Places of Worship*, Heinemann.

Reading/Writing/Language/Discussion

Make different shaped books i.e.
The vicar is
The font is
Individual books of what to look for inside/outside a church i.e. windows or kneelers. Class books recording the visit. Concertina books developing a sequence of events – order of Christmas service, baptism. Make a people book. Read parish records, notices, inscriptions, baptismal roll. What do our names mean?

People who go to church

Vicar   Congregation
Curate   Carpenters
Sidesmen   Builders
Stone masons   Gardeners
Cleaners   Flower arrangers
Church wardens   Organist
Bellringers   Church Council
Sunday School   Youth Club

Story/Poetry

Brown, A. and Seaman, A. (2000) *My Christian Faith*, Evans.
Daly, N. (2000) *Jamela's Dress*, Frances Lincoln (A wedding) 5–7 year olds.
Mattingley, C. (1985) *The Angel with a Mouth-organ*, Hodder and Stoughton – 7–8 year olds.
Oakley G. (1989) The Church Mouse, Macmillan – 7 year olds.
Shilson-Thomas, A. (1996) *First Picture Book of Stories from World Religions*, Viking/Puffin.
Wood, D. (2001) *Grandad's Prayers of the Earth*, Walker Books (Deals with death and remembering all the wonderful things Grandad taught about the beautiful world).

Maths

Look for different shapes – circles, triangles squares, etc. Count doors, windows.
Arbitrary measurement i.e. handspans, cubits Goliath was six cubits and a span high (10ft tall; 1 Sam 17:4)
Time: day, night, winter, summer, etc
Clock face
Money – how is the church money used?
Symmetry – look for patterns

Science

Water – what is it used for?
Sound – who or what makes the sound?
Heat – Some objects feel warmer/colder than others, ie wood/brass. Make comparisons in church structures – look at shapes: squares, rectangles, circles, roof, spire, pillars, columns, arches.
Property of materials – what is it made of?
Wind – weathercock – which way is the wind blowing?
Air and burning – candles
Patterns in the environment – day and night, Seasons, clocks.
Weather – snow and ice, sun, rain, wind.
Nature study – what does the churchyard look like at different times of year?

Music

Listen to church music – organ, piano, instruments
Learn hymns. Make own instruments.

Displays in the classroom

A bell display – encourage children to bring in different bells.
Christening gown display
Photographs of babies – guess who?
Christmas card display

Figure 1 Developing the Theme

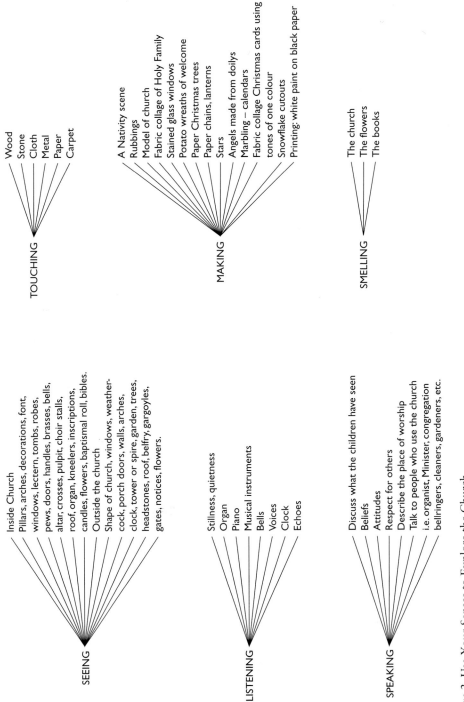

TOUCHING
Wood
Stone
Cloth
Metal
Paper
Carpet

MAKING
A Nativity scene
Rubbings
Model of church
Fabric collage of Holy Family
Stained glass windows
Potato wreaths of welcome
Paper Christmas trees
Paper chains, lanterns
Stars
Angels made from doilys
Marbling – calendars
Fabric collage Christmas cards using tones of one colour
Snowflake cutouts
Printing: white paint on black paper

SMELLING
The church
The flowers
The books

SEEING
Inside Church
Pillars, arches, decorations, font, windows, lectern, tombs, robes, pews, doors, handles, brasses, bells, altar, crosses, pulpit, choir stalls, roof, organ, kneelers, inscriptions, candles, flowers, baptismal roll, bibles.
Outside the church
Shape of church, windows, weather-cock, porch doors, walls, arches, clock, tower or spire, garden, trees, headstones, roof, belfry, gargoyles, gates, notices, flowers.

LISTENING
Stillness, quietness
Organ
Piano
Musical instruments
Bells
Voices
Clock
Echoes

SPEAKING
Discuss what the children have seen
Beliefs
Attitudes
Respect for others
Describe the place of worship
Talk to people who use the church i.e. organist, Minister, congregation bellringers, cleaners, gardeners, etc.

Figure 2 Use Your Senses to Explore the Church

Skills	*Concepts*
Observation	Size
Describing	Shape
Thinking	Church artefacts
Reflecting	The church in the community
Assessing information	Sense of awe and wonder
Presenting	Awareness of meaning of words
Working cooperatively	
Speaking	*Attitudes*
Listening	Willingness to ask questions
Reading	Respect for the belief of others
Writing	Respect for the craftsmen and workers of all
Understanding	kinds, who are motivated by their love of God
Imagining	Sense of care and responsibility
Understanding use of symbolism	Enjoyment in using all the senses for exploring
Computing	and discriminating
Experimenting	

Figure 3 Skills, attitudes, concepts developed by activities relating to a church

The Christingle Service

5–11
Assembly
Christianity

It is usually a good idea to alternate a mammoth Christmas production with a 'quiet' event. In this way teachers and children do not try to out-do each other each year and the Christmas event becomes really enjoyable. Parents enjoy it too, especially when they can join in by singing the well known carols. Parents and carers might also be asked to read the lessons.

A lovely service, which does not require masses of costumes, but simply an orange, a candle, some fruits or sweets and a red ribbon for each child, is the Christingle service. The Christingle originated in Czechoslovakia and is now held for children all over the world.

Briefly, each child needs a decorated orange as a reminder of what Christmas is all about for Christians. The round orange represents the world. A candle is placed into the top of the orange to represent Jesus, the Light of the World. Four cocktail sticks with sweets or raisins are pushed into the orange to represent the four corners of the earth – north, south, east and west – where the Light of the World reaches. The sweets or raisins represent all the good things of the earth that come to us from God. Finally, the red ribbon is tied around the orange to remind us that Jesus came to die for us.

In a proper Christingle service all the lights in the church would be turned off and each child holding a Christingle would have their candles lit. However, in cramped and difficult conditions with few adults to supervise, it may be sensible just to let the older children stand at the end of each row and have their candles lit. The service is very simple: carols interspersed with readings, an explanation about the orange, a final carol and then the candles are all blown out.

People Who Use the Church

This activity is designed for a class assembly involving every child. The props are simple: headdresses and labels could be worn to indicate each character:

Vicar
Sidesmen
Choir
Bellringers
Flower arrangers
Gardeners
Cleaning ladies/men
PCC
Parents and baby for baptism
Couple for wedding
Mourners for funeral (this could be left out if very young children are present)
Congregation

The scene could be built up gradually as each child enters with a brief description of what he or she does:

First child as vicar: I am the vicar; it is my job to care for all the people in this neighbourhood and to oversee every aspect of church life. These are the people who help me.

Sidesmen: We are the sidesmen; we welcome the people and show them to their seats. We also help to look after the building and see that everything runs smoothly.

Choir: We are the choir. We praise God through our singing. We not only sing at all the services, but we have to do a lot of practices during the week. In small churches a choir may be made up of just a few people, but in a cathedral the complete choir may be sixty people or more.

Bellringers: We are the bellringers. We also have to practise during the week. Before services on Sunday, we ring the bells to tell the people that the service is about to begin. We also ring our bells after weddings in celebration, and on other special occasions like the birth of a royal baby.

Flower arrangers: It is our job to decorate the church and make it look beautiful. We make sure that there are fresh flowers in all the vases. At festivals like Christmas, Easter and Harvest we do special floral displays.

Gardeners: We are the gardeners. We have to mow the lawns and keep the flower beds free from weeds.

Cleaners: We clean the church (*each child could describe a different aspect of the work*): I polish the brasses; I clean the windows; I scrub the floors; I dust the pews; I sweep the paths.

PCC: I am a member of the Parochial Church Council. I help the vicar with difficult decisions and I look after the church funds. I am called the PCC Treasurer.

Parents, baby and godparents: We are bringing our baby to be baptised. We are going to call her Georgina (*or insert the name of a new baby brother or sister of one of the children in school*).

Couple for wedding: The minister is going to perform our wedding ceremony. We know the minister well because he has talked to us about what marriage means and the promises we shall make to each other and to God.

Mourners: We feel very sad because our old friend has died. But the vicar has arranged a joyful 'Thanksgiving Service' for our friend. We shall remember all the good things he did and give thanks to God for his life.

(*Last child points to the school*)

Congregation: Finally, any one of us can make up the congregation. Without us the church would be empty. Lots of different people come to the church: young and old, short and tall, different coloured people. God loves each one of us.

Prayer

Heavenly Father, help each one of us to discover our own talents, whether it is gardening or singing, or caring for others, and enable us to offer this talent back to you by using it to help others. Amen.

Hymn

No 37, 'Working together' in *Every Colour under the Sun* (Ward Lock Educational).

Music

No 2, 'I'd like to teach the world to sing' (traditional) in *Apusskidu* A. and C. Black 1996 (double cassette pack available).

A Gurdwara or House of God

Try to arrange a visit to a Gurdwara, or House of God, but remember, shoes must be removed and heads must be covered.

What to look for inside the Gurdwara:

The Guru Granth Sahib	the Sikh's Holy book.
Palki	a sort of throne on which the Guru Granth Sahib is placed.
Cushions	the Holy book rests on beautifully decorated cushions in the Palki.
Offerings	money or food is placed in front of the Guru Granth Sahib by each member of the congregation.
Seating arrangements	everyone sits on the floor. Men usually sit on one side of the Gurdwara, women sit on the other side.
Karah Prasad	the Sikh's holy food is distributed to all the members of the congregation at the end of a service.
Kitchen	a very important room in the Gurdwara, as a communal meal called langar is prepared in the kitchen and offered to all worshippers after the service.

Make a list of questions to ask the Granthi or reader. (There are no priests or ministers).

1 Which day is the day of worship? (In Britain, it tends to be Sunday).
2 In what language is the service conducted? (Usually Punjabi, but sometimes parts of the service may be conducted in English in this country).
3 How long does a service last? (Usually three or four hours but worshippers are free to come and go as they please).
4 Are hymns sung? (Hymns from the Guru Granth Sahib, called Shabads are sung).
5 Are musical instruments used in worship? (Often a harmonium and a pair of small drums are used).
6 What does the reader do? (The reader reads short passages from the Guru Granth Sahib and may give an explanation of the reading).
7 What sort of training would a Granthi need? (He will have a great knowledge of the Holy book and be able to teach others).
8 What provision is there for children? (There are Sunday Schools for children in Britain. Children are taught verses from the Guru Granth Sahib and will also learn the Gurmukhi script).
9 Are there special services for initiation, weddings and funerals? (See pp. 252–8).
10 What other meetings take place during the week? (Some Gurdwaras hold special meetings for young people and community meetings).

Gather all the information together and finally let one group of children draw a ground floor plan of the inside of the Gurdwara and another group draw the outside of the building. Is the building purpose-built or is it a building that has been converted from another building?

All the information can then be written up and presented to the rest of the school in an assembly, making use of short descriptions, paintings and drawings.

Prayer

Father God we have seen the importance of sharing a meal in the Gurdwara. Make us ready to share with those who do not have enough to eat. Amen.

Hymn

No 74, 'Sad, puzzled eyes of small hungry children' in *Come and Praise 2* (BBC).

A Visit to a Mosque

5–11
Activity/Assembly
Islam

For this assembly you will need a large line drawing or poster of the inside/outside of a mosque (see p. 42). If there is a mosque in your town, of course it would be preferable to make a visit, working along similar cross-curricular lines to those outlined on pp. 28–29 (exploring a synagogue). Perhaps the class could visit the Central London Mosque in Regent's Park (Tel: 0208–830–6214 for an appointment.) Prepare a list of questions to ask, and look out for special features, based on the information given below.

Pin the poster to an easel. You will also need some large labels with the following words:

Outside

Dome	architectural feature to denote that the building is a mosque.
Minarets	vertical towers with small domes at the top. In Islamic countries, worshippers are called to prayer by the prayer-caller from the top of the Minaret. Muslims everywhere are called to prayer five times a day.
Muezzin	the prayer-caller.
Fountain or **Pool**	In Islamic countries this is provided for washing before prayers, and for drinking.
Islamic arches	these can be seen above the windows and doors or in the court-yards surrounding the mosques. See picture below.

Patterns	beautiful geometric designs and Arabic Script can often be seen as decorations on the Minarets and walls.

Inside

No pictures, no seats, no statues, no music, no singing; shoes must be removed.

Shoe-rack	everyone takes off his or her shoes before entering the mosque
Washroom	ritual washing always precedes prayers. In some mosques there is a separate washroom for women.
6 Clocks	the times when Muslims should pray are displayed on the clocks. A Muslim prays five times a day so the clocks denote the appropriate times. Of course, prayer times vary in winter and summer months as sunset/sunrise varies. The sixth clock shows the time of the main Friday prayers.
Mihrab	an alcove in the mosque showing the direction of Makkah.

Minbar	the flight of steps from the top of which the Imam speaks to the people.
Prayer mats	beautiful mats or rugs on which to pray.
Prayer hats	most Muslims always cover their heads when they pray.
Agarbattis	incense sticks usually burned during Friday worship.
The Qur'an	this is the Muslim Holy Book.
Wooden stand	the Qur'an is raised above the floor and placed on a simple wooden stand.
Imam	this is a prayer leader.
Women	generally women worship at home, although young girls in Britain, before the age of twelve, will come to the mosque to participate in Islamic classes. There is a special part of the mosque, away from the men, where women may pray.
Mosque classes	in some mosques in Britain, children attend mosque classes, between the ages of 5–12 years, on five nights a week, from about five o'clock until eight o'clock. Islamic studies are taught in the Pakistani language of Urdu. Arabic is also taught because the Qur'an is written in Arabic. Stories about the life of Muhammad 鑫 are also studied.

Using the large picture of the mosque and the words on cards, the teacher takes each word in turn, and after giving a brief explanation, fixes the word in the appropriate position on the poster. When the picture has been completed, the teacher can talk about the wonderful Islamic designs and ask the children if they know how to tell a real Persian carpet from a fake one. Briefly, it is this; in a genuine Persian carpet, there is always a tiny deliberate mistake, because Muslims believe that only God can create perfection. Therefore, a tiny flaw reminds the carpetmakers of their inequality with God.

Let the children experiment with geometric designs, and show the work that they have produced as a result of their research.

Prayer

God, we know that only you are perfect. Forgive our imperfections. Amen.

Outline of a Mosque

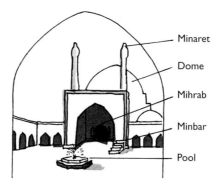

Source: Islam in Words and Pictures, S. Thorley, 1982. RMEP Reproduced by kind permission of SCM-Canterbury Press Ltd. (RMEP is a division of SCM-Canterbury Press Ltd.)

Interview a Buddhist Monk or Nun

7–11
Assembly
Buddhism
(Preparation needed)

Invite a local monk or nun into school, to tell the children about his or her life, work and the monastery where he or she lives. This assembly could be extended to leaders of other faiths. However, it is important to prepare the children first by thinking out some interview questions that they might like to ask their visitor during the assembly. The teacher should ascertain whether the monk or nun follows the Theravāda tradition, or the Tibetan tradition, before asking the following questions. For instance, it is appropriate to ask a Tibetan monk about prayer flags, but not a Theravāda monk, and it is appropriate to ask a Theravāda monk about the number of meals per day, but not a Tibetan monk. (See pp. 206–11 for further information and useful references.) Provided below is the address of the Buddhist Society in London, which may be able to help with names of local regional contacts. Another idea would be for the children to research the questions below and to inform the rest of the school as to their results.

1 Why did you choose to become a monk? Is there a special ceremony? What age do you have to be?
2 What rules do you live by? (See the basic precepts of a monk or nun on p. 208.)
3 Describe a typical day at the monastery.
4 Why do you wear a special robe? (See also p. 208).
5 How many meals do you eat a day? What kind of food do you eat? (Theravāda monk).
6 What is meditation?
7 What are Mantras? (Prayers). What do you say? Do you use prayer beads to help you pray? How many prayer beads are there? What do you write on prayer flags? (Tibetan monk).
8 Do children come to the monastery?
9 Do you have services?
10 Do you have a special day of worship?

It would be a nice idea if the children could bake a special dish or make a special salad that could be given to the monk at the end of his visit, to be taken back and shared with his fellow monks.

These are the basic precepts of a monk or nun. (They also apply to novices).

1 Not to destroy or harm life
2 Not to steal
3 Not to commit adultery or to have irresponsible sexual relations
4 Not to tell lies
5 Not to take intoxicating drinks or to take drugs
6 Not to eat other than at mealtimes
7 Not to go to entertainments like shows, with dancing or music
8 Not to wear perfumes or scents or wear ornaments and decoration

 9   Not to sleep on comfortable raised beds
10   Not to accept or handle gold or silver

(From: pages 33–34 *Buddhists and Buddhism* by M. Patrick (Wayland), East Sussex, 1982).

A time for quiet reflection can be kept to think about perhaps one or two of these basic precepts, i.e. not to steal, or not to tell lies.

Hymn

No 18, 'My mind to me a kingdom is', in *Every Colour Under the Sun* (Ward Lock Educational).

Useful Address

The Buddhist Society
58 Eccleston Square
London SW1V 1PH
Tel: 0207 8345858
website: www.thebuddhistsociety.org.uk

Christianity Around the World

7–11
Assembly
Christianity
(Preparation needed)

Read Romans 12: 4–5 (*RSV*) 'For as in one body we have many members, and all the members do not have the same function, so we, though many, are one body in Christ, and individually members one of another.'

Before this assembly, the teacher will need to study pp. 212–21, Background Information for Teachers, on different Christian denominational faiths and practices. Christians around the world share the same basic belief, that there is one God and Jesus Christ is His Son. Therefore, Christians everywhere, despite their differences in styles of worship, are all members of the world-wide body of Jesus Christ.

This assembly could focus either on each denomination in turn and therefore be spread over many weeks, or be the culmination of many weeks' work, to show what has been learned about each style of worship. Either way, much careful preparation is needed, and each denomination should not only be looked at from the point of view of worship in Great Britain, but how the faith is practised, say, in the West Indies – what it means to be a Pentecostal in Jamaica, or a Roman Catholic in Italy, or an Orthodox Christian in Greece.

If possible, an attempt should be made to display pictures, maps, artefacts, traditional costumes, etc., from the country 'visited' each week. Draw on children's own holiday experiences abroad or use pictures from travel agents. Set up a display table depicting each country that can be changed each week. Finally, let each member of the class dress up in the traditional costume of different countries or wear a simple label and say a brief word about the Christian 'Church' he is representing.

Prayer

Father God, we thank you that we are all part of your world-wide family, united through our Lord, Jesus Christ. Amen.

Hymn

No 19, 'He's got the whole world in his Hands', in *Every Colour under the Sun* (Ward Lock Educational).

Resources

Books

(P) = Pupils
(T) = Teachers

Bates, J. (1986) *Visiting a Methodist Church*, The Lutterworth Press (P & T)
Blackwell, M. (1985) *Visiting a Salvation Army Citadel*, The Lutterworth Press (P & T)

Brown, A. (2001) *Religions of the World: Christian World*, Hodder Wayland (P & T)

Brown, A. and Seaman, A. (2000) *Rainbows, Red, My Christian Faith*, Evans Brothers Ltd. (P)

Caldwell, J.C. (1983) *Let's Visit the West Indies*, Burke (P)

Campbell, K. (1983) *The Caribbean*, Macdonald Educational (P)

Collins, M. and Price, M.A. (1999) *The Story of Christianity*, Dorling Kindersley (T)

Currie, N. (1999) *2000 Years. The Christian Faith in Britain*, Lion Publishing (P & T)

Hackel, S. (1993) *The Orthodox Church*, St Stephen's Press (P & T)

Hall, S. (2003) *Who is Jesus*, Lion Publishing (P)

Killingray, M. (1993) *I am an Anglican*, Franklin Watts (P)

Long, R. (1994) *The Lutheran Church*, RMEP (Chansitor) (There are many more books in this Christian Denomination series) (P & T)

Lye, K. (1988) *Let's Go to Jamaica*, Franklin Watts, (P) (There are many more books in this series)

Owen, G. and Seaman, A. (1998) *Looking at Christianity: Special Occasions*, Hodder Wayland (P)

Penney, S. (1999) *Christianity, Discovering Religions Series*, Heinemann (P & T)

Penney, S. (2001) *Christianity, World Belief and Culture Series*, Heinemann (P & T)

Penney, S. (2002) *Religions of the World: Christianity*, Heinemann (P)

Pettenuzzo, B. (1993) *I am a Pentecostal*, Franklin Watts (P)

Pettenuzzo, B. (2001) *I am a Roman Catholic*, Franklin Watts (P)

Robson, G. (1999) *Places of Worship: Orthodox Churches*, Heinemann (P)

Richards, C. (1999) *Places of Worship: Catholic Churches*, Heinemann (P)

Roussou, M. (1993) *I am a Greek Orthodox*, Franklin Watts (P)

Thomas, R. and Stutchbury, J. (1986) *The Pope and the Vatican*, Macdonald (P)

Thorley, S. (reprint 2003) *Christianity in Words and Pictures*, RMEP (Chansitor) (P & T)

Watson, C. (1997) *Christian Beliefs and Cultures*, Franklin Watts (P)

Watson, C. (2001) *What Do We Know About: Christianity?* Hodder Wayland (P)

Wood, A. (1998) *Where We Worship: The Christian Church*, Franklin Watts (P)

Audio-visual Aids

Posters on Christian Festivals (Christmas, Easter, Whitsun, Harvest), Places of Worship, Religious Belief (with a CD-ROM), My Neighbour's Religion etc. Available from *Pictorial Charts Educational Trust*, 27 Kirchen Road, London W13 OUD.
Tel: 0208 5679206
Fax: 0208 5665120
Web: www.pcet.co.uk

(NB. For a full list of Books and Resources see pp. 212–221.)

3 FRIENDS

Choosing Friends: Rogues' Gallery

5–11
Assembly
All

Ask all the children in the class to study their best friend very carefully and to paint a picture of him or her. Explain that the paintings will be used as a 'Rogues' Gallery', so that each one can be identified. The teacher may need to help the child who is friendless, and encourage other children to paint him or her.

Then ask the children why they chose a particular person. What qualities does a friend have? Give some examples of the kind of things they do together. How does one keep friends? What should you do after a quarrel? Write a brief account. The children could hold up their pictures and read a short extract from the descriptions of their friends.

Now tell and mime this story (based on an idea by R. Wood (1972) in *Activity Talks with Boys and Girls* (NCEC) You will need:

> A rich man sitting at a table
> Some shoppers
> Pile of coins
> A beautiful robe
> A thief
> A mother
> Her son

(Read Matthew 6: 19–21). There was once a man who became very rich by selling things to other people. (*Rich man sells articles to shoppers.*) He became so rich that soon he had piles of money. (*Rich man counts money.*)

He was able to buy himself a beautiful robe. He stored up all his money and he treasured his lovely robe [rich man holds up the robe, puts it on, twirls round in it].

But one night, when he was fast asleep, a thief came and stole his lovely robe and all his money. (*Thief creeps in and steals the robe and money.*)

When the rich man woke up he had nothing left. He had spent all his life getting rich for nothing. (*The rich man wakes up, sees that his robe and money have gone. He buries his head in his hands.*)

Now in that same town there was a wise mother and she told her son that she did not mind what he did as long as he made the world a better place to live in. (*Mother mimes talking to her son.*)

'How can I do that, Mum?' he asked. His mother told him that he must be truthful, kind, gentle and make friends, because no one could steal away kindness, gentleness, truthfulness or friendliness.

Prayer

'Heavenly Father, help me to see not so much of what I can get out of my friends, but more of what I can give to them. Help me to be kind and gentle and truthful because no one can steal these things away. Amen.

Hymn

No 31, 'Thank you for my friends', in *Tinder-box: 66 Songs for Children* A. and C. Black.

Losing Friends

5–9
Assembly
All

To demonstrate how our hands can be welcoming or rejecting. You will need:

    4 children to demonstrate hand positions
    Folded newspaper (two pieces)
    Pair of scissors

The teacher could begin in the following way. Using the scissors she cuts out the shape of some paper dolls and explains that she wants to make a paper chain of friends joining hands together.

For the first demonstration, she deliberately cuts through where the hands should join. The paper children fall to the floor.

She asks the children what has gone wrong.

She takes a second piece of newspaper and this time she is very careful to ensure that the hands will remain joined.

Two children can hold up the chain of dolls between them.

The teacher should go on to explain that friendship is a bit like the joined hands. When hands are joined together, it generally means love, friendship, fun and games. When hands are not joined together, it generally means broken friendship. The friends become a bit like the paper dolls on the floor – alone, sad and lost.

Now ask the four children to come forward and using their hands, mime the following actions:

    punching
    hitting
    pinching
    smacking

The teacher should explain that these actions are all hurtful, unkind and the quickest way to lose friends.

Now the four children can demonstrate ways of using their hands in a kindly way:

Caring hands   – putting their hands round their friend's shoulder;
Helping hands   – lifting a heavy bag;
Fun hands   – playing cat's cradle or turning a skipping rope;
Beckoning hands – welcoming new children to join a game of 'Ring a Ring
                    o' Roses'.

Now read the poem written by a 10-year-old girl entitled 'Loneliness' from R. Deadman and A. Razzell (1977) *Awareness 2* (Macmillan Education).

Loneliness

I sit on the side of the pavement,
watching.
How I wish I hadn't broken friends
She's got everybody on her side
I wish, I wish she'd let me play
The lump in my throat aches
It feels as though its going to burst
Any moment now.
My eyes are swimming with tears –
I opened my mouth to shout,
'Susan, can I play?'
No sound came out.
I couldn't stand it any longer,
I buried my face in my hands
And quietly wept.

(Tracey Stevens, aged 10)

Prayer

'Heavenly Father, grant today that we do not quarrel with our friends or make anyone as unhappy as the little girl in the poem. Help us to stretch out our hands and join them in friendship. Make our hands kind and helpful and caring. Amen.

Hymn

No 30, 'You'll sing a song and I'll sing a song', in *Tinder-box: 66 Songs for Children* A. and C. Black (this hymn encourages the children to add further verses of their own) or No 36, 'Look out for loneliness', in *Someone's Singing Lord* A. and C. Black.

Making-Up	5–7
	Assembly
	All

Tell the following story before encouraging the children to make their own paper bag puppets.

For the puppets you will need:

Large paper bags
Material scraps
Paints and paint brushes
Strong glue
Dowling rods
String

Three usually good friends, Sonam, Idris and Goutam were doing nothing but fighting and annoying each other. The three boys originally all came from different parts of the world. Sonam came from Tibet, Idris came from Saudi Arabia and Goutam came from India, but now they were all in the same class at school and usually, they were the best of friends, except on this particular day.

The teacher had been cross with the boys for being so noisy and for not getting on with their work and now it was time to go home and they were still fighting when their parents came to collect them. The teacher had asked all the children in the class to make a paper bag puppet over the weekend for a puppet play that she wanted them to perform on Monday morning.

She had promised that she would give a prize for the best puppet. As the three friends were being so naughty, the teacher jokingly said to them, 'I think you had better make monster puppets as you are all behaving like little monsters.' Everyone giggled, except for the three boys who remained sullen and cross. Goutam said, 'I don't know how to make a puppet.' Idris said that he had not got any paints and so he could not possibly make one either. Sonam just looked like a crosspatch. The teacher said that they had better do as they were told, or else they would miss the special treat that she had planned for *all* the children the following week.

Sonam, Idris, and Goutam had left school still grumbling and returned home. They did not know how they were going to do what the Teacher had asked and they became just as naughty at home as they had been that day. Each boy quarrelled with his small brothers and sisters about which television programmes they were going to watch. They flicked the food on their plates at tea-time and they squirted water in the bathroom. In the end all three sets of parents had had enough and sent each boy to bed early and told them that they had better get up in a more suitable frame of mind the following morning.

Goutam's Mum and Dad had a grocer's shop and sometimes on a Saturday morning, Goutam would help his Dad put out all the fresh vegetables. On this particular Saturday morning, Goutam started to help his Dad as usual, when suddenly, he saw his Dad empty a new paper sack of potatoes into the display box. 'Dad,' he said, 'Could I have that large paper sack to make a puppet?' 'Of course you can', said his father and picked up the bag for his son.

Sonam's Mum made beautiful clothes and she would often go to the market and buy a few metres of brightly coloured material to make dresses or blouses for the girls or for herself. On this particular Saturday morning, Sonam was watching his mother sew and he said that he was bored and did not know what to do with himself. His Mother said, 'Why don't you sort out my material box for me? Put all the same colours together. For instance, all the blue materials in one pile and all the red materials in another pile and so on.' She asked him to put all the large pieces of material together and place all the small scraps in a bag. Sonam had a wonderful time sorting out all the materials and made a huge pile of scraps. There were silvery-gold materials, sparkly reds, browns and yellows; iridescent blues and shiny mauves and beautiful shades of green scraps.

Idris in the meantime, had decided that he had better try and be good on this particular Saturday morning, as his Mum and Dad had been so cross with him the night before. So he played really nicely with his younger brothers and sisters. They played with the cars and the Lego and the farm set and the jigsaws and when Dad came home for lunch, Idris' Mum told his Dad that Idris had been so good that she would like to buy him a small present. 'What would you like?' They asked him. 'Well, I would really like some paints,' he said. So that afternoon, Idris' Mum bought him a set of lovely thick paints and some paint brushes.

It was then that Idris remembered that he was supposed to make a paper bag puppet over the weekend for school on Monday. 'But I can't make a puppet,' he said miserably, 'because I haven't got a paper bag.' His Mum offered him a plastic bag, but he said that would not do. 'Why don't you go and see Goutam, I'm sure his Dad will have a few paper bags to spare in his shop.' Idris thought for a minute and he said, 'No, I couldn't possibly do that, we were fighting yesterday and we are not friends any more.' 'Well, that's a pity,' said his Mum, 'as I don't see how you can make a paper bag puppet without a paper bag.'

Meanwhile, Goutam had taken the paper bag upstairs that his father had given him, but he was feeling very cross, because he only had a pencil at home and he could not make a face for his puppet. He screwed up the bag and threw it on the floor. He thought that it did not even look like a monster with just a pencil face and no hair.

Sonam in the meantime, had finished sorting out his mother's materials and his mother said that he could have the bag of brightly coloured scraps to take to school and to give his teacher on Monday. Sonam thought that this was a very good idea, but suddenly, he remembered that he was supposed to be making a paper bag puppet over the weekend and that although he had lots of lovely material that he could use for clothes and hair, he did not have any paper bags. 'Why don't you go and ask Goutam for a bag,' his mother said. Sonam remembered that he had broken friends with Goutam and Idris the day before, so he could not possibly ask Goutam for a paper bag. 'That's a pity,' said his Mum, 'as I don't know how you can make a paper bag puppet without a paper bag.'

It was then that the three friends came to their senses. Idris thought that if he did go and see his friend Goutam and say that he was sorry, he could ask Goutam if he would let him have a paper bag to make a puppet and he would let Goutam use his paints. Goutam too, had been feeling very sorry for quarrelling with his two best friends and so he too, thought that if he asked his Dad for *two more* paper sacks, he could make amends by giving each of his friends a bag. Perhaps they could all make the puppets together. Sonam also decided that it was silly to remain at logger-heads with his two best mates, when he could share his huge bag of materials with them to make things.

So it was that each boy set out clutching their gifts for the others. Goutam took three paper sacks, Idris took his set of paints and brushes, Sonam took his bag of materials. They met in the middle of the street and when they realized that they had all set out with the same idea of helping each other, they burst out laughing and became friends once more. They went back to Sonam's home as Sonam's Mum had a huge work table. They cut Sonam's material scraps and stuck them onto Goutam's paper bags and they painted huge eyes and mouths with Idris' paints, amidst peels of laughter. After working together for the whole afternoon, they decided that they had created the three best puppets they had ever seen.

On Monday morning, they could hardly wait to show their teacher the results of their efforts and to tell her how they had all helped each other. The teacher said that the puppets *were indeed*, the best ones produced, so they tied for the First Prize. 'You have cooperated so well by making the puppets together. I wonder if you can cooperate by sharing the prize?' 'Whatever is it?' they asked eagerly. 'A huge box of chocolates,' the teacher said. They put their heads together and whispered for a moment, then they smiled. 'Yes, we will share the prize and we will give everyone in the class a chocolate for making their lovely puppets too.' Everyone smiled and clapped.

Prayer

Father God, help us to make friends quickly after a quarrel and to share our things with each other. Help us to know that when we cooperate with each other, we can achieve so much more. Amen

Hymn

No 148, 'Let the world rejoice together' in *Come and Praise 11* (BBC).

Muhammad ﷺ Shows a Way to Remain Friends

(It should be noted that when speaking Muhammad's ﷺ name, Muslims pay respect to him, by saying the words 'Peace be upon him' or writing the sign for this ﷺ).

The Ka'aba in Makkah is the most sacred shrine of Islam. It is a cube-shaped building which has stood in the centre of the great mosque's courtyard in that city for many centuries. It is believed to date back to the time of Ibrahim. Muslims, during Hajj or pilgrimage, always walk around the Ka'aba seven times and touch or kiss the Black Stone which is set into one corner.

Traditionally, it is believed that the stone, then white, was given to Ibrahim by the Angel Jibra'il. It turned black with all the sins of the world. It is very sacred to all Muslims.

There is a story told about Muhammad ﷺ and the Black Stone, which showed his wisdom in dealing with people and helping them to avoid strife.

In the Sixth Century, the Ka'aba was flooded and had to be rebuilt. The rebuilding work began, and when it was nearly finished, the moment came when the black stone had to be reset into the wall of the Ka'aba. There were many eminent Arabian chiefs helping with the work and they each felt that they should have the honour to replace the stone. They argued and grumbled about who was the most important amongst themselves and therefore, who should have this honour.

Tempers flew, nerves became tattered and everyone shouted and argued at once. First one chief pushed forward and then another, and another and another and so on, all claiming to have the right to do the honours. Eventually, one chief said, 'Since we cannot decide who should have this honour, let us wait and ask the first person who comes to the Ka'aba to settle our dispute'. The first person to walk through the courtyard at that very moment was Muhammad ﷺ .

Once again voices rose in anger as various chiefs tried to explain the problem to Muhammad ﷺ and each laid claim to the honour of replacing the stone.

Muhammad ﷺ was absolutely silent for a moment and the noise died down, as everyone waited expectantly for Muhammad ﷺ to choose the most favoured person. In a strong voice Muhammad ﷺ asked for a sheet to be brought to him. 'A sheet, a sheet', the word whistled around the perplexed onlookers. Eventually, a sheet was found and brought to Muhammad ﷺ . He told all the chiefs to take hold of the sheet and carefully edge the stone into the middle of it, without touching the stone. The chiefs did as they were told and soon the stone was safely in the middle of the sheet. Then Muhammad ﷺ told the chiefs to raise the sheet to the level of the wall where the stone was to be replaced and to gently ease it into position. This they did with great care and the stone fell into place in exactly the right spot. As the chiefs lowered the sheet they were all beaming and smiling and shaking hands. Muhammad ﷺ had turned a ferocious argument into a moment of friendship. How wise he was. Could we turn a problem like that into a solution?

Prayer

Almighty God, help us to turn difficult situations into pleasant ones, arguments into friendships. Amen.

The Unforgiving Servant

(From P. Burbridge and M. Watts (1979) *Time to Act* (Hodder and Stoughton).

Act out the following play to demonstrate the need to forgive one another in all sorts of relationships. You will need the following characters: Two narrators, King, Servant, Wife, Children, Friend and Two Armed Guards.

One:	The disciple Peter said to Jesus:
Two:	How often must I forgive someone who hurts me?
One:	And Jesus said to Peter:
Two:	Think of a number too big to think of.
One:	And while Peter was thinking,
Two:	Jesus told the following story:
One:	The Kingdom of Heaven
Two:	Is rather like
One:	This.
Two:	There was a king.
	(*Enter KING computing accounts with a notebook and pencil.*)
	Settling accounts with his servants.
One:	And there was a servant
Two:	Settling accounts with the king.
	(*Enter SERVANT with enormous debt hung round his neck.*)
One:	And the servant owed the king some money.
Two:	Quite a lot of money, really.
One:	Loads and loads of it, in fact.
Two:	Hundreds!
One:	Thousands!
Two:	Millions!
One:	Well anyway, it was a lot of money.
Two:	For a chap like him.
One:	A massive great big debt.
Two:	Hanging round his neck.
One:	And he knew that he couldn't pay
Two:	And the king knew that he couldn't pay
One:	And he knew that the king knew that he knew he couldn't pay.
Two:	Which was pretty bad news.
One:	So the king ordered him to be sold as a slave.
Two:	And his wife
One:	And his children
Two:	And all that he possessed.
One:	To go to the liquidators.
Two:	Five quid for his shirt!
One:	Six quid for his shoes!
Two:	Twenty five 'p' for his socks!
One:	(*Holding his nose*). No, leave the socks, mate.

Two: Stop! He shouted.
One: And he fell on his knees – clunk!
Two: And he implored the king to have patience with him.
One: Have patience with me!
Two: He implored.
One: And I will pay you everything!
Two: A likely story.
One: But seeing the poor man's distress
Two: The king was deeply moved.
(*The KING removes a handkerchief, wipes tears from his eyes, wrings out the handkerchief and replaces it.*)
One: In one short moment he forgave the man the whole debt!
Two: The whole lot.
(*The KING strikes out the debt and leaves.*)
One: Forgiven
Two: In a moment.
One: Just like that.
Two: Wow!
One: Cor!
Two: Incredible!
One: Too much!
Two: Needless to say, the man was very pleased
One: And he went on his way, merrily
(*NARRATOR ONE whistles nonchantly*).
Two: On his way, he bumped into a friend.
(*Enter FRIEND*)
One: Who owed him a fiver.
Two: Aha! You owe me five quid.
One: Seizing him briskly by the throat.
Two: What do you say to that?
One: (*Strangled noise*).
Two: That's no excuse!
One: But the man fell on his knees – clunk!
Two: And implored the servant to have patience with him.
One: Have patience with me!
Two: He implored.
One: And I will pay you everything!
Two: But, ignoring the poor man's distress,
One: He flung him into jail
Two: Until the debt was paid in full.
(*The SERVANT drags his friend by the scruff of the neck and throws him off stage.*)
One: But the king
Two: Who kept his ears to the ground
(*Enter KING, listening to the ground.*)
One: Heard about this
Two: And what he heard made him extremely angry.
One: In anger he summoned the servant before him.

Two: 'You wicked servant!'
One: He said, angrily.
Two: 'Think of all that I forgave you.
One: Think of what you refused to forgive.
Two: I showed you mercy.
One: You showed him none.
Two: Therefore I will show you none'.
One: And the servant was sent to jail.
       (*Enter TWO ARMED GUARDS who remove the trembling SERVANT.*)
Two: Where he would be very well looked after.
One: (*He laughs knowingly*). Nya, nya, nya, nya . . .
Two: Until his debt was paid in full.
One: And the king said:
       (*The KING comes forward, as if to address the audience.*)
Two: 'Think carefully.
One: This will happen to you as well,
Two: If you do not forgive your brother
One: From your heart.'

(N.B. Permission for a *public* performance of this sketch should be obtained from P. Burbridge and M. Watts, P.O. Box 223, York, Y01 1GW.)

Prayer

Father, you always forgive us when we do wrong, and you go on loving us in spite of our misdeeds. Help us to be forgiving to others when they wrong us. Amen.

Hymn

No 35, 'I'm forgiven', in *Songs of Fellowship* (Kingsway).

Giving and Sharing   7–11
                                                     Assembly
                                                          All

(Written by E.C. Peirce, the play was first broadcast on BBC Radio Programme *Discovery*, 3 December 1987).

Children need to develop an awareness of others being worse off than themselves. They need to see the value of sharing whatever they have. They might like to consider the question of whether it is right that half the world is starving and the other half has too much to eat.

This assembly is designed to consider people in the Third World and perhaps offer children an opportunity to give up some of their time, talents and money to help someone in need.

Much material could be displayed showing the needs of the homeless and hungry in other parts of the world. A scrapbook showing children in need and organizations that help could be made by the children. Many or a few children could act this story. If the whole class participates, the children should be divided into two groups. Two main characters are needed: an English boy and a West African boy (or a child from another disaster area). Approximately half the class should stand behind each boy, and as the story develops these children could mime the appropriate actions. Simple labels could be worn to assist with characterization, e.g. mother, father, shopkeeper, school children, West African people. Simple props can be used such as knives, forks, spoons and bowls for meal times, a Coca Cola tin, nurse's headdress, knitting needles, newspaper. Spot lighting could be used to highlight the different sides of the stage.

The teacher introduces the activity: 'As young as we are, we can all share what we have with others. The story that we are going to act for you today is about one boy who has too much and another boy who does not have enough.'

English boy: When I woke up this morning, my mum gave me sausages, eggs and beans for breakfast. I didn't want the eggs, so I left them on my plate. (*Munches food and pushes plate aside. Mother seen cooking.*)

West African boy: I couldn't sleep last night because I felt so hungry and thirsty. There is a drought and the waterhole has dried up, so I couldn't have a drink. (*Curls up and tries to sleep. Mother and father sadly shake heads.*)

English boy: We had fish fingers, chips and peas for school dinners today. I don't like peas, so I told the dinner lady I didn't want them. (*All the children eat their dinners. The dinner lady takes plate away.*)

West African boy: Every day we are told to report to a camp, ten miles from our home. I am tired and weary and my feet are sore. When we arrive at the camp there is no food left. (*Turns hands, palms upwards, in despair. Long queue of children with empty food bowls trudge up to the nurse, who shakes her head. Then queue sits down.*)

English boy: On the way home from school I spent £5.00 on chocolates, crisps, fruit gums and a fizzy drink. (*Shopkeeper gives items to boy. Boy drinks from Coca Cola tin.*)

West African boy: My father has not got any money. We had some cows, but they died when the drought started. We stand in the queue all day, waiting for a little powdered milk. (*Queue lines up again. Nurse starts to give out some food.*)

English boy: Tonight we had roast chicken and roast potatoes and I went to bed feeling full and ready for sleep. (*Family sits round enjoying evening meal.*)

West African boy: I try to go to sleep but I feel cold and hungry. It is now three days since I have eaten any food. (*Mother cuddles children for warmth.*)

English boy: Princess Anne is on the TV. She is asking us to give some money to help save the children in the Gambia (or other appropriate country). I don't think I'll bother. The people are so far away and I'm sure the money will never get there. I think I'll watch *Star Trek*. (*Sits down and watches TV; Father reads newspaper. Mother does her knitting.*)

West African boy: Some lady has promised to try and get us some food. But we are told it will take many weeks, months, even. Many of us will die before then. (*The rest of the class lie down quietly.*)

English boy: I look around and I see people eating and laughing and growing fat. My Mum's on a diet. (*Lots of people eating, drinking, laughing.*)

West African boy: I look around and I see crying and dying and sad people.

Teacher: We can't all send our pocket money to help the West African families, but perhaps we can have a collection in school for Save the Children Fund, or a charity that helps children (see below), or our local Children's Home. Perhaps we can join a scheme to sponsor a West African child. By sending regular amounts of money to that country we can save one person from starvation. Let us pray for all people in this country and abroad who do not have enough to eat.

Prayer

Heavenly Father, help each one of us to be ready to share what we have with our neighbour. We pray especially for all those people who do not have enough to eat and we ask that those who have plenty will be ready to share whatever they have with those who have nothing. Amen.

Hymn

No 35, 'When I needed a neighbour', in *Someone's Singing Lord* A. and C. Black.

Charities That Help Children

BBC Children in Need
Christian Aid
Dr Barnardo's
National Children's Home
NSPCC
Oxfam
Save the Children Fund
Scope (Children with cerebral palsy)
Shaftesbury (Supporting children with disabilities)
Tearfund
UNICEF
Word Vision (Sponsor a child) Free phone: 0800 501010
    General Enquiries: 599 Avebury Boulevard, Milton Keynes MK9 3PG
    Tel: 01908 841010 for work in Africa, India, Cambodia, Armenia, Romania, etc.

Website for Top 100 Charities
BUBL UK: UK Registered Charities: Children
Http://bubl.ac.uk/uk/charities/kid.htm

The Lion and The Mouse

This mime demonstrates that everyone can help each other. You will need:

Characters	*Props*
A lion	A lion mask, or neck ruff made out of crêpe paper, a long tail
A mouse	A mouse mask, or a simple pair of ears; whiskers can be painted on face.
Four hunters	Anoraks or camouflage jackets can be worn
Three (or more) trees	Twig headdress, or crêpe paper attached to arms; brown paper wrapped round trunks
One narrator	Large piece of netting (fisherman's or garden netting will do)

The main elements of the story are as follows. The narrator sets the scene by telling the children that the stage is the jungle; he points to the trees as they take up their positions (*enter trees*). The narrator introduces the lion, who lies down, stretches out and goes to sleep in the sun (*enter lion*). The narrator introduces the little mouse who scurries across the stage several times before finally stepping on the lion's tail (*enter mouse*).

The lion jumps up and shouts, 'How dare you wake me up – I will kill you for this!' (*Raises paw about to kill the mouse. The mouse cowers.*) The little mouse pleads with the lion. 'Oh please don't kill me! Some day I might be able to help you.' The lion roars with laughter, 'Oh don't be so silly, how can a little thing like you help me? But, as you are such a funny little mouse, I will let you go this time – only don't wake me up again!'

Narrator: The lion lets the little mouse go (*mouse scampers off stage*) and the lion goes back to sleep. Just then, four hunters came into the jungle. They were hoping to catch a lion to send to the zoo. They were hoping to get a great deal of money. The hunters set a trap using a huge net. (*The hunters hang the net from branches of the trees, then go off stage.*)

Narrator: The lion wakes up. Stretches, yawns and goes for a walk. By accident, the lion walks straight into the trap. (*The trees throw the net over the lion, who collapses onto the ground.*) The lion struggles and struggles to try and get out and at last he gives up, feeling exhausted. The whole jungle could hear his pitiful cries. Suddenly, the little mouse scampers up to the lion and says, 'Let me help you. I can set you free' (*enter mouse*).

The lion says, 'How can you possibly set me free? If a strong lion like me can't get out of this net, you couldn't possibly help me.' 'Oh yes, I can', says the little mouse.

Narrator: The little mouse began to gnaw through the net, first in one place, then another, then another. Suddenly, the lion is free. The lion thanks the mouse. They shake hands and both scamper off.

The teacher needs to draw the threads together by saying something like: 'Who would have believed that a little tiny mouse could have helped a great big lion? However small we are, we can still do helpful and kindly acts for others. Can *you* think of ways that you can be helpful today?'

Perhaps the teacher could remind the children about those youngsters who received bravery awards at Buckingham Palace. But it is important to stress that small and simple acts of helpfulness are just as important as those seen on TV and that if children make an effort to do the small things in life, they will be ready to do the big things, when the situation occurs.

Prayer

Heavenly Father, help us to be ready to do a thoughtful deed or a kindly action whenever the opportunity arises. Amen.

Hymn

No 38, 'Think, think on these things', in *Someone's Singing Lord* A. and C. Black.

The Enemy Who Became a Friend

7–11
Assembly
Christianity

This true story from World War II is suitable for older children.

A minister in Burma was preaching about Jesus and helping many people to hide and escape from the Japanese soldiers. One day the minister himself was captured and when he would not give the names of the people who had helped him, he was brutally tortured. Although he was in a great deal of pain, the minister said to his torturer, 'My God has taught me to love my enemies; therefore I forgive you for hurting me.'

After the war was over the minister went back to England and he did not return to Burma for many years. However, one day a group of his old friends wrote to him and invited him back to the small church where he used to preach and from where he had helped so many people during the war. To his great surprise, he came face to face with the torturer of long ago. But what a changed man he saw before him! The man had become a very great Christian, who was helping many, many people. He had become a minister himself and the church was filled with people who wanted to learn more about God.

When the minister from England recognized the Japanese minister, he hugged him and rejoiced with him about all the wonderful things that were taking place. When they were alone together, the minister from England asked, 'But why did you become a Christian?' The Japanese minister said, 'But surely, *you* know. After the war, I couldn't forgive myself for all the terrible things that I had done. I couldn't ask forgiveness of the people that I had hurt, as many were dead or missing. One day I came across this small church – your church – and I found a people here who were so loving and forgiving. They took me into their homes and told me about how Jesus could forgive wrongs, however bad. At last I found peace and happiness and I began to study the Bible. Then I was baptized and confirmed and now I am a Minister.'

Prayer

Heavenly Father, we thank you that Jesus taught us how to forgive others. Help us to be forgiving too. Amen.

Hymn

No 51, 'The Lord's Prayer', in *Come and Praise*, (BBC).

True Love

5–11
Assembly
All

This adaptation of the classic O. Henry story is a lovely story about selflessness. Four main characters are needed to mime the actions as the story is read aloud:

    A little old man
    A little old woman (with beautiful long hair)
    A hairdresser
    A jeweller

Some simple props are needed:

    A hairbrush
    A 'gold' clasp for hair
    A ribbon
    A hairnet and scarf (to hide hair 'cut off')
    A 'gold' watch
    A 'gold' chain
    A large pair of scissors
    An empty purse
    Two pieces of wrapping paper

Before the story begins, the little old couple sit in the centre of the stage; the hairdresser sits on the left with simple props and large scissors; the jeweller sits on the right of the stage with the 'gold' chain and 'gold' clasp.

   As the story unfolds the main characters mime the actions. The little old lady brushes her beautiful long hair; the little old man takes out his watch and admires it. The hairdresser makes huge cutting movements as the hair is cut off and later ties the child's real hair up with the aid of a hairnet and scarf. The jeweller holds up the beautiful clip and the gold chain for everyone to see and later sells the presents to the old couple.

The old couple wrap the presents and exchange gifts.

Once upon a time there lived an old man and an old woman. They were very poor and hardly had enough money to buy food. But they loved each other dearly and would do anything for each other. They loved God and had learned much about His ways.

The little old lady had beautiful long hair which she brushed every day (*brush hair*). It was her proudest possession. She longed for a bright clip to tie back her hair. She had seen one in a jeweller's shop (*jeweller show clip*), but she knew it was far too expensive, and so she made do with a ribbon (*tie with a ribbon*).

She never told her husband that she wanted the clip so badly, but he knew and understood because he had seen her gazing longingly at the beautiful hair clip in the jeweller's shop.

The little old man owned a beautiful gold watch; it had been given to him by his grandfather (*show watch*). He loved this watch as it was the most precious thing he owned. Every day he would take it out and look at it. He loved it so because it kept such perfect time. He badly needed a chain to hang it on instead of carrying it about with him (*show chain*). He had seen one in a jeweller's shop, but he never told his wife. Somehow, she knew and understood, because she loved him so.

Soon it was near Christmas, and the little old man and the little old lady began to think and think about what they could buy each other for Christmas. Sadly, the little old lady looked in her purse, but found she had no money left for presents (*look in purse*). The little old man looked in his pockets, but alas, they were empty (*turn out pockets*). Suddenly, the little old lady had a wonderful idea. She knew exactly how she could get some money to buy her husband the very present that he would like best of all.

She knew how she could buy the beautiful gold chain. Often, when she had visited her hairdresser, he had told her that if she ever wanted to sell her hair to make wigs, she could make a great deal of money. So quietly she slipped out of the house without telling her husband and she went to the hairdressers. He took out an enormous pair of scissors and began to cut off all her lovely hair (*cut hair with scissors and disguise hair with hairnet and scarf*). The hairdresser gave her the money that she needed to buy her husband the gold chain (*give money*). She went straight to the jeweller's shop and bought the beautiful gold chain. She hurried home to wrap up the present for her husband (*wrap present*).

In the meantime, the little old man thought and thought about how he could buy the beautiful hair clip for his wife. Suddenly, he had a wonderful idea. If he could sell his beautiful watch, he would get enough money to buy the lovely hair clip for his wife. So he hurried to the jeweller's shop and sold his watch (*give watch to jeweller*). In return, the jeweller gave him the beautiful hair clip (*jeweller give clip*). The little old man hurried home to wrap up the present for his wife (*wrap up clip*).

On Christmas morning the little old man and the little old woman could hardly wait to give each other their presents. The little old man gave his present first (*give presents*). Carefully, she opened the parcel and saw the beautiful clip. She stared down at it and then she pulled off the scarf and she showed him what she had done to her hair. She gave the little old man his present, and when he saw it was the beautiful gold chain, he told her that he had sold his precious watch to buy her the clip. The two old people hugged each other and laughed because they knew that each had sold their most precious possession in order to show each other their great love (*all go and sit down*).

A time for quiet reflection can be kept.

The Chess Game

7–11
Assembly
All

(Based on a story called 'The Chess Match' in R. Brandling (1977) *Assembly Poems and Prose*, Macmillan. The following adaptation by E.C. Peirce was first broadcast on the BBC Schools' radio programme *Discovery*, 1987.)

Darren kicked the tin can between two cars. 'Goal', he shouted. He continued running, kicking imaginary goals, using bits of rubbish that lay scattered along the streets. He no longer noticed the slogans painted on the walls of the flats, or the windows boarded over where the occupants were tired of replacing broken glass.

He continued running until he reached his own block of flats. He used to live on the fourteenth floor. He smiled when he remembered how, as a little lad, he couldn't reach the lift button for Floor 14, so he had to press the button for the sixth floor and walk the rest of the way up. Now he lived on the sixth floor, ever since his mum had told the Council man that she couldn't get three children down the stairs when the lift wasn't working. The Council man had been very sympathetic, but he said there just wasn't another flat available, and they would have to wait; and anyway the bottom flats were reserved for the elderly, those old people who couldn't walk any distance at all.

Suddenly, Darren remembered one old lady in particular, Mrs Naylor. Darren had done a dreadful thing. He had broken into Mrs Naylor's downstairs flat. He had smashed a small kitchen window and had climbed in to see what he could steal. He would never forget what happened next; he crept silently through the kitchen, looking in pots on top of cupboards, opening drawers and doors – but found nothing. It was then that he decided to creep through to the sitting room. The room was badly lit and was freezing cold, he was certain that there was no one there, so he continued to search for anything valuable.

Quite suddenly, a boney finger curled around his throat and Darren found himself looking into an old wizened face.

A cracked, broken voice pierced his eardrums, 'You'll not find anything here lad', and then a cackle of laughter followed. Darren was rooted to the spot. He couldn't move.

'Now I've had a good look at ye face, I'll recognize ye again. So what's it to be eh? – the police – or never do anything like this again, come on lad, speak up.' Darren couldn't move. Suddenly the peal of cackling laughter echoed around the room again, filling Darren with fear.

'Do ye play chess?' came the eerie voice. Darren nodded, 'well sit down then.'

Darren found himself sitting opposite a chess board with beautifully carved chess pieces all laid out as if the old lady had been playing with someone else.

In the hour that followed everything else was forgotten, as a battle of skills raged, until the old lady wheezed 'checkmate'. Dareen was beaten.

Darren had never been any good at anything at school. His mum had said that if he didn't mend his ways, he would end up in prison.

He smiled now as he remembered his promise to the old lady. He would never break into another flat again, if she didn't tell the police what he had done. In addition, she would teach him to be better at chess than anyone else at school, if he came once a week to play the game with her. He had contemplated never going near the old woman again, but something drew him back each week.

He knew his game was improving. This week he had been picked for the school team to play against a large primary school down the road. The smile on his face broadened into a deep grin as he remembered how he had beaten all his opponents and was now the school champion. He had never told anyone how he had managed to do so well, and he still went to see Mrs Naylor every week.

She had kept her part of the bargain. Now he was looking forward to tonight's match with her. He pressed the lift button for the sixth floor. The lift doors remained tightly closed. No movement. Broken again. He started to climb the dirty, echoey stairs. He would have his tea first and then go and see Mrs Naylor.

He let himself into the flat, his younger brother and sister were fighting and screaming over which TV programme to watch and his mum was washing up at the sink. 'That you Darren? There's a parcel for you on the table.' 'That's odd', thought Darren, 'it's not my birthday, or Christmas.' He rushed over to the table and saw an old, brown paper parcel tied up with string, with his name on it. He quickly undid the knots and then stared down in astonishment. There lay the beautiful chess pieces that had belonged to the old lady. She had left them for him to keep.

> *Teacher*: Why do you think the old lady gave Darren her most treasured possession, especially after the wicked thing he had done to her? Do you think she had forgiven Darren and enjoyed his company? Do you think that she needed his help? Or did Darren need her help in changing his bad behaviour?
>
> What a pity Darren had to learn how nice the old lady was through doing something so dreadful. Still, we can all make mistakes; it is better to say you are sorry and try to put things right than to stay alone, frightened and isolated or even to continue doing those wicked things.

Ask the children to try this week to put right something that they have done wrong, or to make someone else's day worthwhile by being thoughtful or kind to a lonely person.

Prayer

Father, forgive us when we do wrong and help us always to try to put things right. Help us to realize that it is always better to own up, rather than to remain alone and frightened and end up in worse trouble. Amen.

Hymn

No 36, 'Look out for loneliness', in *Someone's Singing Lord*, A. and C. Black.

Study of a Neighbourhood

Many fiction books can be read in an assembly to provide a starting point for bringing a topic sharply into focus. Two such books, which show whole neighbourhoods pulling together in the face of disaster, are: Otto S. Svend (1982) *Children of the Yangtze River*, trans. by Joan Tate, Pelham Books and Shirley Hughes (1997) *Alfie Gets in First*, Red Fox Picture Books. (See overleaf for additional books.)

Children of the Yangtze River is a lovely story about children who are made homeless by a flood. They rebuild their homes and everyone lends a helping hand. This story has proved to be a good discussion starter, particularly for children who have been made homeless for one reason or another. Children can come to terms with disaster when they see how others cope and come to the rescue. The story can also be used to discuss ways in which children in school can collect funds for disaster areas, such as Ethiopia or Armenia.

The second story, *Alfie Gets in First*, shows neighbourhood concern and co-operation when Alfie races home, shuts himself (and his mother's keys) indoors and he cannot get out or let his mother in. First Mrs MacNally tries to help, then Mrs MacNally's Maureen, then the milkman and the window cleaner, all conspire to set him free; but Alfie solves the problem himself by fetching his chair, standing on it and lifting the catch to open the door. Mum repays the neighbourly kindness by inviting everyone in for a cup of tea. This delightful story can be read to the very youngest children to make them aware of how kind neighbours can be.

The assembly could be concluded by asking the children to take a closer look at their neighbourhood and write down a list of ways that they could be more helpful. Examples could include picking up litter, saying a friendly 'hello' to the next-door neighbour, postman, dustman or milkman. Older children could be asked to consider, 'Who is my neighbour?', not necessarily in the vicinity of their home. Examples could include the lady who drops her purse at the supermarket, the child who is lost, disaster areas at home and abroad. What would each child do? Who would be considered the neighbour in each case?

Prayer

Father, we thank you for good neighbours. Show us how we can be neighbourly ourselves. Help us not to miss opportunities to be helpful and caring today. Amen

Hymn

No 37, 'Working together' in *Every Colour Under the Sun* (Ward Lock Educational).

Other Useful Fiction Books on this Theme

Ahlborn, J. (1987) *Jonathan Of Gull Mountain*, R & S Books.
Although this is an imaginary tale about a boy who is born without wings in a world where everyone has wings, it has a serious message regarding handicap. Jonathan's best friend Sara and his Mum and Dad together make him a pair of wings that enable him to fly like his peer group and to participate in school activities. This story has important lessons for us all and how we treat those who have different bodies from our own, or those who are in wheelchairs. It is a lovely narrative about how people can help to solve a desperate problem.

Beresford, E. (1997) *The Smallest Whale*, Orchard.
A wonderful story about cooperation and help from a whole town to save a baby whale that gets separated from his mother and is stranded on a beach. Josh calls the Fire Service and all his friends and neighbours to get buckets of water to help keep the baby whale wet and alive until the tide turns. Eventually all ends happily, with everyone working together and finally managing to push the baby out to sea where he is rejoined by his mother.

Boyd, L. (1988) *The Not-So-Wicked Stepmother*, Puffin.
This has a very important message for all children who are separated from their natural parents and who find themselves being looked after by a 'new' Mum or Dad. The little girl in the story goes to stay with her stepmother and dad for a holiday. She is tearful and determined not to like the new person who has married her dad, or to eat, or to cooperate in any way. However, little by little, she discovers just how wonderful her new stepmother is and she cannot help enjoying herself or joining in and above all, laughing again.

Hoffman, M. (2002) *The Colour of Home*, Frances Lincoln.
Briefly, it tells the story of a little boy from Somalia, remembering the horrors of war from which he and his family fled, and his coming to terms with his new country and neighbourhood.

The Good Me and the Bad Me

5-11
Assembly
All

Each child will need:

>   One piece of card to make a round face
>   (both sides will be used)
>   One piece of paper (with space for five to ten statements on each side;
>   less space will be needed for younger children)
>   Pencil or pen with which to write
>   Felt-tip pens and collage materials to make the face.

Make a model for demonstration purposes:

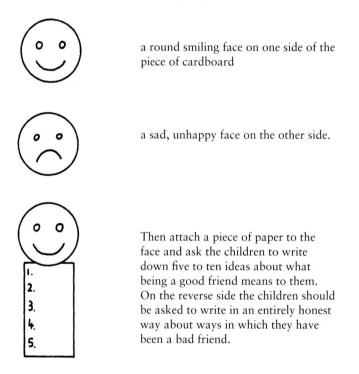

a round smiling face on one side of the piece of cardboard

a sad, unhappy face on the other side.

Then attach a piece of paper to the face and ask the children to write down five to ten ideas about what being a good friend means to them. On the reverse side the children should be asked to write in an entirely honest way about ways in which they have been a bad friend.

   The faces can be decorated with felt-tip pens, wool, string or material for the hair, etc. Select a number of children to read first the good side and then the bad side of friendship to the rest of the school. End with a short prayer of thanks for all our friends.

Hymn

No 43, 'Stick on a smile', in *Every Colour under the Sun*, (Ward Lock Educational).

Jonathan and David

A group of children could act out part of the story of Jonathan and David's friendship. You will need the following characters and props:

Characters	Props
King Saul	Cloak
David	Armour
David's wife	Sword
Jonathan	Belt
Boy Servant	Spear
Chorus	Pile of stones (cardboard boxes)
Narrator	Harp (made out of cardboard)

Narrator: Do you remember the courageous story of how David killed the giant Goliath? Well, King Saul wanted to know who the young boy was and to employ him in his service.

King Saul: Who are you young man?

David: I am David, the son of Jesse, Sir.

King Saul: I want you to work for me; you have proved to be very brave and courageous. I want you to meet my son Jonathan, he is about your age.

Jonathan: I am Jonathan. David, you have shown such courage and bravery that I want to be your friend forever. As a sign of my friendship, I will give you my cloak, armour, sword and belt.

(He puts each item on David.)

David: Thank you Jonathan. I, too, will be your friend forever. Nothing will ever spoil our friendship.

Narrator: David became so successful on all the King's expeditions, that the King made David an officer in his army.

Chorus: Saul has killed thousands, but David has killed *tens* of thousands.

Narrator: Then a very sad thing happened. The King became so jealous of David that he wanted to kill him. You see, the people were singing and praising David for his successes in battle, and King Saul was very afraid that the people would make David King, instead of himself.

Chorus: Saul has killed thousands, but David has killed *tens* of thousands.

Narrator: One day when David was playing his harp, the King threw his spear at David and tried to kill him, but the spear missed David by inches. King Saul told his son Jonathan that he was going to kill David, but, because Jonathan loved David, he told his friend to hide, until he could make his father see sense.

(The actions are mimed in the background)

Jonathan: David, my friend, you must go away and hide, until I can stop my father from trying to kill you.

David: I do not know why your father wants to kill me, but I will do as you say.

(David goes off-stage)

Jonathan: Father, why are you trying to kill David? He has never done you any wrong; on the contrary, he has done nothing but good. Look how he saved us all from the Philistines by killing the giant Goliath.

King Saul: Yes, I suppose you are right, but I am afraid David will take the throne away from you, my son. But because of you, I will not kill him.

Chorus: Saul has killed thousands, but David has killed *tens* of thousands.

Narrator: But King Saul did not keep his promise. He sent his men to kill David in his bed. David's wife overhead the plot to kill David, and helped David to escape. She put a bundle of material in the bed, so that the men would think it was David. When the King found out, he was furious. David went to find his friend Jonathan.

David: What have I done to your father? Why does he want to kill me?

Jonathan: I'm sure he doesn't want to kill you, really. Look, I'll tell you what we'll do. We will make a plan. You go and hide in that large field behind that pile of stones. I will bring my servant into the field to collect the arrows that I shoot. If I shout out that the arrows have fallen *in front* of the stones, you know that you are quite safe and that my father does not want to kill you. But if I shout out that the arrows have gone *beyond* the stones, you will know that my father *does* want to kill you and so you must run away and escape. It is the New Moon festival tomorrow, and if you are not at our dinner table, my father will notice. I will say that you have had to return to Bethlehem. Now look, hurry and do what I say, go and hide.

Narrator: So David went and hid in the field and Jonathan went off to his father's house for the feast. King Saul asked where David was and Jonathan said that David had returned to his home town of Bethlehem. The King was furious and said that as long as David lived, Jonathan would not be king. So King Saul said that he would kill David. Just as Jonathan had promised, he took his servant with him to the fields to shoot arrows. He called out in a loud voice.

(The action is mimed)

Jonathan: Boy, run and fetch my arrows, look they have gone *beyond* those stones.

Narrator: The boy fetched the arrows but could not understand why Jonathan had said that the arrows had gone beyond the stones, because they were in front of the stones. However, he did as he was told and picked up the arrows. Then Jonathan sent the boy back to the city. When he was safely out of the way, he called to David to come out of hiding.

(The action is mimed)

Jonathan: You can come out now, my friend, it is quite safe. But you must get away from this place, you were right, my father does intend to kill you.

Narrator: So Jonathan kept his promise and protected David. They hugged each other and said good-bye. They promised that in spite of their difficulties, they would always remain friends.

(The action is mimed)

King Saul pursued David and tried to kill him many more times, but David always managed to escape. One day David crept up on King Saul as he was resting in a cave, and he cut off a piece of the King's cloak to show the King that he could have killed him, but that he had spared the King's life. When King Saul heard this from David, he broke down and cried, and he said:

'You are more worthy to be King than I'. So eventually David was crowned King.

(The action is mimed in the background)

The teacher needs to draw the threads together by emphasizing the fact that Jonathan's love for his friend, David, saved David's life. Could we be such a true friend in the face of parental opposition?

Prayer

Father God, we thank you for the gift of friendship. Help us not to quarrel or break friends. Help us to be quick to make friends again after an argument. Amen.

Hymn

No 35, 'Take care of a friend', in *Every Colour Under the Sun* (Ward Lock Educational).

4 FESTIVALS

Ramadan and The Festival of Eid-ul-Fitr

7–11
Assembly
Islam

Ramadan or the month of fasting, is a very important month in the Islamic calendar. It is the ninth Islamic month and Muslims believe that it was during this period, that the Angel Jibra'il spoke the sacred words to Muhammad ﷺ, who ordered them to be written down and later collected as their Holy Book, the Qur'an. (See p. 247 for a note regarding the date of the festival.)

During the hours of daylight, Muslims must not eat or drink anything. The fast begins when the new moon is seen at the beginning of the month and ends when the new moon is seen at the end of the month. Muslims can have a drink and a meal from sunset to dawn but not during daylight. Very young children and old or sick people are excused the fast. Muslims keep this time as a reminder of what it is like to be poor and hungry and because God commands it in the Qur'an.

At the end of the period, the Eid-ul-Fitr Festival is held. It is a time of great joy and feasting. New clothes are bought, cards and presents are sent to friends and relations, and money is given to the poor. But the day always begins with prayers at the Mosque.

Prayers are always preceded by the usual pattern of washing. Hands, mouth, nose, face, arms, head, ears, neck and feet must all be washed before the prayers can begin. Every Muslim has to learn the set pattern of prayers and prayer positions and must face towards Makkah (Mecca). Shoes must be removed as a mark of respect for God. Women pray in a special part of the Mosque, away from the men.

There are three aids to prayer that are used; a prayer mat, (obligatory) prayer beads to remind Muslims of the 99 names for God in the Qur'an, and a compass to show the direction of Makkah.

Find out about making Eid sweets, or design Eid cards using Arabic calligraphy (not people or animals). Ask Muslim children in the class to write about what they do at the Festival and perhaps show their new clothes to the school.

Prayer

There is a video cassette about prayer available from the Islamic Cultural Centre and Central Mosque
146, Park Road,
London
NW8 7RG
Tel: 020 7724 3363
email: Islamic200@aol.com
website: www.islamicculturalcentre.co.uk

Resources

There are some useful books in the Information for Teachers section on pp. 248–9.

Harvest: A Loaf of Bread

5–11
Assembly
All

This harvest thanksgiving service is about all those involved in the production and distribution of bread. (Based on an idea given to the author by Revd D. Jennings, Eastbourne. Reproduced with the kind permission of G. Jennings.)

Buy a large farmhouse loaf. Cut the top off very carefully so that it can be replaced. Hollow out the centre of the loaf. Put the following miniature toys inside, representing those involved in the processes of breadmaking:

> parent or carer
> supermarket worker or shopkeeper
> van driver
> factory worker or baker
> lorry driver
> mill worker
> driver of combine harvester
> farmer
> seed

Show the children the loaf of bread and explain that the aim of the service is to give thanks for all those involved in the production and distribution of bread. Ask the children whom they think that they should thank. Now take the top off the loaf and take out the characters with a brief description of their work. Pause and give thanks for each concerned. Finally, give thanks to God, for only He can make a seed and provide the right conditions for the seed to grow.

Hymn

No 56, 'We plough the fields', in *Infant Praise* (Oxford University Press) or No. 55, 'When the corn is planted', in *Someone's Singing Lord*, A. and C. Black.

Sukkot

7–11
Assembly
Judaism

Build a sukkah (a small hut) for the Jewish Harvest Festival of Sukkot.

The school indoor or outdoor climbing frame would be ideal for building a sukkah. Sukkot (plural of sukkah) takes place in the Jewish month of Tishri, about the same time as Christians celebrate Harvest Festival.

Jews often build their sukkah (or tabernacle) in their gardens, or decorate a special garden shed with all sorts of harvest gifts like oranges, apples and grapes. The roof, although covered with branches, should be open to the sky as a reminder to the Jewish people of the tents in which their ancestors camped, during the forty years they spent wandering in the wilderness, over 3000 years ago.

Many families today build their sukkah not only to thank God for His goodness in providing the food we eat, but also as a reminder that God has taken care of His people throughout history. The festival lasts for eight days and Jewish families try to eat many of their meals outside in their tabernacle.

There are four important symbols related to Sukkot. The first is the etrog or lemon. The second is the lulav or branches from a palm tree. The third is a branch of myrtle and the fourth, a willow branch. There are many interpretations of these symbols, one might be to represent the four elements, fire, air, earth and water, respectively. These symbols are then tied together and carried by the worshippers as a reminder of the good things that God has provided. The worshippers then point the branches in every direction showing God's goodness is all around us.

Perhaps four children could hold up the symbols and say in turn what they represent. Then the whole school could learn Psalm 117 and say it together:

Psalm 117

Praise the Lord, all nations!
Praise him, all peoples!
His love for us is strong
and his faithfulness is eternal.
Praise the Lord!

(From the *Good News Bible*)

Activity

Divide the class into four groups representing earth, wind, fire and water. Simple costumes could be made to indicate each element, i.e. Flaming headdresses for fire; strips of blue/green crêpe paper hanging from shoulders to hands for water; green leaf-shaped hats for earth; and filmy sheets of chiffon for wind.

Let each group say who they are and how they help people and then dance or move to their piece of music. (Suitable pieces of music can be found on many classical CDs. Or use pop music). End with a simple prayer.

Prayer

Thank you God for all your precious gifts to us. Especially for the good earth, the wind, fire and water. Amen.

Hymn

Sing the song 'Hodu L'Adonai Ki Tov', 'Thank the Lord, for He is good', printed below from *Sephardic Songs of Praise*, by Abraham Lopes Cardozo (Tara Publications).

Hodu L'Adonai Ki Tov

This is from the Hallel (Praise), Psalms 113–118 which are sung, among other times, on Sukkot, Pesah and Shavuot. (See pronunciation guide on pp. 229–33.) This is part of Psalm 118.

> *Hodu l'Adonai ki tov, ki l'olam hasdo.*
> *Yomar na Yisrael, ki l'olam hasdo.*
> *Yomru na weyt aharon, ki l'olam hasdo.*
> *Yomru na yirei Adonai, ki l'olam hasdo*

Thank the Lord, for He is good,
    for His love is everlasting.
Let Israel now say:
    'For His love is everlasting.'
Let the house of Aaron now say:
    'For His love is everlasting.'
Let all who fear the Lord now say:
    'For His love is everlasting.'

Harvest of Ourselves

5–11
Assembly
All

This harvest festival presentation progresses from giving the usual harvest festival gifts to the more unusual idea of offering our own talents as our harvest gifts.

Narrator: We are going to praise God for the many different kinds of harvest. We shall present this in music, movement and mime. The first kind of harvest that we thank God for is the *harvest of the land*. Watch the seeds unfurling and growing.

> (*A group of children slowly unfurl and grow tall. Simple costumes can be worn – green jumpers and tights, perhaps some thin strips of crêpe paper attached to the hands and elbows to represent unfurling leaves. The children uncurl slowly to the sound of tambourines played by a small group of musicians or tape-recorded music can be used.*)

Narrator: We thank God for all the men and women who work in the factories processing the food that we eat. Here are some of the machines.

> (*A group of children move like robots or machines. Robot masks can be worn or different sized cardboard cogs can be attached to ordinary clothing. Tape-record some 'machine' music.*)

Narrator: We praise God for the *harvest of the sea*. Watch the fishermen haul in their nets, bringing us fish to eat.

> (*A fisherman's net could be borrowed, or use a few metres of vegetable netting to depict the fishermen hauling in their catch. Brightly painted paper fish could be attached to the netting. The children could wear oilskins, wellington boots or warm clothing and knitted hats. Musicians could play some 'sea' music, or use the water music from* Carnival of the Animals *by Saint Saëns.*)

Narrator: *Miners* go deep into the earth to bring us coal to give us warmth and heat and light, as well as many other things that we use daily. Years ago women and children hauled the coal out of the mines.

> (*A group of children could mime the miners at work. Faces should be made dirty and smudged. Dark clothes, balaclava hats and a real miner's lamp would help to add authenticity. Xylophones or tape-recorded music could assist the action.*)

Narrator: Finally, we are going to show our thanks to God for his rich harvest by offering our own talents, big or small, as our harvest gift.

> The children will show either what they can do *now*, or what they would like to do when they *grow up*. (*Each child takes his or her turn to mime something useful – putting a caring arm around a child who is crying; carrying a heavy basket of shopping for an old lady; doing the washing*

up for Mum or Dad; singing in the choir; taking part in the school sports; playing a musical instrument. Appropriate costumes, or a simple label can be worn to depict the particular talent being offered, e.g. leotard for the gymnast. Suitable music could be tape-recorded for each child's action.)

Narrator: This is the harvest of our school. We are all working together, so that we can produce a rich harvest of talents.

(*The children could make up their own prayers about striving for excellence in all things.*)

Prayer

Father God, we thank you for your wonderful harvest gifts to us. We thank you for the harvest of the land, the harvest of the sea, the harvest of the mines, and the harvest from the factories. We offer ourselves today, to live and work for you. May our school produce a rich harvest of talents. Amen.

Hymn

No 56, 'The farmer comes to scatter the seed,' in *Someone's Singing Lord* A. and C. Black.

Animals and Insects Giving for Our Harvest   5–9
Activity/Assembly
All
(Preparation needed)

Choose four or five animals or insects to study in depth, e.g. sheep, cows, chickens, goats, bees. Classbooks, pictures, posters, real life examples (if possible) can be gathered together to form the final assembly after many weeks of careful study and preparation. Each animal could form the basis of one assembly before the finale when all the work is shown. Take each animal in turn and find out as much as possible.

Sheep

Write to The British Wool Marketing Board for information on different breeds of sheep:

Education Department
Wool House,
Roysdale Way
Euroway Trading Estate
Bradford
West Yorkshire BD4 65E

Tel: 01274 688666
Fax: 01274 652233
email: mail@britishwool.org.uk

If possible, invite a farmer to bring a sheep into school. (You will need to check your school's *Health and Safety Policy*, for guidance.) Collect some sheep's wool from fences around fields or send for the *fleece sample cards* and *processing samples* from the address above. Ask the children to make a list and paint or draw all the things that are made of wool. If possible, try to dye some wool using natural dyes like beetroot or other vegetables. Try to find pictures of old spinning wheels. If you know someone who can spin, invite him or her into school or perhaps visit a mill. Make a classbook about all the things you have learned about sheep. (See page 155 for a story about sheep).

   Let the children tell the whole school something that they have learned about sheep; or let the children hold up their pictures or experiments with wool; or invite the farmer into school to talk about the sheep's year from lambing to shearing. (See page 154).

Resources

Bell, R. (2001) *Sheep*, Farm Animals Series, Reed Educational and Professional Publishing Ltd.
Birch, B. (1990) *Discover a Shepherd's Year*, Simon and Schuster Young Books.
Doughty, S. (1990) *Let's Visit A Sheep Farm*, Hodder Wayland.
Moon, C. (1983) *Sheep on The Farm*, Hodder Wayland.
Potter, T. and Bailey, D. (1989) *Sheep*, Macmillan.
Royston, A. (1992) *Lamb*, See How They Grow Series, Dorling Kindersley.
Royston, A. (1989) *The Sheep Farm*, Animal Stories, Kingfisher Books.

Hymn

No 48, 'The Lord's my Shepherd' in *Come and Praise* (BBC).

Cows

Write to the Dairy Council for lots of free information about the different breeds of cow, fact sheets, dairy leaflets/booklets, posters (small charge), Early Years Teaching Pack (small charge), video (small charge), CD ROM, etc. All the information is carefully graded for different Key Stages of Education:

The Dairy Council
Education Department
5–7 John Princes Street
London W1G 0JN

Tel: 0207 74997822
Fax: 0207 4081353
e-mail: info@dairycouncil.org.uk
website: www.milk.co.uk

Milk, cream, butter, and cheese all come from cows. Find out about the different breeds of cows. What do they eat? Find out how cows are milked. How many pints could one cow produce in her lactation period? (Answer: 24,000 pints). How is milk measured? What happens to the milk at the dairy? Find out about the different uses for milk; cream, butter, skimmed milk, yoghurt, cheese, etc. Conduct research on old-fashioned milk pails, shoulder yokes and churns. Learn about George Barham, who in 1566 became the first man to start a dairy company in London. Make a map of England and put a flag on the spot where these cheeses come from: Wensleydale, Lancashire, English Cheshire, Derby, Leicester, Stilton, Caerphilly, Double Gloucester, English Cheddar. Do you have a local cheese? Perhaps the cheesemaker could come to the school and explain the process of cheesemaking, or better still, visit the place where it is made. Try to find out about cheeses from around the world.

Resources

Doughty, S. and Bentley, D. (1989) *Let's Visit A Dairy Farm*, Hodder Wayland.
Moon, C. (1986) *Dairy Cows On The Farm*, Hodder Wayland.
Palmer, J. (1989) *Dairy Farming*, Hodder and Stoughton.
Patterson, G. (1996) *Dairy Farming*, Farming Press Books.
Pepper, S. (1985) *Dairy Farmer*, Franklin Watts.
Potter, T. and Bailey, D. (1996) *Cows, My World Series*, Heinemann.
Powell, J. (2001) *How do they Grow? From calf to cow*, Hodder Children's Books.
Royston, A. (1989) *Farm Animal Stories: The Cow*, Kingfisher Books.
The Duchess of Devonshire (1991) *Farm Animals*, Kyle Cathie.
Wood, T. (1988) *Spotlight on Farm Animals*, Franklin Watts.

Hymn

No 53, Verse 3, 'The cows and sheep in the meadows', from 'The flowers that grow in the garden', in *Someone's Singing Lord* A. and C. Black.

Chickens

Write to Poultry World for charts about all the different breeds of chicken, etc. There is a small charge for these:

> Poultry World
> Quadrant House
> The Quadrant
> Sutton
> Surrey SM2 5AS
>
> Tel: 0208 6524031
> Fax: 0208 6524042
> e-mail: poultry.world@rbi.uk.co

If possible, set up an incubator in the classroom and hatch your own chickens. It takes 21 days at carefully controlled temperatures; the eggs have to be turned three times a day. Children will learn far more from real experience. Find out about different breeds of chicken. Make a list indicating as many ways as possible that we can use eggs. Make a large diagram of what an egg looks like inside. Show the children how to test whether an egg is fresh or not. Try some egg recipes; perhaps make some meringues. Find out about grading eggs. What is meant by large, standard, medium, small? Is there any difference between brown and white eggs? Try decorating hardboiled/blown eggs. Make an eggshell collage. Explain how some broody chickens make very good foster-mothers and can hatch out ducks or geese as well as chicks. Try and visit a farm and take note of any rare breeds.

Resources

Bell, R. (2000) *Chickens*, Farm Animal Series, Heinemann.
Burton, J. and Taylor, K. (1994) *Egg. A Photographic Story of Hatching*, Dorling Kindersley.
Foster, J. (1991) *Egg Poems*, Oxford University Press.
Moss, M. (1990) *Threads: Eggs*, A and C Black.
Powell, J. (1996) *Eggs*, Hodder Wayland.
Powell, J. (2001) *How Do They Grow Series: From Chick to Chicken*, Hodder Wayland.
Spilsbury, L. (2001) *Eggs (Food)*, Heinemann.

British Egg Information:
Website: www.britegg.co. uk

Hymn

No 2, 'The golden cockerel', in *Someone's Singing Lord* A. and C. Black.

Honeybees

How can honey be used? We can eat it on bread; use it as a substitute for sugar; use it as an antiseptic for cuts; use it to soothe sore throats and coughs; put it in cakes; make honey drinks. Find out all you can about bee-keeping, hives, queens, drones, workers, eggs, larvae and pupae. How can beeswax be used? Make large scale drawings of the queen, workers and drones. Learn about the honeybee's dance: the 'round-dance' and the 'waggle-tail dance'. Perhaps the children could make bee headdresses and show the rest of the school some of the bee dances. How much honey could we expect from one hive? (Answer: approximately 33–44lbs/15–20 kg) Find out how many different coloured honeys there are. Why are they a different colour? Why not set up a small observation hive in school?

Tell the Aesop tale, 'Jupiter and the Bee'. It is a cautionary tale about how the queen bee gets her sting, which if used to sting others, will cause her own death.

Resources

Bailey, J. (1989) *The Life-cycle of a Bee*, Hodder Wayland.
Butterworth, C. (1988) *My World Series, Bees*, Macmillan.
Chinery, M. (1997) *How Bees Make Honey*, Marshall Cavendish.
Claybourne, A. (1994) *How Do Bees Make Honey?* Usborne Starting Science.

Cross, G. (1991) *Bees*, Simon and Schuster.

Free, J.B. (1984) *Honeybees*, A and C Black.

Glease, H.E. (1991) *Bees*, Learning Tree 123, Cherrytree Press Limited.

Hartley, K. and Macro, C. (1998) *Bee*, Bug Book Series, Heinemann.

Jeunesse, G., Fuhr, U., Sautai, R. (1993) *The Bee*, First Discovery Series, Moonlight Publishing Limited.

Ramsay, H. (1997) *How Bees Make Honey*, Blue Rainbows Science Series, Evans Brothers Limited.

Smith, A. (1989) *Bees and Wasps*, Hodder Wayland.

Watts, B. (1989) *Honeybees*, A and C Black.

Woodward, K. (2001) *Honeybees*, Brown Partworks.

Hymn

No 42, 'I love God's tiny creatures' in *Someone's Singing Lord* A. and C. Black.

From a Seed to a Chair

5–11
Assembly
All

The following props are required for this assembly:

    infant wooden chair (or antique chair)
    display of carpenter's tools
    children's display of wooden toys
    acorn
    oak seedling

The assembly could be developed over several days. Start with the chair and describe the process from a seed to the finished product (see brief description below). On the second day invite a carpenter into school to describe each tool and its purpose. Link this with Jesus learning the carpenter's trade and discuss what he might have made. Finally, encourage the children to learn about different woods and appreciate their beauty and versatility. Invite the children to bring wooden items or toys from home to set up a 'wooden' display in school. End the series with a general thanksgiving for trees, timber, skill of the craftsmen, useful and beautiful wooden items. Warn them of the dangers of the mindless destruction of trees and the ruination of the rain forests.

As the first day's activity, look at a wooden chair. Have you ever thought where the wood came from and who made it? One of our most treasured timbers comes from the oak tree, which can grow to the height of 100 feet. However, the oak tree begins its life like this [show acorn]. It grows from a tiny seed. It takes many, many years for an oak tree to grow to the size necessary for cutting down and making into timber for the use of a craftsman. When it has reached maturity, the tree is cut down and sent to the sawmill, where it is cut into smaller pieces of timber. Then it is stacked and allowed to dry for a very long time, otherwise it would twist and warp and be useless. Finally, it can be used by the carpenter, the craftsman who has the tools and the skills to shape the wood (show carpenter's tools). Once the shapes have been made, the carpenter fits all the pieces together with great care and makes a thing of beauty that will last for years and years.

Perhaps the children could try to find out which is the oldest known chair in England, or make a scrapbook depicting different types of chairs, or visit a museum to find out about the various woods from which chairs have been made, or visit a modern furniture factory.

Prayers

Father, we thank you for the wonder and beauty of trees. For the miracle of growth from a tiny seed to a tree such as the mighty oak. May we be preservers of trees, not destroyers. May we each play our part in planting trees for the future. We thank you for the many things that come from wood and the skill of the craftsmen, who shape the wood for our use. Amen.

Or 'The Prayer of the Tree'.

The Prayer of the Tree

You who pass by and would
raise your hand against me,
hearken ere you harm me,
I am the heat of your hearth
on the cold winter night,
the friendly shade screening
you from summer sun,
And my fruits are refreshing
draughts quenching your thirst
as you journey on.
I am the beam that holds your house,
the board of your table,
the bed on which you lie,
the timber that builds your boat,
I am the handle of your hoe,
the door of your homestead,
the wood of your cradle,
the shell of your last resting place.
I am the gift of God and the friend of man.
You who pass by, listen to my prayer,
Harm me not.

Anon.

Hymn

No 18, 'Give to us eyes', in *Someone's Singing Lord* A. and C. Black.

Sharing Our Harvest Gifts: A Bowl of Rice

5–11
Assembly
All

(Adapted from a lesson in M. Ashby (Ed.) *R.E. Handbook: A Resource for Primary School Teachers* (Scripture Union, 1983) (It is reproduced with the kind permission of Scripture Union).

The following props are required for this activity talk.

> A bowl of cooked cold rice
> Spoon
> Nine plates
> Selection of appetizing harvest gifts such as tin of baked beans, ham, peaches, etc.

Choose nine children to come and stand out at the front in a line. Give each child a plate. Give every third child a spoonful of rice. Ask for the children's comments. Do you think that is fair? What about those who haven't got anything? Go back down the line and give those children who had nothing as many tins of good food as can be fitted on their plates. Ask the children if it is fair now? Explain to the children that two-thirds of the world have good things to eat, while one-third has only very little.

Ask the children in the line who have the good things what they should do with their food to make it more fair for those children with only some rice. Let the children share out their tins with each other. Look carefully at how the children decide what to keep and what to give away. Comment if necessary. Finally, explain how the harvest gifts will be distributed to those who do not have very much.

Prayer

Father, you have made us deeply conscious of those who do not have enough to eat. Help us always to be generous. Amen.

Hymn

No 31, 'Because you care', in *Every Colour under the Sun* (Ward Lock).

Holi, The Hindu Festival of Colour

5–7
Assembly
Hinduism

As India is such a vast country, Holi is celebrated in many different ways, which vary from region to region. This riotous festival takes place in March or early April and marks the beginning of Spring. People or revellers squirt coloured water or paint at each other. For some, this is a reminder of the story about the playful way that Krishna threw coloured water at a beautiful girl called Radha. (For further information about Lord Krishna, the god Vishnu and pronunciation guides, see pp. 235–44). In some areas, like Gujarat, it is a time for bonfires, fun and playing tricks on one another. Other regions use the festival to celebrate the start of a new farming year and to give thanks for the anticipated new growth and the harvest to come.

One way of expressing this riotous celebration of colour in class, is to squirt paint onto a huge sheet of paper and then allow the children to make a massive, collective finger painting. This painting can be pinned up and shown to the rest of the school. The class can then show the rest of the assembled children how they can dance to the movement of the paint, pretending to be the squiggles and swirls and explosions of colour. (This is far 'safer' than squirting paint at one another in school!).

Many different stories are told at Holi. One story that is told, is the exciting narrative about Holika and Prahlad. The story varies slightly in detail in the different regions, but basically it is about *good* triumphing over *evil*. Perhaps a class of children could act out this story. One way of telling the story might be as follows. There are rich opportunities for dance as well as drama.

You will need the following characters:

Prince Prahlad
Father, King Hiranyakashipu
King's sister, Holicka
Herd of Elephants (plus masks)
Snakes
Children dressed as flames
Taped music to which to dance

The story for dramatization and ideas for dance

Prince Prahlad is very devout and prays to the god Vishnu every day (*mime the action*).

His father, King Hiranyakashipu issues a proclamation to all people, that states that they must worship him, instead of worshipping Vishnu (*proclamation is read*).

Prince Prahlad refuses to obey and continues to pray to Vishnu, so his father throws him into a pit of snakes (*action is mimed*).

Prince Prahlad asks the god Vishnu for protection.

Snakes do their snake-dance, but the Prince walks through them, unharmed (*tape-recorded music is needed*).

The King is furious, so he orders a herd of elephants to trample on Prince Prahlad. Once again, the Prince prays to the god Vishnu.

Elephants (*wearing their masks*) dance to their music. Prince Prahlad walks safely through the middle of the herd.

The King is now so enraged that he asks his evil sister, Holika to help kill the Prince.

Holika builds a huge bonfire; she has special powers that protect her from the flames.

She persuades Prince Prahlad to walk through the centre of the bonfire with her.

Once again, Prince Prahlad prays to the god Vishnu for protection (*the action is mimed*).

The flames dance to their music (*tape-recorded music is needed*).

Holika is completely consumed by the fire. Her special powers desert her (*the action is mimed*).

Prince Prahlad walks free (*the action is mimed*).

Some people build bonfires and some will burn effigies of Holika. They remember Prince Prahlad's trust in Vishnu and good triumphing over evil.

Prayer

Thank you God, for the return of Spring and for all that this means to us. Thank you too, for the joys of festival and the promise of new life.

Hymn

No 98, 'You shall go out with joy' in *Come and Praise 2* (BBC).

Carnival before Lent

5–11
Assembly
Christianity

Before this carnival assembly, the children need to know something about the importance of Lent in the Christian calendar. Lent today is remembered as the forty days before Easter, when Jesus went into the desert and was tempted by the devil. (see Matthew 4: 1–11). Jesus went without food during this period, and three times the devil tempted Jesus with riches rather than sacrifice. But Jesus rejected the devil. Christians try to follow in Jesus' footsteps and go without something that they particularly like during Lent, giving the money saved to charities.

Ash Wednesday marks the beginning of Lent, but is immediately preceded by Shrove Tuesday. 'Shrove' comes from the word 'shriven', which means to be forgiven.

Christian people traditionally ask God's forgiveness on this day for all the things that they have done wrong. Shrove Tuesday is also known as 'Pancake Day', because people used to use up all their luxury foods like fats and sweet things, making pancakes before they gave up those foods during Lent. Ash Wednesday is so-called because Christians used to mark their foreheads with ashes to show their repentance for their sins. Some Christians still do this today.

Other Christians, like many in the Caribbean, hold a carnival before Lent before the strict self-denial that Lent brings. People dance to beautiful steel bands and calypso music, a carnival king and queen are chosen and people wear fantastic costumes. All sorts of themes for the costumes can be chosen, such as beautiful flowers, birds, fish, animals.

For this assembly children could have great fun making masks and headdresses and hold a carnival dance. But a simpler assembly could be arranged by playing some good steel band music and allowing each class to dance in turn. (Warn them beforehand that when the music stops, they must return to their places.)

Prayer

Father God, help us to be generous in our giving, not only during Lent, but all through the year. Amen.

Hymn

No 64, 'Everybody loves carnival night', in *Tinder-Box: 66 Songs for Children* A. and C. Black.

Easter: The Ugly Man
5–11
Assembly

Explaining the meaning of Easter to 5-year-old children is exceedingly difficult. I have told the story first as it is in the New Testament, spending each day of a week talking about the events that led up to the death of Jesus (see Luke, Chapters 22–24). But I was always left wondering if the children really understood the story, particularly why any man should want to give his life for others.

The story of the ugly man solves this problem and helps explain why a man should wish to die for someone else. It is based on a story called 'He Died for Us' by Dee Moss in *Today's Talks for Today's Children* (Chester House Publications, 1967). Having told the story for many years to infant children, I adapted it for the BBC Radio Programme *Discovery* in 1987 for 7–9-year-olds. (See also p. 127, 'Celebration of New Life after Death.)

Gary was very excited. After school he was going to meet an uncle who had been living in India, that he had never met before. He wasn't a real uncle, but someone his mum and dad had known for a very long time and they called him 'uncle'. He knew all *about* his 'uncle', because every Christmas and birthday he had received fantastic toys from him, as well as long amusing letters throughout the year, since he had been a very small child.

Gary's parents were always talking about Gary's uncle – what fun they used to have with him when Gary was a baby; they talked about his uncle's marvellous sense of humour and his great love of life. So Gary couldn't *wait* to meet him. The day at school seemed to drag on forever as he struggled with his French and then his mathematics, and all the other subjects. At last the bell went. Gary raced out of school, to start the long walk home. A group of Gary's friends took the same route home, and they always walked together, laughing and joking along the way. But this time something happened, something dreadful that had never happened before. Ahead of the children was an old, bent crippled man with a burnt, scarred face. The scars were livid red and twisted and contorted the man's face. Along the man's arms and neck and hands more lumps and scars could be seen. Part of the man's hands had been eaten away. The man looked *so* ugly.

'Scar-face', shouted one of the boys. 'Uagghh, isn't he ugly', shouted another. 'Look at his hair – he looks as if he's seen a ghost.' Then one of the boys did a most despicable thing, he picked up a stick and started poking the man, and another boy pulled the man round in circles, ripping his coat. Gary, led on by the others, began to shout rude names and to jeer and to laugh. When they had had their 'fun', they left the poor man hobbling along the road, and they continued to shout rude names over their shoulders, as they raced home until they were out of sight.

Gary ran on home, pushed open the garden gate, called out to his mum that he was home and rushed upstairs to change out of his school uniform. Just then, he heard the garden gate click and so he rushed to the window to catch a first glimpse of his uncle. Oh no, who do you think was coming up the garden path? None other than the bent, scarred man that he had taunted on his way home. Gary felt devastated, surely this man couldn't be *his* uncle, *surely* there was some mistake. But his mother's call confirmed that his uncle had arrived, and told him that this was no mistake.

'I've got to hide', Gary whispered, 'I can't possibly meet him. He will recognize me. Oh, what have I done?' Gary's mother continued to call, and eventually she came upstairs to get him. White as a sheet, Gary went downstairs and was introduced.

If the scarred man recognized Gary as one of the rude boys who had ill-treated him, he never said, and as they talked and Gary's uncle began to tell some of his exciting stories over tea, Gary soon forgot about the terrible scars and his own dreadful behaviour earlier.

Soon it was time for Gary's uncle to leave, and Gary felt very sad because he knew this man was truly a great person. When Gary's dad came to say good-night that night, Gary said, 'Dad, how did my uncle get those terrible scars on his face, arms and hands? You never mentioned them to me before.' Gary's dad said, 'Well, your uncle never talks about it, but when your mum and I were much younger, we went on holiday. We stayed in a caravan. We took our tiny baby with us. It was such a lovely evening that first night, so we just stepped outside the caravan for a few minutes and we were talking to some other people who were staying on the same camp site. Suddenly, we heard someone yelling 'fire! fire!' We turned round and saw that our caravan was on fire. The fire spread quickly throughout the caravan, thick smoke and flames came pouring out the windows and doors. Your mum screamed, 'Our baby is in there.' We began running, other people began running and yelling, 'Go back, go back. You will be burned.'

Ahead of us, a young man ran out of the crowd and into the flaming van. Seconds later he re-emerged, like a blazing torch, his arms, hair and clothes were all on fire, but he was using his body to shield something, to shield our tiny baby. Our baby was unhurt, but the man was badly burnt and he was rushed to hospital. He stayed in hospital for many months while surgeons fought to save his life and rebuild his burnt body using plastic surgery. 'That's when we became very great friends, because you see we were so grateful to him.'

Gary was silent. Then he whispered, 'That baby was me wasn't it, and that man is now the man I call 'uncle'. His bravery saved my life. His courage cost him his good looks. He was turned into an ugly man for my sake, and I have hurt him.' Gary turned away and quietly cried.

Prayer

Dear Lord Jesus, we know, that just like the man in the story, you were hurt for our sakes. Help us to use the new life that we have been given in your service. Amen.

Hymn

No 51, 'We have a king who rides a donkey', in *Someone's Singing Lord* A. and C. Black or No 69, 'At Easter time', in *New Child Songs* (Denholm House Press).

Video

As an alternative to the above story, the S.U. video 'The Champion' gives a most moving account of the Easter story, with some original songs by Garth Hewitt. Retold in 'picture form', it is suitable for the oldest children, although the part where Jesus washes the disciples feet is very suitable for younger children.

Pesah or Passover

This exciting story can be found in the Bible, in Exodus, Chapters 5–12. However, the teacher needs to summarize the main events and retell the story in her own words. The story provides a marvellous opportunity for dramatic movement, accompanied by music from home-made instruments. Opportunities for children to wear frog, locust, gnats and fly masks are afforded, as children act out the plagues sent by God in order to persuade the King of Egypt to let the Israelites go free. The beat of hailstones, the whisper of death, the eery sounds of darkness covering the land, the rushing water of the red sea, can all be musically interwoven into the story.

Then the Passover meal itself. The Jews of old were told by Moses to mark their door-posts with lamb's blood, so that the Angel of Death would pass over their homes, thus sparing them the death that was intended for the Egyptians.

Every year since then, the Passover meal or Seder is commemorated by Jewish families the world over. The meal takes place on the first evening of this seven-day Festival in the Spring. (See picture on p. 227).

The table is set with various special items as a reminder of what Passover means. For instance, Matzot or unleavened bread is eaten as God commanded. Lamb is roasted and eaten with bitter herbs (Horseradish) (see Exodus, Chapter 12, verse 8).

For the assembly, choose a Narrator to tell the story, and divide the children into groups representing the different plagues, the Jewish people, the Egyptians, animals and dancers, and then let the children mime their parts as the story is retold.

The Passover Play

You will need the following characters:

> Moses
> Aaron
> King of Egypt
> King's Advisers
> Frogs
> Gnats
> Flies
> Locusts
> Various animals (cattle, sheep, horses, camels, etc).
> Hailstones (children dressed in white shifts with paper balls to throw)
> Darkness Dancers (children dressed in black tights and leotards)

Narrator: Moses goes to the King of Egypt and asks him to free the Jewish people from slavery.

Moses: The Lord God of Israel, says, 'Let my people go'. (*Good News Bible*)

King: No. I will not let your people go. They must work for me, making bricks. I will beat them and make them work harder.

Narrator: Moses complained to God that the Jewish people were even worse off than before. God promised to set His people free and told Moses to go back to the King.

Moses: You *must* let my people go, or God will turn this River Nile into a river of blood.

Narrator: The King refused, so Aaron (Moses' brother) held out his stick over the Nile and the river turned to blood. But still the King refused to let the people go.

> (*Two children waft a long piece of red material into the air to represent the river of blood*). See suggestions for dance music on p. 94)

Moses: Let my people go, or the Lord God will send a plague of frogs to cover your land.

Narrator: But still the King refused to let the people go.

> (*Frogs leap and jump all round the hall*)

Moses: Let my people go or the Lord God will send a plague of gnats all over your land.

Narrator: But still the King refused to let the people go.

> (*Gnats dance round the hall making snapping movements with their mouths*)

Moses: Let my people go or the Lord God will send a swarm of flies over your kingdom.

> (*Flies buzz round the hall.*)

Narrator: But once the flies had gone, the King refused to free the people again.

Moses: Let my people go, or the Lord God will send a dreadful disease that will kill all your sheep, cattle, donkeys and camels.

> (*Sheep, cattle, donkeys and camels stand up and walk round and then gradually fall to the ground, dead*)

Narrator: But still the King refused to let the people go.

Moses: Let my people go or the Lord God will send a plague of boils on all your people.

> (*Boils are quickly painted or stuck on the King's face and the faces of his advisers*)

Narrator: But still the King refused to let the people go.

Moses: Let my people go or the Lord God will cause a heavy hailstorm to fall on the country, such as you have never seen before.

Narrator: Thunder, lightning and hailstones struck the ground.

> (*The children can make a cacophany of sound with their instruments at this point*)

King: All right Moses, this time I have had enough, I will let your people go.

Narrator: But once the hailstorm stopped, the King changed his mind.

Moses: Let my people go, or the Lord God will send a swarm of locusts to eat up all your crops and destroy all your trees and fill all your homes.

(*Locusts swarm round the hail pretending to eat everything*)

Narrator: But once the locusts went away, the King still refused to let the people go. So God sent a terrible darkness over all the land which lasted for three whole days and nights.

(*Eerie music may be played by the children. Other children wearing black tights and leotards do a darkness dance*)

King: All right, you may go this time.

Narrator: But the King went back on his word once more and refused to let the people go.

Moses: Let my people go, or the Lord God will send *one final* punishment on you and all your people. He will kill all your first-born children, including your *very own* son.

Narrator: God told Moses to mark the door post of the homes of all the Jewish people, so that when the Angel of Death passed through Egypt, He would not harm the Jews. This was done, but the Angel of Death killed all the first-born sons of the Egyptians including the King's *very own* son. Then the King sent for Moses once more.

King: Get out of my country, you and all your people. Leave at once, go and worship your God, and leave me alone in peace. I have had enough. I can't bear any more.

Narrator: So the Jewish people left quickly, taking with them unleavened bread to eat (i.e. dough that has not had time to rise, because of the need for speed) bundles of clothes and the gold and silver given to them by the Egyptians. And God told Moses that the Jewish people must hold a Passover Festival every year in remembrance that God had set them free.

The assembly could end quite simply at this point with the hymn and prayer below, or the next episode, crossing the Red Sea could be retold and re-enacted.

Prayer

Father, we pray for all people everywhere who are bullied or teased by others. Help us, in our own small way, to right any wrongs that we see. Amen.

Hymn

Sing the classic Pesah song 'Ma Nishtana'. It is about the four questions that the youngest child or children ask early on in the Seder meal: Why is this night different from every other night? It can be found on the excellent CD *The Real Complete Passover Seder, 35 Songs and Blessings of the Haggadah*' by David and the High Spirit. It is available from *Jewish Music Distribution* (address below). It is worth listening to the whole CD and learning some of the Hebrew songs. Each song is accompanied by an English explanation.

'Ma Nishtana' and other Passover songs can also be found in *Favourite Hebrew Melodies* by Elisheva Myers (The Pelican Press).

'Ma Nishtana' is also in *Sephardic Songs of Praise* by A.L. Cardozo (Tara Publications).

Some Suggestions for Dance Music for the Pesah Story

(Taken From the double cassette tape entitled *Essential Classics; 33 of the Greatest Classics* by Polygram Record Operations Ltd.)

River of blood	Orff, 'Carmina Burana' – O Fortuna (Side 3 no. 1)
Frogs	Johann Strauss, 11 'Emperor Waltz' Extract (Side 2 no. 5)
Gnats	Vivaldi, 'The Four Seasons' – Spring – First Movement (Side 1 no. 4)
Flies	Wagner, 'The Ride of the Valkyries' (Side 3 no. 3)
Sheep die	Massenet, 'Thais' – Meditation Extract (Side 3 no. 2)
Thunder and Lightening	Sibelius 'Karelia Suite' – Intermezzo (Side 4 no. 3)
Locusts	Bizet, 'Carmen' – Prelude (Side 3 no. 5)
Death	Mahler, – Symphony No. 5 – Adagietto (Side 4 no. 6)

(Modern, popular music can be used just as effectively.)

Address

Jewish Music Distribution
PO Box 67
Hailsham
East Sussex BN27 4UW
Tel/Fax: 01323832863
Email: jmduk@hotmail.com
Website: www.jmi.org.uk/jmd

Pentecost or Whitsunday

Ten days after Jesus' ascension into heaven and fifty days after his resurrection came Pentecost (the Greek word for fiftieth). Jews celebrate 'Shavout' on this day, or the giving of the law at Mount Sinai, fifty days after their Passover Festival, 'Pesah'. (See p. 226 for information about Shavout).

For Christians, this is the day when God sent his Holy Spirit to empower his disciples to preach the gospel to all nations. For information regarding Pentecostal Christians, see pp. 218–19. (The following activity is based on an idea given to the author by Revd. R Mann, Oxfordshire).

Ask for twelve volunteers from the floor to come out and help you. Whisper to these children that they must go back and choose just one person to whom to whisper something that Jesus taught. For instance, God loves them, or Jesus is alive, etc. Then they should go and sit down.

When everyone is quiet, explain to the rest of the children that the twelve volunteers have just become the first missionaries to the school. This is how the gospel spread throughout the ages, with each person telling somebody else the good news that Jesus broke the power of death, can forgive sins and is alive through His Spirit within us.

The name 'Whitsunday' comes from the words 'White Sunday' because, as people heard the good news, they wanted to be baptised at Pentecost or Whitsunday, as an outward sign of turning from their old life to a new life and a tradition grew up to wear white for baptism. In England today, there are still some street processions on Whitsunday, when children and adults wear white to commemorate the first coming of the Holy Spirit.

Prayer

Lord Jesus, thank you for sending your Holy Spirit to live with us and to teach us to become more like you. Amen

Hymn

No 16, 'For all the strength we have' in *Somebody's Singing Lord*, A. and C. Black.

The Twelve Days of Christmas

5–7
Assembly
All

The problem of how to involve every child in an infant school, with approximately five classes of 30 children per class in the Christmas production, is beautifully solved by dancing, singing and miming to the song 'The Twelve Days of Christmas'. Additional parts can be found for many angels and shepherds, oxen and asses, wise men and pages, plus Mary and Joseph, by simply adding a final verse using the same tune, but with the words:

> But the best gift of Christmas,
> I am sure you will agree
> Is God's gift to everyone
> Of a ti – ny ba – by.

For this activity you will need:

One announcer with scroll containing the words of the song
'The Twelve Days of Christmas'
Two 'true loves'
One partridge
One pear tree
Two turtle doves
Three French hens
Four colly birds
Five gold rings
Six geese a-laying
Seven swans a-swimming
Eight maids a-milking
Nine drummers drumming
Ten pipers piping
Eleven ladies dancing
Twelve Lords a-leaping

(Different versions may vary as to who does what.)

This makes a total of 82 children to be involved. To this number approximately 63 (or more) further children can take the parts of the Nativity tableau, making a total of approximately 150 children to be involved altogether: i.e.

Two for Mary and Joseph
Twenty angels
Twenty shepherds
Three wise men
Three page boys
Five oxen
Five asses
Five sheep

The Dramatic Movement

The drama takes place in-the-round. All the children come into the hall and sit in a huge circle, dressed as the different gifts in the order of the song – true loves, partridge, turtle doves, etc. The parents also sit in a circle around and behind the children, so that they can see the whole production. The announcer reads the following: 'On the first day of Christmas my true love sent to me . . . [pause]. Here are the two true loves.' Announcer sits down. Two children dressed in huge red hearts sewn onto white shifts stand up and move to the centre of the circle. Popular music is played for a few minutes to which the two children dance. (See below for suggestions for different music for the different dances of the gifts.) The true loves then stand at one end of the circle and the announcer reappears).

> *Announcer*: On the first day of Christmas my true love sent to me a partridge in a pear tree.

The announcer sits down. A child dressed as a pear tree stands up and walks to the centre of the circle. The child dressed as a partridge also stands up, bows to the true loves and dances to his piece of music, before coming to rest and returns to his seat. Both actors then sit down.

The whole operation is repeated, with the announcer announcing each gift, who dances in turn before the true loves, until the final verse of the original song. Then all the children *sing* the original song (encourage the parents to sing as well). As each child hears their part sung, they can stand up and take a bow.

Finally, the children *only* sing the new verse, 'But the best gift of Christmas, I'm sure you will agree, is God's gift to everyone of a tiny baby.' At this point the Nativity pageant stand up, and in turn walk round the circle with dignity, to make a central tableau of Mary, Joseph and Jesus, angels holding their wings high, shepherds kneeling, oxen and asses and sheep crouching around the outer edges of the circle. There are many appropriate Christmas hymns, in *Carol, Gaily Carol* (A. and C. Black) which can be sung as each group plays its part.

Then all the children, parents and teachers can be invited to sing 'Silent Night', or 'Away in a Manger' before Mary and Joseph lead the whole cast quietly out of the hall.

The Music for Dancing

Some well-known pieces of classical music that are also very popular are suitable. The following pieces were taped. The children mime their parts – pipers piping, drummers drumming, etc. – and improvise their dance to the music.

> *True loves* danced to Mozart, *Piano Concerto No. 21*, 'Elvira Madigan' Theme.
> *Partridge* danced to Tchaikovsky, *Piano Concerto No. 1*.
> *Two turtle doves* danced to Offenbach, 'Barcarolle' from *The Tales of Hoffman*.
> *Three French hens* danced to Ponchielli, 'Galop' from *The Dance of the Hours*.
> *Four colly birds* danced to Tchaikovsky, *Waltz from the Serenade for Strings*.
> *Five gold rings* danced to Boccherini, *Minuet*.
> *Six geese a-laying* danced to Bizet, *March of the Toreadors from Carmen*.
> *Seven swans a-swimming* danced to Chopin, *Prelude in A Flat*.
> *Eight maids a-milking* danced to Chopin, *Grand Waltz* from *Les Sylphides*.
> *Nine drummers drumming* danced to Chopin, *Military Polonaise*.

Ten pipers piping danced to Schubert, *Marche Militaire*.
Eleven ladies dancing danced to Johann Strauss, *Blue Danube Waltz*.
Twelve lords a-leaping danced to Brahms, *Hungarian Dance No. 5*.

The Costumes

The costumes were of the simplest type, mainly consisting of a simple headdress and shift made by a working party of mothers and teachers.

True loves: White sheets cut into shifts for boy and girl, with red hearts sewn on back and front, white tights, one red rose which the boy presents to the girl at the end of the dance, tinsel in the girl's hair.

Partridge: Brown jumper and brown tights, with small bird mask (consisting of yellow beak and black eyes), large wings of cardboard attached from the shoulder to the little finger which loops over the finger.

Pear tree: Green sheet cut into half-moon shape, with golden pears (made out of foil) attached, twig or leaf headdress.

Turtle doves: White vests or leotards and white tights, with very soft white fabric attached from middle of the back to little finger (to give wing effect), white ballet shoes if possible.

French hens: Red cones attached to a head-band, tunics with feathers (made out of paper).

Colly birds: Bird masks, black jumpers and black tights.

Gold rings: Yellow jumpers and yellow tights, with gold bands around heads. Dancing with PE hoops covered in gold foil.

Geese a-laying: Yellow webbed feet made out of cardboard or swimming flippers, white shifts drawn together at the throat and just below the knees (can be padded out with soft cushions), hard-boiled eggs to produce at the end of their dance.

Swans a-swimming: Crêpe paper ballet skirts sewn onto a band tied around the waist with white tops and white tights, tiny wings attached to backs.

Maids a-milking: Floral dresses with white aprons and white mob-caps, plastic buckets and three-legged stools if possible.

Drummers drumming: Military uniforms look very smart, but for ease two team-bands can be crossed across the chest of ordinary school clothes, with a military paper hat, drums and drum sticks; paper epaulettes could be added for fun.

Pipers piping: Boat-shaped hats all the same colour with brightly coloured sashes across the chest, tin whistle.

Ladies dancing: Long pretty dresses, long gloves, cone-shaped hats with veil.

Lords a-leaping: Three-cornered hats with a feather, white ruffled shirts, bow-ties, long black trousers cut off at the knee and tightened with elastic, black plimsolls with silver foil buckles stuck on.

The Nativity

Traditional costumes for Mary and Joseph; Shepherds: stripy material tied at the waist; Angels: white shifts with tinsel in their hair; Oxen, asses, sheep: masks can be made out of card.

Hannukah or the Festival of Lights

You will need the following:

> Judah Maccabee
> Jewish Army
> Syrian Army
> Temple Dancers

Props:

> Swords
> Hannukah menorah or eight-branched candle, plus one for lighting, making 9 altogether (a home-made one would do. This could be done by placing 9 candles in pots or jars).

Explain to the children that over 2000 years ago, Judah Maccabee led a small band of Jewish people into battle against the Syrians, who had spoilt their Temple and had tried to stop the Jews from worshipping God.

The drama can commence with a battle between two groups of children portraying the Jews and the Syrians, fighting each other with swords. The Temple dancers, representing the pagan worshippers, dance in and out of the Temple in the background. Judah Maccabee is pronounced the victor. The small Jewish army take back their Temple, banishing the dancers [who go and sit down] and then worship God. [*The Jewish army kneels in prayer*]

Judah lights the first Temple lamp (the menorah) as a symbol of God's presence, and then discovers that there is only enough of the precious oil to last for one day. He dispatches a group of people to get more oil, but while they are gone, by some miracle, the oil lasts for eight days.

Judah now lights the other seven candles in turn.

Explain that Jews today light the special Hannukah menorah in remembrance of the eight days that the oil lasted. The Festival takes place in December. Presents are given on the first day and special food that has been cooked in oil (like doughnuts) and latkes (potato cakes) are eaten. Try to obtain an eight-branched candle to show the children. (The Articles of Faith Catalogue, produce an imitation one. See p. 101 for address.) The Temple menorah has seven branches, it has become a symbol for the Jewish people everywhere.

End the assembly with a simple prayer, or allow a time for quiet reflection. The candles can be lit as a symbol of God's presence, or to accompany the song below:

How Many Candles

A counting song for Hannukah: sing up to 'one' on the first night, up to 'two' on the second night and so on up to eight. It can be very meaningful to sing *while* lighting a Hannukiyah (with a shamash or 'helper' candle). (Angela Wood)

How many candles, how many candles,
How many candles do we light?
On our hannukiyah, on our hannukiyah
On this Hannukah night?

(Chanting) one, one, one, one, one, one

One candle burning, one candle burning,
One candle burning bright
On our hannukiyah, on our hannukiyah
On this Hannukah night.

Chorus: How many candles, how many candles,
Verse: One candle burning, one candle burning,
Two
Three, etc.

How many candles do we light?
One candle burning bright.

On our hanukiyah, on our hanukiyah,
On our hanukiyah, on our hanukiyah,

On this Hanukah night.
On this Hanukah night.

One, one, one, one, one, one.
Two, two, two, two, two, two.
Three, etc.

Address

Articles of Faith Ltd.,
Resource House,
Kay Street
Bury BL9 6BU
Tel: 0161 763 6232
Fax: 0161 763 5366
e-mail: ArticlesFaith@cs.com
website: www. articlesoffaith.co.uk

Diwali

This important Festival of Light reminds Hindus of the triumph of good over evil; light over darkness. It can be seen in the story of Ram and Sita triumphing over the evil demon king.

The festival takes place in October or November. For many Hindus this festival marks the Hindu New Year, although there are other New Year festivals in different regions of India. Greeting cards are sent to family and friends; visits are made to relations, gifts and sweets are exchanged. Diva or small lights are lit and placed in all the windows of the houses as a reminder of the triumph of light over darkness.

The story of Ram and Sita can be retold or presented as a drama or puppet play. It can be retold in the following way: (see p. 244 for a guide to pronunciation).

You will need the following characters:

Narrator
Ram – Handsome Prince
Sita – Beautiful Princess
Ram's Father – The old King
Ram's Stepmother – The old Queen
Bharat – Ram's half-brother
Lakshman – Ram's other half-brother
Vulture – The King of the Vultures
Ravan – The Demon King with ten heads
Old Beggar – The Demon King in disguise
Monkeys – Who help Ram and Sita
Hanuman – The leader of the monkeys

The Narrator introduces each of the characters in turn.

Narrator: This is Ram, the handsome Prince

   (*Ram puppet takes a bow*)

This is Sita, his beautiful Princess wife

   (*Sita takes a bow*)

This is Ram's father, the old King.

   (*King bows*)

This is Ram's stepmother, the old Queen.

   (*Queen bows*)

This is Lakshman, Ram's half-brother.

   (*Lakshman bows*)

This is Bharat, Ram's other half-brother.

(*Bharat bows*)

This is the Vulture King.

(*Vulture king bows*)

This is Ravan, the Demon King. (You can hiss when he comes on to the stage.)

(*Ravan bows. Children hiss*)

Finally, this is Hanuman and the monkey army. (You can cheer.)

(*Hanuman bows – Children cheer.*)

Now we are going to tell you a story about all these characters.

(*Enter the old King and Queen*)

Queen: Listen my dear King, I think my son Bharat should be the next King, and not your son Ram. I think you should send Ram away for a while.

King: I don't want to send Ram away, but I will send him out into the forest to fight many battles and prove that he is worthy of being the next King.

(*King and Queen exit. Enter Sita, Ram and Lakshman*)

Sita: If you are going away from the Palace, Ram, I am coming too.

Ram: No you can't come with me – it will be too dangerous.

Lakshman: Well, I am coming with you. I can help you fight your battles and I will look after you and Sita if you let her come.

Ram: Well, all right, you can both come, but I warn you, we have a very difficult journey ahead of us and I don't know what danger will befall us.

Narrator: Ram, Sita and Lakshman set off. Suddenly, Sita sees a beautiful deer and begs Ram to capture it for her. Ram sets off to catch it, and tells Lakshman to remain behind and look after Sita. But Lakshman thinks he hears Ram cry out for help, so he says to Sita:

Lakshman: Wait here. I will draw a circle in the dust around you to protect you – on no account must you speak to anyone or step outside this circle. I must go and help Ram.

Narrator: Sita agreed, but suddenly, while the two men were gone, an old beggar came up to Sita and begged her for some food. He was really the Demon King in disguise.

Beggar: Please give me some food.

Sita: No I can't, I promised not to step outside this circle.

Beggar: But if you don't give me some food, I shall surely die.

Sita: Oh all right then, just for a moment, here is the food.

Narrator: In an instant, the old beggar changed back into Ravan the ten-headed Demon King and captured Sita. The King of the Vultures heard Sita's cries and tried to help, but Ravan was too strong for him, and struck him to the ground with his sword. Ram and Lakshman returned and saw that Sita had gone and the Vulture King lay wounded on the ground.

(*The action is mimed*)

Vulture: Oh Ram, the Demon King Ravan, has taken away your beautiful wife. I tried to stop him, but he struck me with his sword.

(*Enter Hanuman and monkey army*)

Narrator: Just then Hanuman, the Monkey King, and his army of monkeys came by, and Hanuman promised Ram that he would help him find Sita. Everyone searched and searched, calling out her name. At last Hanuman discovered where she was being held prisoner. She was on the island of Lanka. Hanuman went to find King Ravan.

(*The action is mimed*)

Hanuman: You must let Sita go, or else there will be a fierce battle and you will surely die.

Ravan: Ha, ha, no one is strong enough to kill me. To teach you a lesson – I am going to set fire to your tail.

(*Children hiss*)

Narrator: Poor Hanuman's tail was set alight, but he leapt from building to building, burning the houses with his tail as he went. In the meantime, the monkey army, who had built a bridge across the sea from India to Lanka, arrived and came to help their King fight Ravan. After a fierce battle, it was Ram who killed Ravan with his spear. Ram, Sita and Lakshman returned home, where Ram was crowned King and Sita was crowned Queen by Bharat, Ram's other half-brother.

(*The action is mimed. Children can cheer*)

Hymn

No 62, 'Diwali', in *Tinder-box; 66 Songs for Children* A. and C. Black.

The Festival of Purim

The Festival of Purim or the Feast of Lots is celebrated in the Jewish month of Adar, which is in February or March. The teacher will find the account in the Bible, but it is best read from a children's Bible or an abridged version. It is called the Feast of Lots, because Haman cast lots to 'choose the best day on which to kill all the Jews' (Esther Chapter 4, Verse 7, *Good News Bible*. (For background information it would be useful for the teacher to read the entire book of Esther, Chapters 1–10.)

You will need the following:

King Ahasuerus of Persia
Three Advisers to the King
Queen Vashti and handmaidens
Esther and servant girls
Hathach (Esther's manservant)
Haman (The King's Prime Minister)
Mordecai (Esther's Uncle)

Props:
Two crowns
Gold sceptre (which the King lifts as a sign to enter his presence)
Greggers or rattles (made from plastic bottles filled with rice to be used as shakers)
Labels (to be hung round the neck of each character and briefly introduced before the play begins)
Beautiful cloak
Ring

As the story is read aloud by the Narrator, the children mime or act their parts. The rest of the school can shake their rattles or hiss every time Haman's name is mentioned and cheer at the end for Queen Esther. Each class may like to wear fancy dress to school for the performance.

The story goes like this:

Narrator: King Ahasueras summons Queen Vashti to his banquet, but she refuses to obey.

King: Come to my feast

Queen Vashti: No!

King: Call my Advisers. (*Advisers enter*) The Queen has insulted me, what shall I do with her?

Advisers: You must banish her, and make another girl Queen.

Narrator: So the advisers find a young Jewish girl called Esther. They bring Esther to meet the King. She kneels before him.

King: Esther, you shall be my Queen. I will give you this crown to wear.

Narrator: Haman enters. (*The audience can hiss and shake rattles.*)

Haman: I am Haman, the King's Prime Minister. I'm so important that everyone must bow down to me.

Narrator: The servants and advisers bow down. But Mordecai, Esther's uncle, remains standing.

Haman: But who is this, who refuses to bow down to me?

Mordecai: My name is Mordecai. I am a Jew. I bow down only before God.

Narrator: Haman was so angry that he went to the King and this is what he said:

Haman: O King dear, (*hiss*) there are some very wicked people in your kingdom, who do not obey your laws. You must sign this proclamation to put them all to death. Yes, men, women and children. Kill them all. And not only will you rid yourself of these wicked people, but also you will become very rich because you can take all their gold and silver as well. So do sign here, [*Hiss*] King dear.

Narrator: So the King agreed and signed the proclamation. When Mordecai, Esther's uncle, heard the news, he was so upset and cried out loudly (*Mordecai wails loudly*). The Queen's servant girls heard Mordecai crying and told Esther, so she sent her trusted servant Hathach to Mordecai. Mordecai told Hathach about Haman's wicked plot and begged Esther to go to the King, but Esther said that if anyone went to the King without being invited, they were put to death instantly. However, she sadly agreed.

Esther: I will go to the King, and if I am put to death, so be it. But you and all our fellow Jews must pray for me and eat nothing for three days. My servant girls and I will do the same. Then I will go to the King.

Narrator: On the third day, Esther put on her best clothes and went to see the King. He raised his golden sceptre, which meant that she could enter his throne room.

King: Why dearest Esther, what do you want? You can have anything you want, you know, even half my kingdom.

Esther: Your Majesty, will you and your Prime Minister Haman come to a special banquet tonight?

   (*Hiss*)

King: Of course, we will come.

Narrator: A wonderful feast was prepared and the King and Haman arrived.

   (*Hiss*)

King: Now my Queen, you can have anything you ask for. What do you want?

Esther: Will you and Haman come to dinner again tomorrow night?

   (*Hiss*)

King: Of course, we will come.

Narrator: Haman's friends advised Haman to build a special platform on which to kill Mordecai. But that same night, unknown to Haman, the King remembered that Mordecai had saved his life and so he ordered Haman to give Mordecai a beautiful cloak to wear. Haman was furious. (*Hiss. He puts the cloak on Mordecai*). The next night, the King and Haman went to Esther's banquet.

King: Now my dearest Queen, what do you want from me?

Esther: My Lord, I ask you to spare my life and the lives of all my people.

King: What on earth do your mean? Who says you must be killed? Show me the man who says such a thing.

Esther: This evil man, Haman says so.

(*Hiss, boo, shake rattles, etc.*)

King: Take him away at once and hang him. And bring Mordecai to me, he shall be my Prime Minister.

(*Mordecai enters and kneels before the King. The King gives him his ring*)

Esther: Please stop your proclamation to kill all my people.

King: I'm afraid the order has already been sent out, but Mordecai can write to all the Jews in all the provinces and warn them to defend themselves.

Narrator: So there was much joy and happiness because the Jewish people were saved. Mordecai and Queen Esther said that the people must remember this day forever and have a festival on the same day every year. Let us give Queen Esther a cheer.

End by singing the Purim songs below and let each class, in turn, parade round the hall to show off their Festival Fancy Dress.

Prayer

Thank you God for the bravery of Queen Esther and for showing that you are against tyrants. Amen.

Songs

'Ani Purim' Lyrics: Kipnis, Levin and Music: Nardi, Nachum in *Sefer Hamoadim Vol. 6*, Yom-Tov Levinski (Ed.) (1955) published by Tel-Aviv, Agudat Oneg Shabbat; (with permission of Tarbut-Vechinuch Educational Publishing House and Acum Ltd.) or 'Der Rebbe', a traditional Yiddish East European Folk Song. (See pp. 108–9 for words and music.)

Ani Purim

Purim is a time for silliness and this is a silly song! Masks, fancy dress, street parades, clowning and all-round humour are an effective response to antisemitism: laughing prejudice in the face. (Angela Wood)

Ani Purim, Ani Purim sameah um'vadeah.
Halo rak paam bashanah avo l'hitareah.

My name is Purim, Purim, Purim, festival of gladness.
I only visit once a year (Ha, ha, ha) so throw away your sadness.

* Here there can be a short break in the song for a burst of laughter.

Der Rebbe

It is a custom for anyone who is so moved to act as Purim Rabbi for the day. This light-hearted Yiddish song about 'The Rabbi' is Purim-ish in spirit. Whatever the Rabbi does, it says, his Hasidim also do. (Angela Wood)

En az der rebbe	*zingt (La, la, la) zingen alle die Hasidim. (La, la, la)*
	shluft (snore) shlufen (snore)
	veynt (oi, oi, oi) veynen (oi, oi, oi)
	shveygt (silence) shveygen (silence)
	dovt (ruh, ruh, ruh) doven (ruh, ruh, ruh)
	klept (clap) kleppen (clap, clap, clap)

When the Rabbi sings	(La, la, la) all the Hasidim sing (La, la, la)
	sleeps (snore) sleep (snore)
	weeps (oi, oi, oi) weep (oi, oi, oi)
	is silent (silence) are silent (silence)
	prays (ruh, ruh, ruh) pray (ruh, ruh, ruh)
	claps (clap, clap, clap) clap (clap, clap, clap)

Kathina

7–11
Activity/Assembly
Buddhism

This Theravāda Buddhist festival takes place in October and November. It is a time when gifts are given to Buddhist monks before the onset of winter.

The tradition started during the Buddha's lifetime. A group of monks were making their way in July to spend their annual retreat season with the Buddha. They did not arrive in time and so were obliged to spend the three-month retreat apart from him. When the retreat was over, the Buddha suggested that they make a new robe together, as a unifying, compensatory activity. People round about willingly gave cloth and dye and a frame called a Kathina, on which to stretch the cloth to make the new robe.

Since that time, it has become the custom to give cloth for new robes to the monks in Buddhist Monasteries. Many other basic necessities are also given to the monks and nuns during this festival.

The day begins early, with people arriving at the monastery. The Three Refuges and the Five Precepts are chanted:

> I go to the Buddha for Refuge
> I go to the Dharma for Refuge (Teaching)
> I go to the Sangha for Refuge (Order of Monks)

(M. Patrick, *Buddhists and Buddhism*, (Wayland), East Sussex, 1982, page 25).

The Five Precepts are the rules by which Buddhists promise to live:

1   Not to destroy or harm life
2   Not to steal
3   Not to commit adultery or have irresponsible sexual relations
4   Not to tell lies
5   Not to take intoxicating drinks or to take drugs

On this festival day, there follows a communal meal and the offering of gifts takes place. The cloth is then made into a robe and the festival ends when the finished article is presented to the chosen monk.

For this assembly, all this historical information can be given to the children, followed by an activity in empathy with the tradition of making and giving.

With so many natural disasters throughout the world, it would be a worthwhile activity to make a blanket or bedcover to be sent to one of the disaster areas perhaps bearing the name of the school. A quick and easy activity is for everyone to knit a square of wool that can be joined together to make a colourful blanket. The teacher could ask everyone at the assembly to contribute.

A time of silence could be kept to think about children in need around the world and what we can do to help them.

Hymn

No 31, 'Because you care', in *'Every Colour Under the Sun'* (Ward Lock Educational).

Diwali	5–11 Assembly Sikhism

Sikhs as well as Hindus celebrate Diwali, or the Festival of Light, but for different reasons. As we have seen on pages 102–4 Hindus remember the story of Ram and Sita and good triumphing over evil. Sikhs remember a very important event in their own history, the release of the sixth Guru, Guru Hargobind from prison. However, both festivals are celebrated at approximately the same time of year in October or November. As Sikhism developed out of Hinduism, it is natural that Sikhs have retained some of the Hindu festivals, and the release of Guru Hargobind, actually occurred at the time when the Hindus were celebrating Diwali, in the year 1620.

This lovely story of the Guru's ingenuity, could be re-enacted by the children. However, it is important to remember that some Sikhs do not like to see their Gurus portrayed in drama, and so it is as well to seek approval from the local Sikh community before performing the following play. If there are objections, Piara Singh Sambhi suggests that the part of Guru Hargobind could be spoken by the narrator or from behind a curtain. The reason for this should be explained to the children.

You will need the following:

Characters

>   Guru Hargobind
>   Muslim Emperor, Jehangir
>   52 Hindu Princes (10 could be a representative number)
>   First Prince
>   Second Prince
>   Third Prince
>   Sikh followers (10 or more)
>   2 Prison Officers
>   2 children to make an archway
>   Narrator

>   *Props*
>   Hargobind's cloak (with tassels)
>   Bundle of Food

Narrator: (The Narrator sets the scene) This is a story that happened a long time ago. The Muslim Emperor Jehangir had been told that the Sikh Guru, Guru Hargobind, had attracted many followers and that the Guru had built a fort in the city of Amritsar. He was afraid that the Guru might plot against him and try to kill him, so he decided to have Guru Hargobind thrown into prison at a place called Gwalior.

Emperor Jehangir: What is all this I hear about you building a fortress at Amritsar, is it true?

Hargobind: Yes Sir.

Emperor: So you are plotting to kill me are you, and to take my place as Emperor?

Hargobind: No Sir, of course not.

Emperor: I don't believe you, throw him into jail.

Narrator: Poor Hargobind was taken by two armed prison officers and thrown into jail.

   (*Prison Officers come forward and push Hargobind into jail*)

Narrator: Once inside the jail, Hargobind looked around him and found that there were many others there, accused of the same crime. In fact there were fifty-two Hindu Princes all wanting to talk at once.

Princes: (*All talking at once*)
Look here,
Let me tell you,
Did you know,
We are so badly treated, etc., etc.

Hargobind: Stop, stop, I can't hear you, if you all talk at once. Will somebody tell me why you are here, and why you are so angry?

First Prince: We are so badly treated. We are not even given enough food to eat.

Hargobind: Well then, you must have some of mine. Some of my friends gave me this bundle of food, please take some and share it, all of you.

Narrattor: So the princes sat down and shared the food between them.

   (*Group sit in a circle and the bundle is passed around*)

Hargobind: Now, will someone tell me why you are here?

Second Prince: We are all accused of plotting to kill the Emperor.

Third Prince: And it is all untrue.

Narrator: Hargobind listened to their grievances and day by day, he continued to share his food with them. Many days went by and Hargobind was still kept a prisoner, even though he was innocent. Each day, more and more of his Sikh followers came and stood outside the jail in a silent protest about his imprisonment.

   (*Sikh followers get up, one by one, and form a semi-circle around the group sitting in the jail*)

Narrator: The prison officers began to get worried about this and decided to go and see the Emperor.

Officers: Your Highness, we do not know what to do, we fear that there will be a riot unless you free this man Hargobind. Every day, more and more of his followers are standing outside the jail.

Emperor: Let me look into his case and see if I can release him. It may be better for all concerned if I set him free.

   (*He shuffles through some papers*)

Well, looking at these papers, the case against him seems a bit thin. Perhaps we had better let him go.

Officers: Yes Sir, thank you Sir, we will go and tell him at once.

Narrator: So the officers left the Emperor and hurried to tell Hargobind that he was free.

Officers: Hargobind, we are here to tell you that the Emperor has set you free. You can leave right now.

Princes: (*Together*) What about us? What about us? Set us free too. Why can't we leave? This is unfair. It's unjust. It's criminal.

Hargobind: Thank you for your message from the Emperor. But please, will you tell his Highness that I cannot possibly leave prison without my 52 friends here.

Officers: He won't like it, he won't like it, you know. He will be very angry, and may not release *any* of you.

Narrator: However, the officers went back to tell the Emperor. (*The officers and Emperor put their heads together and mutter.*) Then the officers return to the jail.

First Officer: Hargobind, the Emperor has said you may go, and as for these princes here, the Emperor will only free those princes who can pass through this narrow doorway with you at the same time as you leave. Only those princes who can actually touch your clothes, will be released with you. Ha, ha, ha, they will have to be jolly thin to pass through this doorway with you. Ha, ha, ha.

Narrator: The Guru, bowed with thanks and called all the princes together. Then he spoke again.

   (*The action is mimed*)

Hargobind: I am now ready to leave officer, and so are the princes who are coming with me.

   (*Hargobind stands up and passes through the archway made by the two children holding their hands together. As he does so, he undoes his cloak and each of the princes grasp hold of a tassle and so passes through the archway*)

Officers: (*Scratching their heads*) Well I'm blowed. We can't stop them, they *are* touching the Guru's clothing, but who would have thought that this could happen?

Narrator: So the Guru and the princes all passed through the archway to freedom. The Guru went back to Amritsar and saw many little lights or divas lighting up the fortress. Today, Sikhs everywhere light divas as they remember this lovely story about their Guru.

Prayer

Holy God, help us to see the needs of others as well as our own, and to be always ready to help others in distress. Amen.

Hymn

No 127, 'Diwali time is here', in *Come and Praise 2* (BBC).

Navratri (or Nine Nights) and Dussehra

5–11
Activity
Hinduism

(Pronounced Nav/ra/tri; first 'a' is short; the second 'a' is long as in far'; 'tri' rhymes with 'see'. Duss/eh/ra, 'Duss' rhymes with 'thus', 'e' as in let, 'ra' rhymes with 'far'. See p. 244 for further guide to pronunciations.)

The festival of Navratri and Dussehra is celebrated by Hindus all over the world, during late September or early October. The mother goddess or devi is worshipped, and the triumph of good over evil is celebrated. The festival takes different forms in different parts of India.

In one of her many forms, the mother goddess is called Durga and she is depicted defeating the Demon King. During each of the nine nights of the festival, Durga's different powers are remembered, culminating on the tenth night or Dussehra, with a terrific bonfire on which the huge effigy of Ravan, the Demon King, is burnt. (See pp. 102–4 for the story about Ram and the Demon King).

Indeed, in some parts of northern India, the emphasis is not so much on the goddess Durga, as on the victory of Ram (the incarnation of Lord Vishnu) over the Demon King Ravan. The story is retold and re-enacted, culminating with Ram defeating Ravan. There are great bonfires and firework displays.

But the message is much the same, goodness triumphs over evil, and many Hindus use the festival time as a time of rejoicing and goodwill.

The festival provides a wonderful opportunity for art and craft work in school. The children could either make a huge effigy of the demon king for a bonfire of their own, or make the mother goddess Durga, with her ten arms. (It should be noted that it takes years to train a proper sculptor to make the mother goddess, as skills are handed down from generation to generation. Sculptors adhere strictly to the guidelines in the Hindu Scriptures).

Prayer

Almighty God, we remember that this festival commemorates goodness triumphing over evil. May this be true, both in our own lives and in our schools. Amen.

Hymn

No 134, 'I planted a seed', in *Come and Praise 2* (BBC).

Eid-ul-Adha

5–11
Assembly
Islam

(See p. 247 for a note regarding the date of the festival)

This is the festival that takes place at the end of Hajj or pilgrimage in the twelfth month of the Muslim calendar. If they can, each family will sacrifice a sheep or cow, giving part of it to families who cannot afford to make the sacrifice. This is done in remembrance of Prophet Ibrahim's willingness to sacrifice his son, Isma'ail. Isma'ail was the son born to Ibrahim and Hagar. Muslims believe that Ibrahim was a great Prophet who was asked by Allah (God) to sacrifice his son as a test, to demonstrate his willingness to obey Allah in everything. (The story can be read in the Qur'an or in the Bible. If the story is read in the Bible, it is Isaac who is to be sacrificed by Abraham, not Isma'ail. See Genesis, Chapter 22, verses 1–19. In the Qur'an it is Chapter 2, verses 126–87 and 37, verse 102).

There is a problem over presenting this exciting story in dramatic form, as Muslims are not allowed to present God or his Prophets as persons. Therefore, out of respect for the Muslim people, the story should be simply retold by a storyteller.

One day, when Ibrahim was alone, he heard Allah speaking to him in a dream. Allah asked Ibrahim if he was willing to be completely obedient to Him, in every detail of his life. Of course, being a righteous man, Ibrahim told Allah that he would do anything that Allah asked him to do. So Allah put Ibrahim to the test. He told Ibrahim to take his son to the land of Moriah, where Allah would show him the place where Ibrahim must sacrifice his son.

Poor Ibrahim was devastated, but he knew he must obey Allah. The next morning, he cut up some firewood and took his son to the place that Allah had told him about. Ibrahim told Isma'ail what Allah had asked him to do, and Isma'ail said, 'O my Father, I do that which thou art commanded (Qur'an, 37:102). Sadly, Ibrahim looked at his beloved son and he ordered him to lie down on the wood, ready to be sacrificed. He was just about to kill Isma'ail, when suddenly Ibrahim heard the Angel Jibra'il's voice, telling him not to touch or harm the boy. The Angel Jibra'il told Ibrahim, that God knew now, that Ibrahim was completely obedient to Him in all things and as a reward, Allah would richly bless Ibrahim. God provided a sheep for the sacrifice. Ibrahim quickly untied his son and sacrificed the sheep instead. Ibrahim invited everyone to share in the festivity.

That is why at the festival of Eid-ul-Adha families sacrifice a sheep or cow in memory of this event, and they give part of the sheep away to the poorer families, who cannot afford to make their own sacrifice. This shows God's provision for them too.

Prayer

Almighty God, help us to be obedient to you in all our doings. Thank you for providing for all our needs. Amen.

Hola Mohalla

7–11
Activity/Assembly
Sikhism

As we have seen on p. 86, this was a Hindu festival. But the tenth Guru, Guru Gobind Singh, wanted Sikhs to have their own celebration. So in 1700 CE he introduced the festival of Hola Mohalla in Anandpur, in the foothills of the Himalayas.

The festival was to be a time when all Sikhs gathered together to celebrate all kinds of sports and gamesmanship; Guru Gobind Singh wanted a time to display the strength and ability of his army. So with this in mind, he arranged displays of 'swordsmanship, horsemanship, archery and wrestling competitions'. (J.G. Walshe, *Celebrations across the Cultures*).

Today too, Sikhs continue to celebrate Hola Mohalla by having athletic tournaments and other sporting events such as horse riding. The festival is still celebrated in Anandpur, in remembrance of Guru Gobind Singh's command to meet together for this Spring festival. Today in the West, after the sporting events, Sikhs usually go to their Gurdwaras and pray for health and strength and the ability to keep their bodies fit.

For this assembly, groups of children could display their prowess in all forms of movement, gymnastics, etc. Perhaps the importance of keeping one's body healthy could be stressed. It might also be a good opportunity to warn the children against smoking, drinking and drug abuse. Perhaps a small group of children could research these topics and present some statistics in graph form, written work and art work. Close the assembly with a simple prayer.

Prayer

Father God, help each one of us to keep our bodies fit and healthy. May we never spoil our bodies by drug abuse. Amen.

Hymn

No 16, 'For all the strength we have', in *Someone's Singing Lord* A. & C. Black.

5 RITES OF PASSAGE

Baptism

Before the subject of baptism is discussed in assembly, it is most helpful if the theme of water has already been studied – (see pp. 132–33) the lovely feeling of being clean after a particularly dirty job, the life-giving drink of water to a thirsty person, the uses of water in our daily lives, etc. This can lead to a most natural thanksgiving service to God for his daily provision. Strong links can then be drawn between being made clean, receiving life, daily living and baptism.

Perhaps the class could visit a church and look at the font, or make a study of different fonts, or baptismal pools in the free churches. It is most helpful if a minister is invited into school to explain the meaning of baptism and the service itself. A display of Christening gowns could be set up. Perhaps some Christening presents could be displayed (Anglican).

The most important aspect of baptism for the children to understand is that it is the outward sign of the beginning of a new life with God. The links then are clear: the symbolism of washing away sin; receiving the life-giving gift of the Holy Spirit; and daily living with Jesus.

It needs to be explained that when a baby is baptised, it is the parents or godparents who undertake the responsibility to bring up the child as member of the 'church' family and teach him all about faith in God. But, as we have already seen, this is only the beginning. Once the child can make decisions for himself or herself and is willing to take responsibility then he or she must come to confirm his or her beliefs. There also needs to be some explanation of adult baptism as practised by the Baptists and Pentecostalists. (see pp. 217–19) This can be seen on the video *Aspects of Christianity* available from RMEP SCM-Canterbury Press (RMEP is a division of SCM-Canterbury Press Ltd), St. Mary's Works, St Mary's Plain, Norwich, Norfolk NR3 3BH.

Prayer

We thank you Father, that we are all part of your world-wide family. Amen.

Hymn

No 113, 'Family of man' or No 63, 'Sing hosanna', in *New Life* (Galliard).

A Hindu Naming Ceremony

In Hindu culture there are lots of different ceremonies for naming a baby. Ceremonies may differ for a variety of reasons. For instance, variations occur according to the caste into which the baby is born, or the region in which the family resides.

However, most Hindu babies' names are determined by their horoscopes. The Brahmin or family priest works out the child's horoscope from the exact moment that the baby was born. Then, based on this information, the priest will often choose the initial letter for the baby's name. Hindu names usually have a special meaning. For instance, if a boy's initial letter is 'R', he might be called Ram, after one of the gods. This naming ceremony usually takes place ten days after the baby is born and it is a very special occasion when the baby is welcomed into the world. It is called the nām Samskār ceremony.

For this assembly, having given the children the above information, hold a competition and write down as many names as possible beginning with a certain letter. Children from different cultures should be given the opportunity to explain the meaning of their names if they know them. Of course, many young children may not know the meaning of their name, and so this could become a project to be researched at home.

Once the children have understood the concept that calling people by their proper name is important and that everyone is unique and valuable, perhaps the teacher could use the occasion to discuss the improper use of name-calling and so discourage prejudice of any kind.

Compare and contrast other name-giving ceremonies (see Chapter 9).

Prayer

Lord God, we thank you that each one of us is special and precious in your sight. Amen.

Song

'Today's a special day', in *Sing a Song of Celebration* by M. Martin and V. Stumbles (Holt, Rinehart and Winston).

Junior and Senior Soldiers

5–11
Assembly
Christianity

There is a turning point for young children in many faiths when children must profess their faith for themselves. The age at which this decision is taken varies from faith to faith, but usually takes place between 7 and 14 years. Roman Catholic children, for instance, make their first Holy Communion at about 7 or 8 years old; Salvation Army children do not have a communion service, but there is a special service for children to become 'Junior Soldiers'.

Generally, the children who will become Junior Soldiers will have attended primary church first. This is the class for 3–7-year-olds and teaches the children about the Bible through music, movement and mime. At 7 years of age the Salvation Army children are considered old enough to attend Junior meetings, where they learn more about the Bible and Salvation Army doctrines. When they are ready to make their promises to God for themselves, they are made Junior Soldiers at a special service at the Salvation Army citadel. They have to sign a card to show that their intentions are serious and that they promise to read their Bible and pray every day.

These Junior Soldiers then go on to an award scheme, where they have to work hard at various activities to obtain the bronze award. They have to pass eight activities in all to receive their badges. There are four compulsory sections such as reading the Bible, writing prayers, knowledge of the Army and being helpful; and there is another section from which children can choose four more activities, e.g. learning a musical instrument, becoming proficient in art and craft, etc. Parents have to sign the cards to say that their children have done these activities. Then the children can work towards their silver and gold awards.

Junior Soldiers sometimes join the singing group or the junior band which sings and plays instruments to people in old people's homes or hospitals. Junior Soldiers can only become Senior soldiers by attending special classes and studying the Bible. Then at about 15 years of age there is a special swearing-in ceremony. The young people have to sign the 'Articles of War', which sets out all the beliefs held by Salvation Army members and which these children must profess in front of the full company, solemnly standing in front of their Army flag.

Either invite an Army officer into school for this assembly to explain the passage from Junior Soldier to Senior Soldier, or tell the children about it. Listen to some 'Army' music. Perhaps a 'helpful' scheme could be introduced into school, with teachers noting when children have been especially kind and helpful.

Useful address

The Salvation Army, 101 Newington Causeway, London, SE1 6BN.
Tel: 0207 367 4500.

Hymn

No 21, 'Hands to work and feet to run', in *Someone's Singing Lord* A. and C. Black.

Bar Mitzvah/Bat Mitzvah

Boys become Bar Mitzvah at around the age of twelve years. Girls become Bat Mitzvah at around the age of thirteen years. Bar Mitzvah means 'Son of the Commandments', Bat Mitzvah means 'Daughter of the Commandments'. Before boys and girls can take part in this joyful ceremony, they will have received special lessons from their Rabbi or teacher. They will have had to learn how to read a special portion of the Scriptures. It is quite difficult.

Before the age of twelve or thirteen, the children's parents are responsible for their behaviour and actions; but at this special ceremony, the children themselves take on responsibility for their own actions. That is, they promise to obey God's Commandments and to keep the Jewish laws for themselves. They are considered to be old enough to judge right from wrong and to act accordingly. This is a turning point in the young people's lives; leaving childish behaviour behind and acting in a more grown-up way.

For this assembly, you could watch one of the excellent videos that are available, such as *Aspects of Judaism* that covers the Bar Mitzvah Ceremony (as well as Festivals such as Purim and Passover). Available from:

RMEP, SCM-Canterbury Press Limited,
St Mary's Works,
St Mary's Plain, Norwich,
Norfolk NR3 3BH.
Tel: 01603 612914
Website: www.scm-canterburypress.co.uk

The video entitled *Believe It Or Not 1* covers the Bar Mitzvah Ceremony (as well as other rites of passage in other faiths), and is also available from RMEP at the above address.

The school children may not have seen a Tallit or prayer shawl, the Shel Rosh and the Shel Yad, that is, the boxes that are worn on the head and arm. Replicas of these items can be obtained from:

Articles of Faith,
Resource House,
Kay Street,
Bury BL9 6BU.
Tel: 01617 636232
Email: ArticlesFaith@cs.com
Website: www.articlesoffaith.co.uk

These replicas do not contain the portions of scripture, as it is not permitted to handle the holy words. If there are any Jewish children in school, it may be possible for them to show these precious items to the rest of the school. But again extreme caution must be observed with the artefacts.

Discuss what it means to be responsible for all one's own actions. Encourage all children to act responsibly. How might children have already had to act in a grown-up way? In what circumstances might responsibility be thrust upon young shoulders? Reflect on these issues before singing the joyful song that many children sing at their Bar Mitzvah.

Song

This is a joyous song which is often sung at weddings or Bar/Bat Mitzvah parties, from *Israel in Song*, compiled, edited and arranged by Velvel Pasternak (Tara Publications, Cedarhurst) N.Y.

> Hava nagilah, Hava nagilah, Hava nagilah, v'nis'm'cha!
> Hava n'ran'na, v'nis'm'cha!
> U'ru . . . achim
> U'ru achim b'lev sameach!

> Come, let us have joy and happiness in it!
> Arise, my friends, with a joyful heart!

A Christian Wedding

5–11
Assembly
All

Everybody loves a wedding, the beautiful clothes, the food and the presents, the excitement and preparation for the big day. A good starting point for this topic is to ask the children to bring in photographs of their parents' wedding or grandparents' wedding, or to cut out pictures of weddings from newspapers or magazines.

Perhaps a real wedding dress could be borrowed and displayed together with shoes, head dress and veil, etc. A bridesmaid's dress and a page-boy's outfit could also be borrowed and displayed. This will provoke much good discussion, written work and artwork. For handwriting practice, wedding invitations could be sent out from one class of children to all the other classes in the school. (Names can be copied from school registers). Older children could draw up lists of wedding gifts that they think are essential items to have in the home. The cost of these items could be explored. Younger children could *draw* the things they think they would need. Food for the wedding could be discussed, written about or painted. Perhaps a model of a wedding cake could be made, or a caterer invited into school to tell the children about the kind of food he or she has prepared for a reception. Transport to and from the ceremony could be considered. How many ways could the couple travel to the reception? Paintings and models could support the answers, i.e. horse-drawn carriages, Rolls Royce cars, wheelbarrows, trains, etc. The ceremony itself should then be discussed. Where do couples get married today? What promises do people make at weddings? Try to find out about as many different places and types of service as possible.

Draw all the threads together by having a wedding assembly. Since the whole school is invited, the children can all make special hats for the occasion, so that they can participate as guests. The class involved in the project (approximately 30 children) can take the following parts and will need some appropriate costumes:

Bride
Groom
Four Bridesmaids
Two Pageboys
Two Bride's Parents
Two Groom's Parents
Friends of the couple
Minister
Fifteen Choir Members

These children could re-enact a simplified version of the wedding service, either by reading the words on cards or by improvization. A real treat for the whole school would be to let all the children share in the 'reception' afterwards by having a biscuit or a piece of cake taken around to all the assembled children, by the 'wedding' class. It is amazing how a surprise piece of food in an assembly is regarded as a huge treat by all children.

End with a simple prayer of thanks for all the joy and fun that weddings can bring.

Hymn

No 15, 'Think of a world', from *Someone's Singing Lord* A. and C. Black.

Resources

Aspects of Christianity features an Anglican wedding on the video (among other topics). It is available from:

RMEP SCM-Canterbury Press Ltd.,
St Mary's Works,
St Mary's Plain,
Norwich,
Norfolk NR3 3BH
Tel: 01603 612914
Fax: 01603 624483
e.mail: sales@scm-canterburypress.co.uk

A Sikh Wedding

Begin by comparing and contrasting a typical English wedding in a church (on p. 123), with a traditional Sikh wedding in a Gurdwara. (Although Sikh weddings can also take place in halls or in the Bride's house.)

You could discuss the pros and cons of choosing a partner for oneself and of having a partner chosen by one's family. Ask the children if they have ever attended a wedding. Make a scrapbook.

As a wedding is such a happy and colourful occasion, it would be more meaningful if a Sikh mother was invited into the school to describe her beautiful clothes and the important aspects of the wedding ceremony.

Deep red is the traditional colour of a bride's clothes in India, whether she is Hindu, Muslim or Sikh. Sikh women wear a tunic or frock called a kameeze, which is a little longer than a mini skirt, and shalwar which are like trousers gathered in tightly at the ankles. She wears a dupatta or veil on her head, which is made to match the kameeze.

The distinguishing feature of a Sikh man is his turban, which may be of any colour, but orange or red is the preferred colour for weddings. He also wears a scarf called a pulla, which is used in the ceremony. He will hold one end, while his bride holds the other end.

Perhaps it might be possible to re-enact a Sikh wedding using all the children in the hall as wedding guests.

The main elements are as follows:

The young man and the male relatives of both couples meet in the Gurdwara.

The groom's father places a garland of flowers around his son's neck.

The groom bows to the Guru Granth Sahib (the Holy book containing the Sikh Scriptures) and then sits down facing the Guru Granth Sahib.

Then the bride enters dressed in red, with her sister or friend or a female relative. She also bows to the Guru Granth Sahib and then sits next to the groom.

The bride's father places a garland of flowers around the Guru Granth Sahib and one around the neck of both the bride and the groom.

There are readings and prayers from the Holy book.

The groom holds one end of his scarf, while the bride holds the other end.

The most important part of the wedding is when the groom leads his bride four times around the sacred book.

A special hymn is sung which tells the couple that true happiness lies in devotion to God.

The ceremony ends with a prayer called Ardas.

Karah prasad (the Sikh's holy food) is distributed to all the members of the congregation at the end of the service.

Other friends and relatives bring garlands of flowers to the happy couple.

After the ceremony, there is a special wedding feast. Gifts of money are usually given to the couple and everyone shares the meal together.

Finally, the bride leaves with her husband to go to his home.

Perhaps every child could be given a small sweetmeat to taste at the end of the assembly.

Hymn

No 6, 'Come to the party', in *Game-Songs with Prof Dogg's Troupe* A. and C. Black.

Resources

Bennett, O. (1985) *A Sikh Wedding*, Hamish Hamilton.
Compton, A. (1995) *Marriage Customs*, Hodder Wayland.
Ganeri, A. (1998) *Wedding Days*, Evans Brothers Limited.
Kaur Singh, K. (2000) *Keystones Sikh Gurdwara*, A. and C. Black (Contains information about weddings).
Sambhi, Piara Singh (1995) *The Guru Granth Sahib*, Heinemann.

Celebration of New Life After Death

7–11
Assembly
Christianity/All

Jesus said, 'I am the resurrection and the life. He who believes in me, though he die, yet shall he live' (John, Chapter 11, verse 25, *Revised Standard Version*). Christians believe this wonderful promise that death is just the beginning of new life.

Let us look at the evidence for the risen Jesus. This could take the form of a series of brief playlets. Begin in the following way: Jesus is dead, his friends are terribly unhappy, confused and frightened.

First Playlet: The women go to the tomb feeling desperately sad and find the stone rolled away (Luke, Chapter 24, verses 1–10). What might they say to each other? How are they feeling? Whom do they meet? What are their feelings now? What happens next?

Second Playlet: The two friends are walking and talking about Jesus' death on the road to Emmaus. (Luke, Chapter 24, verses 13–32). How do you think they are feeling? Who is the stranger who joins them? What do you say to him? What happens next? How do you think they are feeling now?

Third Playlet: The disciples are in the upper room in Jerusalem. (John, Chapter 20, verses 19–30). Jesus appears to his friends. But on this first occasion, Thomas is not present, so when the disciples tell him the good news that Jesus is alive, he does not believe them. Jesus returns a week later, then Thomas believes. How might the disciples have been feeling before Jesus came to them? What did he say to them? What did Thomas tell his friends? What did Thomas say to Jesus?

Fourth Playlet: Simon Peter and some of the other disciples decide to go fishing. (John, Chapter 21, verses 1–14). But that night they catch nothing. Someone calls to them from the beach to cast their nets over the other side of the boat and as a result they can hardly haul in their catch, as there are so many fish. John knows instantly who the mystery person is. Simon Peter rushes ashore to find Jesus already cooking a barbecue of fish and bread and you cannot have breakfast with a ghost! How must the disciples have felt when they caught nothing? What do you think they might have been wondering about recent events? How do you think they felt when they recognised Jesus?

The subject of death needs very careful and sensitive handling with young children. Some children will have experienced death of relatives or friends already. Many others will have no knowledge or understanding. If pupils or the school are able to keep pets, then it becomes an integral part of the child's experience. Eventually death can be seen as the natural order of things, although it does not lessen the pain and anxiety and dreadful feelings of loss at the time. A very helpful book that deals with death in a gentle way is:

Wood, D. (2001) *Grandad's Prayers of the Earth*, Walker Books.
A boy eventually finds he is able to accept his Grandad's death and is even able to smile, by remembering all the wonderful things that Grandad taught him about the natural world. This story could be read in an assembly before one introduces the above subject.

Another very helpful book is:

Wilhelm, H. (2002) *I'll Always Love You*, Crown Publications.

It tells the story of a much beloved dog growing up, through the cycle of his life, describing all his antics, getting older and eventually dying in his sleep. The little boy is helped in his grief by knowing that every night, before he went to sleep, he would tell his old dog friend that he would always love him.

   Grief should not be suppressed. It may be that these two books and the positive playlets above will open up a wider discussion and provide some help to a grief stricken child. A child needs time and space to express his anger, grief, feelings of guilt and pain at the death of a loved one.

Meditation

A candle could be lit to aid a time of quiet reflection, or in memory of loved ones who have died.

Hymn

No 28, 'The journey of life', in *Someone's Singing Lord*, A. and C. Black or
No 28, 'I danced in the morning', in *New Life*, Galliard or
No 35, 'He's back in the land of the living', in *New Life*, Galliard.

The Buddha Teaches About Death

Death is a very difficult subject to deal with in an assembly, and yet some attempt must be made to cover this subject in order to reassure those children who are grieving over the loss of loved ones and perhaps reassure others for the future. It could be argued that the subject is best left until the need for explanation arises, but equally it could be argued, that it is much better to have tackled the subject long before an actual death which inevitably, will be charged with intense emotion.

This story at least, may open the doors for free discussion and bring some understanding to a grieving child, at the necessary time. The story is a dramatized version of how the Buddha dealt with a grieving mother. You will need to prepare the children carefully beforehand, that they are going to see a play about a mother whose baby has died, and who goes to see the Buddha for an explanation.

You will need the following characters:

The Buddha
Mother
First Villager
Second Villager
Third Villager
Narrator

Mother: (*Weeping approaches the Buddha*) Oh Buddha, Buddha, help me, help me, my baby has died. Why should this dreadful thing have happened to me?

The Buddha: My dear, all mankind, everywhere, must suffer at some time or other in their lives.

Mother: Oh, but I hurt so much inside, and I am so full of sadness that I know that I will never be happy again.

The Buddha: I can see you are suffering now. I too, feel your pain, as if it were my own, but one thing I know is true, everything passes in time, even your pain will pass in time.

Mother: I cannot believe you. You do not understand how I feel – nobody understands. (*Weeps*)

The Buddha: (*Gently*) My dear, will you do something for me?

Mother: (*Between sobs*) What do you want me to do?

The Buddha: Go back to your village and knock on every door that you come to. Ask each person first, if they have ever suffered and secondly, whether as time passes, the suffering passes. When you have done this, bring me back a seed from every house, where there has *never* been any suffering of any kind.

Mother: I am sure no one else will have suffered like me, no one has spoken to me about suffering. I will bring you back many seeds, I know.

Narrator: So the weeping mother set off and did as the Buddha had asked her to do. She knocked on the door of the first house in her village.

Mother: I have lost my baby, I shall never get over her death, but the Buddha has asked me to collect a seed from each house where I find there has been no suffering. Will you give me such a seed? I am sure that you have never suffered.

First Villager: I'm afraid I cannot give you a seed. You see, my mother died when I was quite young and the pain was so awful. We all suffered. As children, we helped each other in our grief, but we still suffered greatly. I cannot give you such a seed. However, one thing I can tell you, that as time passed, the pain has lessened and we are now able to talk about our mother without crying. We can even remember some of the lovely things that we did together and sometimes laugh. But we did suffer at the time.

Narrator: The mother hurried on to the next house in search of her seed.

Mother: My baby has died and I am suffering greatly. Have you ever suffered?

Second Villager: Oh we are suffering now, you see our pet dog died this morning and we cannot bear his loss. Perhaps one day, when we feel better we will have a new pet, but not now.

Narrator: The mother did not receive a seed from this family. She could see they were suffering too, in a different way, and so she hurried on to the next house to find her seed.

Mother: The Buddha has sent me to collect a seed from you, if you can tell me that you have never suffered any loss or pain of any kind.

Third Villager: Well, I am afraid you will have to try another house, because you see, I cannot give you such a seed. We have all suffered greatly. You see, we lost our grandad. Oh we loved him so much, he used to do so much about the house. The only thing I can tell you is that the pain was terrible at the time, but it has passed a little now.

Narrator: The mother travelled on and on asking first at one house and then another. But everywhere she went, she learnt that what the Buddha had said was true. Everyone had suffered in some way, but eventually all suffering passed away.

After a time of quiet reflection, give an opportunity for open question and answer discussion, to help allay fears, but also to recognize the need to talk about deep-felt grief.

Hymn

No 140, 'Lead me from death to life', in *Come and Praise 2* (BBC).

6 WATER THEMES

Water Projects

5–11
Activity/Assembly
All
(Preparation needed)

To begin this series of assemblies on water, set the scene by asking the children to think about how water is used in their daily lives. Perhaps each class could focus on one particular aspect of water and be prepared to speak about it when the classes join together for this first assembly. For instance, each class could think about these different activities:

Water in the Home – cooking, washing, drinking, heating, showering, cleaning, etc.

Water Sports – swimming, water-skiing, diving, fishing, canoeing, river-rafting, sailing, punting

Water Holidays – by the sea, on the river, on the canals, visits to ponds and lakes

Water in Industry – canning, laundries, waterworks, power stations

The Weather – rain and measuring rain fall, storms, floods, hurricanes, keeping records, clouds

Water Conservation – how to save water in our homes, schools, gardens

Under-water Creatures – those creatures that live in the sea, ponds, rivers, lakes

Lack of Water – what would this mean at home and abroad? (This could be developed in the second assembly)

At this first assembly *all* the ideas need to be drawn together and shared with the whole school. This can be done in a variety of ways:

The children could be encouraged to make magazine picture collages or paintings and drawings of a particular activity. Related craft ideas could be brought to the assembly to encourage a watery theme. For instance, different shaped fish could be cut out and suspended from the ceiling, or deep-sea tanks could be made out of old cardboard boxes with cellophane panels. Artefacts such as under-water goggles, flippers, arm-bands, etc., could be brought into school and displayed.

When everyone has had a brief chance to contribute, these topics could be further developed back in the classroom. There are some books in the *Resources* section to stimulate further discussion.

Prayer

Father God, we thank you for the gift of water – For the fun it brings and the life it supports. Help us to conserve our water and not waste this precious commodity. Amen

Hymn

No 7, 'Water of life' in *Come and Praise* (BBC).

Resources

Bailey, D. (1991) *What Can We Do About Wasting Water?* Franklin Watts.
Baines, J. (1993) *Links: Water*, Hodder Wayland.
Davies, K. and Oldfield, W. (1991) *Starting Science: Floating and Sinking*, Hodder Wayland.
Davies, K. and Oldfield, W. (1993) *Starting Science: Water*, Hodder Wayland.
Ellis, C. (1991) *Fact Finders: Water*, BBC.
Parker, P. (1990) *Water For Life*, Simon and Schuster Young Books.
Smith, D. (1997) *The Water Cycle*, Hodder Wayland.
Taylor, B. (1993) *Water and Life, Science Starters*, Franklin Watts.
Walpole, B. (1991) *Water, Threads Series*, A and C Black, 1991
Williams, B. (2001) *Water, Environment Starts Here*, Hodder Wayland.

Moses	5–7
	Assembly
	Judaism and Christianity

The whole class can be involved in this assembly, which is based on Exodus 1–2, through movement and music, dance and drama.

Divide the class into *groups*:

Soldiers
Mothers with babies
Reeds
Handmaidens

And main *characters*:

King
Captain of Army
Princess
Mother
Miriam
Moses
Narrator

Narrator: This is the story of how a baby was saved in a basket that floated on a river a long, long time ago. The baby's name was Moses and he had a big sister called Miriam. They lived in the land of Egypt, where one day the King made a very cruel law. He decided to kill all the baby boys that were born to the Israelite people.

(*Enter King who calls his soldiers to carry out his orders*)

King: Call my Army Captains here to me. (*Soldiers come running*) Ah, there you are. I have decided that the Israelite people are becoming far too powerful in my land. So I have decided to kill all the baby boys so that they cannot grow up and rise against me. I want you to carry out my orders for me. Find all the baby boys and throw them into the Nile.

(*The army begins by searching a group of mothers who are holding their babies. They take them away*)

Narrator: Moses' mother heard this terrible news so she called her daughter Miriam to her and together they thought of a plan.

Moses' Mother: Quickly, let us make a basket out of the reeds from the river. If we cover the bottom with tar, it will be perfectly safe and watertight and will float on the water. Then we can hide our baby inside and float the basket between the tall reeds. When the soldiers come to search our house, they will not find our baby.

Narrator: Miriam did as she was told. She helped her mother to make the basket and carefully placed the baby inside. Then she ran to the river to hide the basket amongst the gently waving reeds.

(*The reeds dance as Miriam hides the baby. Tape-record some music to which the reeds can dance. Finally the reeds cover the baby with their arms bent in different positions*)

Narrator: When Miriam was certain that the baby was quite safe in the reeds, she stood close by to make quite sure that nothing happened to him. Just then the King's own daughter came down to the water with all her beautiful maidens to have a swim.

(*The princess and her maidens perform their swimming dance. Tape-recorded music is needed once more*)

Narrator: Suddenly, the princess saw the basket. She asked one of her servants to bring it to her. She opened the basket and saw the baby inside. The baby was crying. Miriam saw what happened and forgetting about being afraid, she ran up to the princess.

(*Miriam runs to the group of swimmers*)

Miriam: Shall I go and find a nurse for you, who can look after the baby?

Princess: Oh yes please do, I think the poor little boy is hungry.

Narrator: So Miriam ran to fetch Moses' own mother.

(*Moses' mother curtsies to the princess*)

Princess: If you look after this baby for me, I will pay you well.

Narrator: Moses' mother was overjoyed to be looking after her own baby and to be protected by the princess. Later when Moses was much older, he went to live in the royal palace with the princess. He grew up into a fine, strong man and he became a very great leader. This was all part of God's plan for him and for the people of Israel. (See page 91 for the dramatic Pesah story).

Hymn

No 17, 'Little Baby Moses' in *Come and Sing* (Scripture Union).

The Man Who Took Seven Baths

5–7
Assembly
Judaism (and Christianity)

This Old Testament story from 2 Kings 5: 1–19 can be read from Rock, L. (2001) The Lion Bible Everlasting Stories, Lion Publishing PLC. A class of children can mime the actions. You will need the following characters:

Captain Naaman
100 captives
King
Several doctors
Naaman's wife
Wife's maid
Naaman's servants
Elisha
Elisha's servant

The story unfolds in the following way. Captain Naaman returns victoriously from war, bringing with him 100 captives. The King richly rewards Naaman by giving him twelve sacks of gold and twelve servants. Suddenly, they notice that Naaman has the dreaded skin disease, leprosy. Everyone runs away from him. Many doctors try to cure him, but all to no avail.

Naaman's wife has a little Israelite maid. The little maid tells her mistress that she knows a prophet in her own country who could cure Naaman. So Naaman sets out to see the King of this country, taking with him many chariots containing his servants and silver and gold to give to the King. The King sends Naaman to the Prophet Elisha. Elisha does not answer his door, but sends his servant out to tell Naaman that he must take seven baths in the River Jordan in order to be cured. Naaman flies into a rage, saying that he could have bathed in his own rivers and that he did not travel all this way just to bathe in the muddy River Jordan.

Naaman's servants plead with him to do what Elisha has commanded him to do. So Naaman decides to obey. He goes down to the Jordan and gets in and out of the water seven times. (*Children can hold a large sheet to imitate the water movement.*) Naaman's skin is healed. Naaman returns to Elisha's house once more and says: 'Now I know there is only one true God. Please accept these gifts.' But Elisha refuses and sends him home. End with a simple prayer of thanks for the little girl who saved her master.

Hymn

No 10, 'Praise Him', in *Come and Sing* (Scripture Union).

Calming of The Storm

5–11
Assembly
Christianity

For those who live near the sea, try and arrange a visit to look at fishermen at work. Collect items for a display table – bits of driftwood, shells, cuttlefish, etc. Others will have to be content with a picture/book display about the sea.

Let the children mime the following story, with these characters:

Jesus
Six friends
Wind
Waves

Jesus had been talking to great crowds of people all day. He beckoned his friends and told them that he was tired. He asked his friends if they would sail him across the Sea of Galilee to the other shore where it was more peaceful. They agreed. All the friends got into a large boat and set sail. It was a calm evening. The fishermen knew the waters well. They had fished them for many years. Suddenly, the wind began to blow and buffet the little boat (*a group of children perform the wind dance*). Then the waves began to beat against the side of the boat. Jesus was so tired that he had fallen asleep. (*The waves dance around the boat.*)

At first the friends did not bother to wake Jesus, they just talked anxiously to each other. But then the waves became larger and stronger and rocked the boat and the friends became very frightened indeed. The friends woke Jesus up and said: 'We are in terrible trouble, the boat is sinking.' Jesus stood up and said, 'Peace, be still.' Immediately the wind ceased and the waves calmed and Jesus said to his friends: 'Why were you so afraid? Don't you know that I will look after you?' But the friends looked at each other and said: 'Who is this man? Even the wind and waves obey him!'

Prayer

Dear Lord Jesus, you protected your friends in that storm on the Sea of Galilee. We ask you to protect all those who work at sea. Amen.

Hymn

No 26, 'A little ship was on the sea', in *Child Songs*, ed. by Carey Bonner (The Pilgrim Press).

Water Poems For Movement

5–7
Assembly
All

The following poems are from a book edited by E.J.M. Woodland (1966) *Poems for Movement*, which has been used by teachers for many years. They are reproduced by kind permission of HarperCollins Publishers, Ltd. The poems could be read to the school to encourage participation in the assembly theme through use of whole body movement.

The Rain

Pitter-patter, pitter-patter,
Little drops of rain,
Pitter-patter, pitter-patter
On the window pane.

Pitter-patter, pitter-patter,
Little drops of rain
Gently falling. Gently falling
To the ground again.

Pitter-patter, pitter-patter,
Little drops of rain
Running quickly. Running quickly,
Dance into a chain.

© S. Holroyd, 1966

Here the children may imitate the rain-drops. Everyone stands up.

Verse 1: With head, arms and hands the children suggest the rain-drops dashing against the window-pane and trickling down.
Verse 2: Arms and hands move gently downward. A whole body movement to the ground follows.
Verse 3: Here the children use the suggestion of running, then join hands to suggest the rain-drops running together into trickles.

The Song of the Waves

We are the quiet, timid waves that gently
    kiss your toe.
We hardly seem to move at all, so softly do
    we flow.
The only sound we ever make is a whisper or
    a sigh,
But inch by inch we creep along until the
    tide is high.

We are the jolly, bubbling waves that laugh and
    splash with glee.
We bustle up the seashore, as merry as can be.
We spill our foam upon the beach, spread like a
    soapy pool,
Then slide back quickly to the sea and leave the
    hot sand cool.

We are the heavy, roaring waves, that burst in
    clouds of spray.
We crash against the cliff-side, and swirl and
    spin away.
As each of us falls backwards, there's another
    close behind
To hammer at the sturdy rock; to smash and tear
    and grind.

© Bernard W. Martin, 1966

Verse 1: Children make soft, flowing movements with hands, arms and whole bodies, while gently moving forward.

Verse 2: Children use brisk, sharp movements of hands, arms and legs. They move forward to suggest the waves breaking.

Verse 3: Here really strong, vigorous movements should be made with all parts of the body.

    (It helps to suggest that one end of the room represents the beach.)

Prayer

Heavenly Father, we thank you for the soft refreshing rain that makes the flowers grow and for all the fun and joy of the seaside. Take care of each one of us during the summer holidays. Amen.

Hymn

No 9, 'To God who makes all lovely things', in *Someone's Singing Lord*, A. and C. Black.

Noah's Ark

This Old Testament story can either be read from a children's Bible or retold from one of the many lovely story books listed on overleaf. Noah's obedience, trust in God and God's promise of a rainbow can be discussed. Children need to know that Noah was a very good man, who was warned by God that there would be a flood and that he should build an ark to save his family and two of every kind of bird, insect and animal (Genesis, Chapters 6–9). The story has rich opportunities for cross-curricular links and for children to feel their way into the story through dance and drama, movement and mime and all kinds of art and craft and musical activities.

Lots of Assembly Ideas:

1 A book that retells the story of Noah's ark for young children, using simple language and large, imaginative pictures, is A. Barber (1998) *Noah and the Ark*, Picture Corgi. It retells the main elements of the story and talks about God washing the earth clean for the animals, as man had spoilt it. Reading the story and pouring over the pictures is a very good way to introduce the subject, especially if it is intended that the story will be used as a drama production for an assembly.

Every child then, can be involved in a class assembly either by pretending to build the ark or by being one of the animals. It is even possible to involve the whole school in the drama by sitting in-the-round, wearing simple masks and getting children to march or dance round the centre when their particular section is called: e.g., all the insects parade round, pretending to board the ark; all the 'cats' show us how they eat; all the birds fly round before roosting. Children can dance to music from the *Carnival of the Animals* by Saint Saëns, or many other classical or popular pieces of music can be used.

2 Other related themes for assemblies could take the form of art work and writing about endangered species; the work of the World Wildlife Organization; descriptions of visits to zoos; bird sanctuaries and wildlife parks; care of pets, protection of birds and bird nests; insects and mini-beasts. One of the most interesting story books that can be used as a discussion starter on this theme is: A. Jonas (1991), *Aardvarks, Disembark*, Julia MacRae Books. It is an excellent picture book about Noah's ark that cuts straight to the rain, rainbow and animals disembarking. The book's distinguishing feature is the rare and unusual animals that are mentioned, most of which are endangered or now extinct species. One would be forgiven for thinking that those named are mythological creatures because of their strange names, but the excellent biographical details at the back of the book record what the animals are and where they come from. For instance, would you know that an *agouti* was a Central American rodent? Or a *fennec* was an African fox? Or a *lammergeier* was a vulture found in Europe, Africa and the Middle East? Lots of other interesting facts.

3 Visitors from various animal sanctuaries or charities could be invited in to school to talk to the children about their work, e.g., PDSA, RSPCA, RSPB, etc. Perhaps the children could make a special collection for a particular charity.

4 In some parts of the country, specialists will come into school and bring their animals, birds or insects for the children to see, e.g. a police horse, owls that have grown up in captivity, or a bee-keeper, who could describe his work.

5 A 'Thank You God for the Creepy-Crawlies that Nobody Likes' assembly could be presented in words and dancing to the song 'The Ugly Bug Ball'.

Noah's Ark Stories

Adams, G. (2000) *Noah's Ark*, Orion Children's Books.

Agard, J. (1990) *Go Noah Go*, Hodder and Stoughton (Delightful illustrations for children to pour over. Rhyming West Indian phraseology).

Allen, J. (1995) *Two by Two by Two*, Orion Children's Books (Very humorous cartoon-like pictures show how the animals amuse themselves on the journey. Noah organizes games; soccer, basket-ball, a giraffe slide, a weekly show, a nose parade, etc.).

Auld, M. (1999) *Noah's Ark*, Franklin Watts (Lovely pictures to hold up in an assembly. Useful information at the back, i.e. Genesis is the first book in the Bible. Hebrew Bible called the Tanakh. Raises difficult questions about death of everything, etc.).

Cousins, L. (1997) *Noah's Ark*, Walker Books.

Frank, P. (1999) *Noah and the Great Flood*, Lion Publishing.

Goodhart, P. (1998) *Noah Makes a Boat*, Methuen (Excellent for humour and scientific/practical boat-making solutions.).

Hawkins. C. and J. (1990) *Noah Built an Ark One Day*, Methuen Children's Books (A lift-the-flap book. Good for counting activities).

Ray, J. (1995) *Noah's Ark*, Orchard Books.

Resnick, J.P. (1995) *Bible Stories, A Treasury for Young Readers*, Courage Books. (Includes Noah, lovely illustrations).

Rose, G. (1985) *Trouble in the Ark*, Puffin Books/Kestrel (Good for animal sounds).

Shilson-Thomas, A. (1994) *A First Picture Puffin Book of Bible Stories*, Puffin Books.

Spier, P. (1998) *The Great Flood*, Mammoth (Winner of Caldecott Medal. A tell-your-own-story from the pictures without words, apart from the opening poem.)

Unwin, P. and Petty, K. (2003) *Wake Up, Mr Noah*, Macmillan Children's Books, (Mr Noah takes up today's issues; oil on birds' wings, poaching and killing animals for their commercial value, destruction of habitats for different species. Noah's answer is to teach the world to protect/respect what we have).

Waddell, M. (2001) *Stories from the Bible*, Frances Lincoln, (Includes Noah).

Williams, M. (1998) *The Amazing Story of Noah's Ark*, Walker Books (Cartoon-like pictures).

Poetry

There are many useful poetry books with the emphasis on animals or counting animals:

Agard, J. (1996) *We Animals Would Like a Word With You*, Random House Children's Books.

Andreae, G. (2002) *Cock-a-doodle-doo! Farmyard Hullabaloo*, Orchard Books.

Andreae, G. (2002) *Rumble in the Jungle*, Orchard Books.

Bennett, J. (Compiled by) (1999) *Green Poems*, Oxford University Press.

Bennett, J. (Compiled by) (1991) *The Animal Fair*, Picture Puffins.

Bradman, T. (Compiled by) (1990) *Animals Like Us*, A Young Puffin Book.

Chichester Clark, E. (2000) *I Never Saw a Purple Cow & Other Nonsense Rhymes*, Walker Books.

Cooling, W. (Compiled by) (2000) *Poems About Animals, What Fun to be a Hippo*, Franklin Watts.

Daniel, M. (Compiled by) (1991) *A First Golden Treasury of Animal Verse*, Macmillan Children's Books.

Edwards, R. (1996) *Moon Frog, Animal Poems for Young Children*, Walker Books.

Foster, J. (1994) *Poetry Paintbox: Minibeast Poems*, Oxford University Press.

Foster, J. and Paul, K. (2000) *Pet Poems*, Oxford University Press (Wonderful illustrations).

Nichols, G. (1998) *Asana and the Animals. A Book of Poetry*, Walker Books.

Puffin Books, (Various Authors) (2001) *The Puffin Book of Amazing Animal Poems*, Puffin Books.

Rice, J. (1994) *Bears Don't Like Bananas*, Simon and Schuster.

Environmental Studies

Birds of Prey (also on video) *Amazing World Series* (1997), Dorling Kindersley.

(Also in the same series, some of which are on CD-Rom or video: *Bats, Beetles, Cats, Crocodiles and Reptiles, Dogs and Foxes, Frogs and Toads, Lizards, Mammals, Poisonous Animals* (video), *Spiders, Snakes, Tropical Birds* (video), *Wolves*)

Bender, L. (1989) *Creatures of the Deep*, Franklin Watts.

Bright, M. (1988) *Giant Panda*, Project Wildlife Series, Franklin Watts.

(Other books in the series include: *Alligators and Crocodiles, Eagles, Elephants, Koalas, Mountain Gorilla, Tiger*)

Eyewitness Guides, Bird, (2002) published by Dorling Kindersley.

(Other books in the series include: *Butterfly and Moth, Cat, Desert, Dog, Eagle, Elephant Gorilla, Horse, Insect, Jungle, Mammal, Pond and River, Reptile, Whale*).

Ganeri, A. (1999) *Creatures That Glow*, Mammoth Paperback, Marshall Pickering Editions.

Ganeri, A. (1999) *Prickly and Poisonous*, Mammoth Paperback, Marshall Pickering Editions.

Greenaway, T. (1996) *The Really Horrible Guides: The Really Horrible Horny Toad and Other Clammy Creatures*, Dorling Kindersley.

Johnson, J. (1999) *Creepy Crawlies*, Marshall Pickering Editions.

Johnson, J. (1997) *Spooky Spiders and Other Insects*, Marshall Pickering Editions.

Ling, M. (1998) *Chick*, See How They Grow Series, Dorling Kindersley.

(There are many other books in this series including: *Penguin, Butterfly* (video), *Calf, Foal, Fox, Giraffe, Kitten, Lamb, Mouse, Owl, Pig, Puppy*)

Morgan, S. (2002) *Butterflies and Moths* Life Cycle Series, Belitha Press.

(Other books in the series include: *Cats and Other Mammals, Crabs and other Crustaceans, Ducks and Other Birds, Frogs and Other Amphibians*).

Crocodile Natural World Series, Hodder Wayland in Association with WWF-UK (2001)

(Other books include: *Chimpanzee, Dolphin, Elephant, Giant Panda, Great White*

Shark, Grizzly Bear, Hippopotamus, Killer Whale, Lion, Orangutan, Penguin, Habitats, Life Cycles, Polar Bear, Tiger).

Parker, S. (1992) *Whales and Dolphins*, Insights Series, Oxford University Press. (Other books include: *Armoured Animals, Bugs and Beetles, Frogs and Toads*).

Pipe, J. (1998) *The Giant Book of Snakes and Slithery Creatures*, Aladdin/Watts Books.

Royston, A. (1992) *Baby Animals*, Eye Opener Series, Dorling Kindersley. (Other books include: *Birds, Farm Animals, Jungle Animals, Sea Animals, Zoo Animals, Minibeasts, Night-Time Animals*).

Savage, S. (2002) *Amphibians*, What's The Difference series, Hodder Wayland. (Other books include: *Birds, Fish, Insects, Mammals*).

Taylor, B. (1998) *Animal Hide and Seek*, Dorling Kindersley (Over 440 animals to find: key to pictures at the back).

Wallace, K. and Bostock, M. (1996) *Imagine You Are a Crocodile*, Hodder Children's Books.

Young, C. (1996) *The Big Bug Search*, Usborne.

Art/Craft

Bulloch, I. and James, D. (1996) *I Want To Be A Puppeteer*, Two-Can Publishing Limited.

Butterfield, M. (1994) *Making Puppets*, Creative Craft Series, Heinemann.

Chapman, G. and Robson, P. (1995) *Making Masks for Children*, Hodder Wayland.

Chapman, G. and Robson, P. (1994) *Making Toys That Move*, Simon and Schuster (includes scurrying spider, jumping bugs, cat, mouse and dinosaur puppets).

Gibson, R. and Tyler, J. (1992) *You and Your Child: Paperplay, Lots of Ideas for Young Children*, Usborne Publishing Limited.

Good, K. (1999) *Moulding Materials*, Design Challenge Series, Evans Brothers Limited (Some excellent ideas, especially for creepy crawlies).

Grater, M. (1987) *Fun Models, A Michael Grater Fun-to-make Book*, Macdonald (Includes Noah's Ark, cats, lions, kangaroo, cows etc.).

Grater, M. (1987) *Fun Movers, A Michael Grater Fun-to-make Book*, Macdonald.

Grater, M. (1983) *Make it in Paper*, Dover Publications.

Grater, M. (1995) *Masks and Disguises*, Dragons World.

Grater, M. (1988) *Papercraft Projects with One Piece of Paper*, Dover Publications.

Grater, M. (1967) *Paper Faces*, Mills and Boon (A classic for masks if you can still find a copy).

Grater, M. (1985) *Paper Mask-making*, Dover Publications.

Lynn, S. and James, D. (1991) *Play with Paper*, Two-Can Publishing (Excellent simple paper-tearing fish; bear, monkey, tiger masks; bear, rabbit paper-chains).

McNiven, H. and P. (1994) *Masks*, Hodder Wayland.

Morrow, J. (1990) *Making Models from Junk*, Longman (Pigs, dogs, caterpillars).

Pitcher, C. (1985) *Masks and Puppets*, Franklin Watts.

Robson, D. (1991) *Rainy Days, Masks and Funny Faces*, Franklin Watts (Excellent elephant and mouse mask).

Smith, A.G. (1990) *Easy-to-make Noah's Ark*, Dover Publications.

Tofts, H. (1990) *The 3-D Paper Book, Fun Things to do with Paper*, Franklin Watts (Very good crocodile and easy bird).

Wright, L. (1991) *Creative Craft, Masks. A Step-by-step Introduction*, Franklin Watts (Excellent).

Music

There are some lovely hymns and songs associated with this theme, including the following:

No 44, 'Who Built the Ark?' in *Someone's Sing Lord*, A. and C. Black, 1973.

No 41, 'All Things Which Live Below the Sky', in *Someone's Singing Lord*, A. and C. Black, 1973.

No 38, 'The Animals went in Two by Two', in *Apusskidu*, A. and C. Black, 1996 (Now available as a double cassette pack for the non-specialist music teacher).

No 39, 'Going to the Zoo', in *Apusskidu*, A. and C. Black, 1996 (Double cassette, as above).

No 1, 'I Have Two Ears', in *Count Me In*, A. and C. Black, 1984.

No 37, 'Two in a Boat' (Action Song), in *Count Me In*, A. and C. Black, 1984.

No 44, 'Mr Noah's Birthday', in *Count Me In*, A. and C. Black, 1984.

No 14, 'Act in Song', in *Game-Songs with Prof. Dogg's Troupe*, A. and C. Black, 2001 (Book and CD Pack).

No 18, 'Walking Through the Jungle', in *Game-Songs with Prof. Dogg's Troupe*, A. and C. Black, 2001, (CD Pack as above).

No 25, 'Colour Song', in *Game-Songs with Prof. Dogg's Troupe*, A. and C. Black, 2001 (As above).

No 38, 'Weather Song', in *Game-Songs with Prof. Dogg's Troupe*, A. and C. Black. 2001.

No 14, 'Who Put the Colours in the Rainbow?' In *Come and Praise*, BBC, 1990 (CD available).

Jonah

5–11
Assembly
Judaism and Christianity

An activity assembly to involve the whole class. Much topic work can be encouraged beforehand to do with the sea, ships, sailors, whales, etc.

You will need the following:

Characters	*Props*
God	Storm effects
Jonah	percussion instruments
Skipper	Cardboard ship
Sailors	Large fish
Large Fish	Crown
King of Nineveh	Dressing-up clothes
King's Courtiers	Swords
People of Nineveh	
Narrator	

Small groups of children can practise their parts beforehand, i.e. the sailors could learn the sailor's hornpipe dance; the people of Nineveh could practise mock fights; the courtiers could do a courtier's dance.

Begin in the following way. The children mime their parts while the narrator reads the story.

Narrator: God spoke to Jonah.

God: I am very angry with the people in the city of Nineveh. They have turned away from my ways and they are very wicked. Go and tell them that they must say they are sorry and try to live better lives, or I shall destroy the whole city!

Jonah: I don't want to go to that evil place. I shall hide from God. I shall go a long, long way away from God. I know, I'll take a ship and go to Tarshish.

Narrator: So Jonah set off to find a group of sailors who would sail him to Tarshish. By some very good fortune, he came across a group of sailors practising their sailor's dance in Joppa.

(*Hornpipe music – sailors have a few minutes to show off their dance*)

Jonah: Please take me to Tarshish. Here is my fare.

Skipper: All right, we are just about to set sail, come aboard.

Narrator: So the ship set sail with Jonah on board. But God caused a huge storm to arise, which tossed the ship high on the waves and threatened to sink the little boat. The sailors, terrified for their lives, began to throw their cargo overboard. Meanwhile, Jonah lay fast asleep below deck. But the skipper soon went and woke him up.

Skipper: What are you doing here fast asleep? Wake up and pray to your God to save us. It must be your fault that this great storm has come upon us. Who are you, where do you come from?

Jonah: 'I am a Hebrew, and I fear the Lord God of heaven who made the sea and the dry land.' (*RSV*)

Narrator: Then he told them about what God had asked him to do and how he had run away. The sailors became exceedingly afraid. The skipper spoke again.

Skipper: What must we do to save ourselves?

Jonah: You will have to throw me overboard.

Narrator: The sailors did not want to do this, but in order to save their ship and their own lives, they took hold of Jonah and tossed him into the raging sea. Immediately, the sea became calm and the storm died down and the sailors were very afraid. They knelt down and prayed to God. Meanwhile God sent a huge fish to save Jonah from drowning. The fish swallowed Jonah with one gulp.

(*Fish swims across the stage and swallows Jonah*)

Poor old Jonah had to stay inside the fish for three days and three nights, but then he prayed to God.

Jonah: Thank you God for saving my life. Now, whatever you ask me to do, I will do.

Narrator: So God caused the fish to carry Jonah to the safety of dry land and the fish spat him out onto the shore. Then God spoke to Jonah again.

God: This time Jonah, you must obey me and go straight to the people of Nineveh, and tell them that unless they say they are sorry and stop doing all these wicked things, they will surely die.

Narrator: So Jonah set off for the city of Nineveh to warn the people that they must turn away from their wicked ways or they would be destroyed within forty days.

   (*People of Nineveh stand up and demonstrate mock fights*)

Narrator: The King and his courtiers were having a party when they heard whispers of what Jonah had been saying.

   (*Coutiers dance, then the dance stops as each couple whispers in the ear of the next couple*)

Narrator: So the King of Nineveh spoke.

King: Listen to me everyone, we must ask God's forgiveness for our sins and try to lead better lives. No more fighting, no more bad behaviour. I declare a day of fasting. We will go without food and drink and put on sackcloths, to show God that we are truly sorry, and we will beg God to forgive us. Perhaps then we will be saved.

Narrator: When God saw all this, he knew that they were indeed truly sorry, so he did not punish the people of Nineveh. But the story does not end quite there. Jonah felt very cross with God because God did not punish the people after all. But God explained to Jonah that he would always forgive people if they were truly sorry.

Prayer

Father God, forgive us when we do wrong things and help us to lead better lives. Amen.

Hymn

'Ose Shalom', lyrics: traditional; music: Hirsch Nurit in *Israel in Song*, compiled, edited and arranged by Velvel Pasternak, published by Tara Publications, Cedarhurst, NY. It is reproduced by kind permission of the author and ACUM Ltd.

Ose Shalom

A traditional refrain which rounds off many set liturgical passages is a recurring motif in Jewish art and a popular chorus for youth groups' singalongs. The alternative form – appearing below in brackets – is favoured by some progressive communities who wish to extend the prayer for peace beyond those present and beyond the Jewish community – to all people. (Angela Wood)

Ose shalom bimromav, hu ya'ase shalom, aleynu v'al kol Yisrael
(v'kol benei adam) v'imru Amen.

May he who makes peace in the highest bring this peace upon us and upon
all Israel (and all the human race) and let us say Amen.

The music is arranged in two parts. The air could be taught to younger children. Older
children might like the challenge of learning the second part.

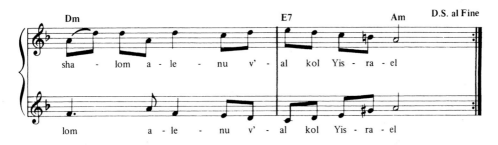

The Money Tree
(A Chinese Traditional Tale Based on a Story by
Ken Ma)

5–11
Assembly
All

For this assembly you will need a deep tray of water, and two small tins of oil paint, (the type used for painting model aeroplanes) two straws, and two or three pieces of paper that have been cut to the size of the tray.

The aim of this assembly is to show the children that the truth will eventually come to the surface, like oil paint always floats to the surface on water. A print can be made of the oil paint by floating the paper on top of the water. This is called marbling. All the children can have a turn in their classrooms after the assembly.

To demonstrate the activity, take one of the straws, dip it into the paint, and swirl it around on top of the water in the tray. Do the same thing again with the other coloured paint. Then simply float the paper on the top of the paint and water and show the beautiful pattern that the oil paint has made. This exercise can be repeated several times to show that the oil will always stay on the top of the water and make a pretty pattern.

Then tell the following Chinese traditional tale about how oil floating on water saved a little Chinese boy and his family from financial ruin. The story could be mimed as the teacher tells the tale.

A long time ago, in a far away country called China, a little boy called Chang made his living for his family by selling oil for people to use in their oil lamps. Each week, when it was market day, Chang would carry his two cans of oil to market, carefully balanced on each end of a long pole that he carried on his shoulders. It was a very long walk to the market and the cans felt heavier with every step. But as soon as he got to the market he would set up his little stall and sell oil to everyone who came to him. It was quite a messy job, and the oil would often spill over his fingers as he poured it from his large cans into the little oil lamps that people would bring for him to fill up. People placed the money into his little oily hands and he put the money carefully into his pockets. When all the oil was sold, he would carry the empty tins back on his shoulders and start walking the long journey home.

On one particular market day, when he had been selling oil all day, he felt so tired that he decided to sit down and rest under an enormous shady tree just outside the market. Before long, his eyelids began to feel very heavy and he fell fast asleep. He must have slept for some time, because when he awoke, most of the people had left the market place and they were going home. He picked up his empty cans, put his hands in his pockets to check that the money was still safe and made ready to set off for home. To his horror, he found that his pockets were quite empty, the money had all gone, it had been stolen.

Poor Chang burst into tears. He got down on his hands and knees and looked all round the base of the tree, just in case the money had fallen out of his pockets. But there was not a coin to be found. Chang put his head in his hands and cried loudly. What on earth would he tell his father? How could he tell him that he had sold all the precious oil and then lost all their money? He cried and cried.

Just then, an old wise man with a very long beard, carrying a water jar and a walking stick, came along and asked Chang why he was crying. Through his sobs, Chang explained that someone had stolen all his money while he had been asleep.

'Oh' said the wise man, 'I know who has stolen all your money, it is this Money tree, under which you have been sleeping'. And taking his walking stick, he said, 'I will make the Money tree give it all back to you.' He set about hitting the Money tree to make it return Chang's money.

Very soon a huge crowd gathered around the old man and the young boy and when they asked what the old man was doing, they started to roar with laughter. 'There is no such thing as a Money tree, you silly old thing. Why not beat the tree a bit harder, it might rain down jewels as well, or pearls, or gold. Ha, ha.'

When everyone had had a good laugh, the old man turned round and said 'You have been watching a show, and for making you laugh, you owe me two coins each.' Everyone stopped laughing, and tried to escape but the old man put up his stick and said, 'No one leaves until you drop two coins into my water-jar.' One by one, the little crowd put two coins into the jar, when suddenly the old man shouted, 'Stop Thief'. A greedy, fat man looked at the old man and said, 'Who me?' 'Yes you,' said the old man, 'Come and look everybody, you can see for yourself that this man has stolen young Chang's money'. As the people crowded round the water jar, the coins had sunk to the bottom, but there was a strange oily film across the top of the water.

'Turn out your pockets at once', commanded the old man. Shaking with fear, the fat man put his hands into his pockets and produced all the missing coins, all covered in oil by little Chang's oily fingers.

He had to give back all the money to little Chang and he was taken away quickly by a passing policeman. So you see, the truth surfaced like the oil floating on top of the water, saved little Chang and his family from losing all their money.

Prayer

Father God, make each one of us completely honest. Help us never to steal anything that does not belong to us. Amen.

Hymn

No 38, 'Think, think on these things', in *Someone's Singing Lord* A. & C. Black.

How the Kingfisher Got its Name
(An Indian Folk Story)

5–7
Assembly
Hindusim

(Adapted from 'How a Bird got its Lovely Colour' by S.G. Pottam in *Indian Folk Tales*, published by Sabbash Publishers).

You will need the following:

Characters:
    King
    Princess
    4 Noblemen
    Brown Bird
    4 Brown Babies
    Crow
    4 Black babies
    Narrator

Props:
    Crown
    Ring
    Cloaks
    5 Brown tunics of feathers
    5 Brown bird masks
    1 Cloak of beautiful Kingfisher feathers
    5 Black tunics of feathers
    5 Black bird masks

Narrator: Once upon a time, two birds built their nests in the trees alongside the river Ganges. One was a little brown bird and the other was a large black crow. (*The brown bird and the black crow mime the building of nests and then sit down*). Very soon, both birds had laid four beautiful eggs each. They were both very proud of their eggs and showed them to each other.

(*The two birds mime twittering movements with their heads and beckon one another to come and look at each others eggs*).

The black crow frowned and scratched her head. She thought that the brown bird's eggs looked distinctly nicer than her own. So one day when the little brown bird was diving in the river to catch fish to eat, the black crow did a most despicable thing. She very carefully swapped each of the brown bird's eggs with her own.

(*The crow mimes the action while the brown bird pretends to dive for fish*).

When the brown bird came back to her nest, she thought her eggs looked a little odd, but she settled down, and waited for her babies to hatch.
    One fine morning, there was the sound of eggs cracking in the brown bird's nest, and out popped four large black birds.

(The action is mimed)

Brown Bird: Oh no, you cannot be my babies.

Narrator: Just at that moment, the eggs in the crow's nest began to hatch, and out popped four beautiful little brown birds.

> *(The eight children mime the action of breaking out of their eggs and make twittering movements around their 'wrong' mother)*

Brown Bird: Crow, there must be some dreadful mistake, I have got your babies, and you have got mine. Please give me back my babies.

Crow: No, No, there is no mistake, these are my babies, I hatched them.

Narrator: Poor brown bird did not know what to do. Suddenly, she had a brilliant idea, she would go and see the King. Surely he could sort out her terrible problem. Brown bird flew off to the palace to seek justice, only to discover that the King had problems of his own. The Princess was in floods of tears, the King looked distraught, and the noblemen were going hither and thither searching for something.

> *(The birds leave the stage; the King, Princess and Noblemen enter)*

Princess: Boo hoo, boo hoo, oh where, oh where can I have lost my ring? Are you sure that you have searched everywhere?

First Nobleman: I have looked all over the Palace.

Second Nobleman: I have looked everywhere in the gardens.

Third Nobleman: I have looked in all the fields.

Fourth Nobleman: The only place we haven't looked is the river. We need that little brown bird that dives into the river to catch fish. She could look and see if you dropped your ring in the river.

King: Bring the brown bird to me.

Brown Bird: I am here Sir, I heard everything because I was coming to tell you that crow has stolen my babies.

King: Well then, if you find my daughter's ring, I will give you a very great reward. But first, let us deal with your problem. Come on everyone let us go down to the river. I shall devise a test to sort out whose babies belong to whom.

Narrator: Everyone went down to the river, where crow was sitting with her brown babies.

King: Now, little black birds, I want you all to dive into the river to see if you can find my daughter's ring.

Narrator: The four black birds lined up and, one by one, jumped into the river. The first one nearly drowned and came up coughing and spluttering; the second one put its toe in the water and then ran away in fright. The third one dipped its wing in the water, fell over, and came out shrieking and squawking; and the fourth one was so frightened at seeing all its brothers' and sisters' mishaps that it held its nose, closed its eyes, flapped its wings and took a running jump. It landed splat on a stone and had to be helped up by everyone else.

(*The four black birds mime these actions in turn*)

King: Now come along, little brown birds, it's your turn. Line up, line up, see if you can find my daughter's ring.

Narrator: The little brown birds lined up beside the river and with one beautiful movement, they dived into the water and came up again.

(*The baby brown birds mime the action and come up smiling*)

Baby Brown Birds: We saw something beautiful and shining down there, but we haven't learned to pick up things yet, we're so little.

Mother Brown Bird: But I can, your majesty, let me go and have a look.

Narrator: The brown bird dived into the water and sure enough, she came up holding the Princess's ring.

(*The action is mimed*)

King: Now it must seem clear to you crow, that these brown birds are not afraid of the water, and those black birds are afraid. You are a very silly mother. You should be proud of your beautiful black babies. It is just that they are not meant to fish in the water like these brown birds. Now return the babies instantly. [The babies swap sides] Brown bird, as a reward for finding my daughter's ring, I shall call you the King's Fisher and I shall give you a beautiful, new, brightly coloured cloak of feathers, fit for a King.

(*The King gives the brown bird the cloak of beautiful feathers*).

Narrator: And so that is how the Kingfisher got its name and beautiful feathers. Water birds are different from land birds, but each play an important part in God's beautiful world.

Prayer

Thank you God for our similarities and our differences. Help each one of us to learn the unique contribution that we can make in your world. Amen.

Hymn

No 39, 'The ink is black', in *Someone's Singing Lord* A. & C. Black.

7 ANIMALS AND BIRDS

Sheep Farming: A Lamb Called Nuisance

5–7
Activity/Assembly
All

Show the children a shepherd's crook and ask if anyone knows what it is? Then ask them whether the crook shown is a neck or a leg crook. Do they know the difference? (Neck crooks are much wider than leg crooks.)

Perhaps some sheep's wool can be taken into school to show the children. Different groups could try dyeing it different colours using vegetable dyes.

Explain the work of a sheep farmer. Stress that it is very hard work. Farmers have to get up very early and in all weathers to feed the sheep. They have to count them to make sure that none are lost and to check that none have fallen over or in a ditch. This twice daily routine is called 'lookering' by farmers.

Remind the children of the sheep farming year:

Lambing in the spring; sometimes bottle-feeding lambs who have lost their mothers in the birthing process (called 'sock' lambs).

Shearing in the summer and rolling the fleece to put into deep sacks called 'sheep sheets'.

Dipping to prevent disease in the summer and autumn.

Regularly clipping and cleaning feet and bottoms against foot-rot and disease.

Changing the sheep from one field to another to give them new pasture and fresh grass.

Rounding up the sheep to inject against various ailments and to drench (that is giving medicine by mouth) against worms or liver fluke.

Going to market to sell young lambs and later, the wool after shearing.

Making hay in late summer for the sheep to eat during the winter snows.

Selecting the ewes to make up the new flock for next year, etc.

Write to: The British Wool Marketing Board for Education Packs, Multi-breed Posters, Fleece Samples, etc.

The Education Department
British Wool Marketing Board
Wool House, Roysdale Way
Euroway Trading Estate
Bradford BD4 6SE
Tel: 01274 688666
Fax: 01274 652233
Email: mail@britishwool.org.uk
Website: britishwool.org.uk

Then tell the following story: **A Lamb Called Nuisance**

Mrs Brown was ill in bed. Farmer Brown had to go out all day to buy new machinery. But it was lambing time and although most of the ewes had lambed successfully, Farmer Brown was extremely worried about one ewe who had had twins early that morning. Although the ewe was feeding the first lamb quite happily, she was neglecting the other lamb because it looked so sick and weakly. Farmer Brown knew that unless the lamb fed from its mother very quickly, the mother would reject the lamb completely and it would die.

'I'm terribly worried about that ewe and her two lambs – she doesn't seem to be feeding the second lamb at all. I know you are not well, my dear', Mr Brown said to Mrs Brown, 'but could you just look out of the window during the morning and see if the second lamb is all right.' 'Oh dear', said Mrs Brown, 'I don't feel at all well, but I will keep an eye on the lamb.'

Mr Brown set off and Mrs Brown went back to bed. At about coffee time Mrs Brown looked out the window. She stood watching silently for a minute or two and then to her horror she saw the ewe that Mr Brown had mentioned, pushing a very sickly lamb away from her. The ewe butted the lamb so hard that the lamb fell over and then the ewe marched off with her healthy lamb. Mrs Brown could hear sad little cries of 'baa, baa' coming from the sickly lamb, but then she saw it get up and follow its mother.

'Oh dear', thought Mrs Brown, 'if I go and get the lamb now, I might frighten the mother ewe altogether and she may never take it. I had better leave the lamb to follow its mother.'

Sometime later Mrs Brown looked out the window again. This time the mother ewe was far more ferocious and butted the lamb into the air. But the brave little lamb got up and followed its mother once more. Mrs Brown didn't know what to do. On the one hand, she could see that the mother wasn't taking to her lamb, but on the other hand, the lamb seemed determined to stay with its mother. So once more Mrs Brown decided not to interfere.

It was about tea-time when Mrs Brown looked out the window again; this time Mrs Brown could see the mother ewe and her healthy lamb, but she couldn't see the sickly lamb anywhere. 'Oh dear, what a nuisance,' thought Mrs Brown, 'I feel so ill, but I will just have to put on my dressing-gown and walk down the field and search for that baby lamb.'

It was a very long way to the bottom of the field and poor Mrs Brown, dressed in her dressing-gown and wellies, tramped over the long wet grass looking everywhere for the lost lamb. 'Where are you?' she called, 'Oh, where are you?' Suddenly, she heard a weak little bleat coming from the patch of grass just ahead of her. She hurried forward and there in the long grass lay the tiny white lamb. It was so exhausted from trying to catch up with its mother and it was so weak from having had no food that Mrs Brown thought that it was dying. The lamb did not move. Mrs Brown bent down and carefully put the lamb inside her dressing-gown. The lamb was so cold and shivery that Mrs Brown was certain the lamb would not live.

'Oh,' she whispered, 'you are such a nuisance. I don't feel well myself and I certainly don't feel like carrying you all the way back to the house. But I will. Come along, here we go.' Mrs Brown trudged back up the field to the house, the lamb felt heavier with every step and Mrs Brown felt more and more tired. When she got indoors, Mrs Brown put the lamb in a box by the kitchen cooker. But the lamb did not move, its head rolled forward and it was too weak even to bleat.

Mrs Brown could not find the baby milk and bottle that was always kept in the farmhouse, so she just did not know what to do to save the lamb. Suddenly, she thought, 'I will phone Mr Brown at the machinery sale, he will know how to save the lamb.' So Mrs Brown dialled the number. 'I am afraid that we ran out of the baby milk yesterday. Can you make up some warm sugar-water and dip a piece of cloth into it for the lamb to suck?' Mr Brown said, 'I hope that will keep the baby lamb alive until I can get home and bring the special milk and the baby bottle.'

Mrs Brown quickly made up the warm water and dipped a clean piece of sheet into it. But the lamb was too weak to suck. So Mrs Brown dipped her finger into the water and the lamb started to suck very gently. But it was a very slow process, and the kitchen floor was cold and hard and Mrs Brown was feeling very ill. 'You are a nuisance,' she whispered, 'but you have just got to drink.' Mrs Brown sat with the lamb for two hours, giving it drips of the sugar-water on her finger and then on the piece of rag. Miraculously, the lamb held on until Mr Brown came home with the milk and the baby bottle. Mr Brown made up the warm powdery milk and after trying very hard, the little lamb started to suck. However, she still looked very weak and sickly and Mr Brown was afraid that she would not live through the night. They made her warm and comfortable for the night and then they went to bed. Mr and Mrs Brown took it in turns to try and feed the lamb every two hours during the night.

In the morning the little lamb was sitting up and bleating. Farmer Brown quickly made up some more milk and to his astonishment, the little lamb sucked very hard and drank half the bottle. Mr and Mrs Brown again took it in turns to feed the lamb throughout that day and the next night and the next day and night, until on the third day the little lamb struggled to get out of her box and began to follow Mrs Brown round the kitchen.

'She doesn't know she's a lamb, she thinks she's our baby', laughed Mrs Brown. And that's when she got her name 'Nuisance'. While it was funny at first to be followed everywhere, it soon became very tiresome, especially when the lamb went to the toilet on the Brown's best sitting-room carpet, and even followed Mr Brown into the shower and then proceeded to put wet hoof marks all the way down the stair-carpet. 'Oh, you are a nuisance', the Browns both said. 'She will have to join the rest of the flock', said Mr Brown two weeks later. She's really becoming a nuisance in the house.

Nuisance didn't want to join the rest of the flock and stayed close to Mr and Mrs Brown, but quite suddenly when she saw all the other lambs chasing round the field and skipping and gambolling, she set off without a backward glance, and ran off to play with them.

It was a very strange thing that Nuisance really knew her name and whenever Mr and Mrs Brown called 'Nuisance', 'Nuisance', she would come running up to them, wherever they were in the field.

But the story doesn't end there. Two or three years later, when Nuisance was a mother ewe herself, Farmer Brown himself was ill, and Mrs Brown had to move the whole flock to a new pasture on her own. It's quite difficult to move sheep on one's own, as any farmer will tell you, because unless you are very careful, they will go off in all different directions. But Mrs Brown shouted, 'Nuisance, come on Nuisance, you have got to lead the way to the new field. If you come, all the others will follow you.' And do you know, that's exactly what they did.

If you know any farmers, perhaps you could feed a sock lamb in school and bring it into the assembly.

Prayer

Heavenly father, we thank you for all farmers and for the work they do. Be with them in times of difficulty and hardship. Give them the strength to work very long hours, for our benefit. Amen.

Hymn

No 14, 'Stand up, clap hands, shout thank you Lord', in *Someone's Singing Lord* A. and C. Black.

Pets	5–7 Assembly All

The aim of this assembly is to encourage children to really look after their pets properly. All pets need feeding, shelter, warmth and care. Children need to learn to take responsibility for their pets by feeding them. They need to learn to keep their pets clean and dry by changing bedding. They need to know that pets have to be taken to the vet when they are ill. And most important of all, pets need to be loved and need time invested in them. In taking responsibility for pets, children begin to understand that an animal cannot buy food for itself, or open a tin, or get its own drink and that neglected pets get lonely, frightened and hungry and may even run away.

The following story may help children to see the need for love, care and persistence with animals that cannot tell you how they are feeling and that caring for animals in the long term brings its own rewards.

It was an icy February, the chilling winds were blowing across the fields of frozen grass and increasing the long icicles that were hanging from buildings everywhere. A very young cat, almost a kitten herself, lost and lonely, tried to find shelter in a freezing shed. Half starved, shivering with the cold and very afraid, she searched for a place to sleep, she needed a place of safety. Through the stiff grass, she could see a light from a kitchen window from a house near-by.

At that moment, the door was flung open, illuminating a little girl who was about to feed the wild birds. In that instant, the terrified little cat was caught in the crossbeam of light and she fled immediately. Running to tell her parents, the little girl discovered, when she returned, that the cat was now nowhere to be seen. 'If we find it, can we keep it, can we keep it?' she pleaded. Her father thought that the cat might be a wild cat, to be so afraid of people, or else it was a cat that had been badly treated. So he gently said that as it was a bitter-cold evening, the little girl could leave some food outside the back door that night, for the cat to eat in case it was hungry.

To her astonishment, by the next morning, the food had all disappeared, but there was still no sign of the cat. This happened the next night and the following night and for a week after that. Each evening the food that the family left completely disappeared, but there was no sign of the one who was eating it. The little girl was getting more and more frustrated as the days went by. 'How can you look after a pet that doesn't want to be looked after or even seen?' she questioned.

The next day, her father made a rather peculiar discovery. He found that one of his old coats that had been hanging in his shed had accidentally fallen on the floor and he could see from the indentations that someone or something had been sleeping on it. So the following night, the family put the food in the shed and managed to stay close enough to see a thin little cat push open the door and come out licking its lips, looking very pleased with itself.

'It is a wild cat', confirmed Dad, 'It must be or else it would have come inside the house by now'. For several months, until early summer, the family patiently left food and milk for the little cat, bringing the dishes closer and closer to the kitchen door. Eventually, the timid little creature showed itself more and more as it gained in confidence, realizing that no one was going to hurt it. One day it came out quite openly to have her supper, but she still would not let the family touch her or stroke her, although they did speak very kindly to her.

One day, as the little girl was looking out of the window she gasped, 'Dad, there are now *two* cats on the lawn.' 'Oh no', said Dad 'the local cats must have told each other that this is a good place to eat!' The cat on the lawn was much larger than the one they were feeding. He was a big, male cat. The family nicknamed him Tom and called the young female cat, Pussy.

Some time later, although Tom and Pussy would not come into the house, as they were still fearful of people, Dad noticed that Pussy was getting fatter and fatter. 'Do you know, I think Pussy is going to have kittens,' he observed one day. One May morning, Pussy could not be found anywhere. She was not in any of her usual places. 'Perhaps she has left us,' thought the little girl sadly. Then quite suddenly, the family heard a cry coming from the hay barn. They rushed over to the barn to discover four beautiful kittens with their eyes tightly shut, mewing and wriggling against their very proud mother.

The family were overjoyed. But then a very sad thing happened. From that very day onwards, the babies completely disappeared. Everyone searched high and low, calling Pussy's name. Where could they be? The family were so upset. Perhaps some predator had taken the babies, like a fox or a crow. Dad reminded everyone that they *were* wild cats and so they might have just moved on somewhere else.

After about a month of searching and just as the family were beginning to give up all hope of ever seeing the baby kittens again, Dad suddenly discovered a nest of babies inside his old shed once more. 'She must have brought them home,' he thought delightedly. He tried to pick up one of the babies to get to know it, but tiny as it was, it was so like its mum, it was very afraid of human beings. It spat and scratched and tried to claw its way to freedom. Dad carefully put the baby back in the nest. 'We are never going to be able to tame these little ones unless we handle them as much as we can,' he said to himself. 'We shall have to tempt them out of their hiding place with food every day until they come to love and trust us and know that we intend them no harm.

Several more attempts were made to pick up the babies, but all to no avail. Until one day, the littlest one, who was also the bravest kitten of them all, thought to herself, 'all this spitting and scratching is doing me no good at all. I might as well try to get to know these humans, they may be alright after all.' So she trotted out of her hiding place and allowed herself to be picked up and stroked. She found out that it was quite pleasant and that she really enjoyed being petted and loved and given nourishing titbits. Gradually, gradually, the little kitten came out more and more often to be loved and fed. The other kittens soon began to follow her lead, very cautiously at first, but soon they too decided that human beings could be kind. The little girl adored all four kittens and found that through her constant love, care and attention, they soon became her special friends and playmates.

Prayer

Heavenly Father, we thank you for all the joy and happiness that pets can bring. May we never hurt or harm our pets. Help us to remember to be loving and kind and to clean and feed our pets every day. Bless those who rescue animals that have been ill-treated and those who look after them. Amen

Hymn

No 42, 'I love God's tiny creatures', in *Someone's Singing Lord* A. and C. Black.

The Lost Sheep

5–11
Assembly
Christianity

(Adapted from an idea in Judy Gattis Smith (1985), *Show Me*, Creative Resources Two, Bible Society.)

Make a happy and a sad mask out of brown paper bags. Tell the story of the lost sheep using the *Good News Bible*, Luke 15: 1–7.

Help the children to explore the feelings of the shepherd; first his *anguish* over one missing lamb after he has counted ninety-nine and recounted them to make quite sure

that one is missing; then his *fear* that a fox might have taken the lamb; then his *concern*, looking in all the likely places that the lamb might be trapped; finally, his *joy* when he hears a weak little bleat and his feelings of great *happiness*, when he finds the lamb unharmed, but stuck in a rocky crevice.

Recount how he rushes home to tell all his friends that he has found the lost lamb and how he decides to invite his friends to a special celebratory party.

Then it is the children's turn. One child puts on the unhappy mask and retells the story in his own words, trying to describe the shepherd's unhappy feelings. Another child puts on the happy mask and plays the part of the joyful shepherd. Variations on this theme include characters from the Bible portraying fear and bravery, nice or nasty.

The book *Show Me* is well worth trying to find. It is intended for 3–13-year-olds, and it is packed with many useful ideas and activities for drama in RE and school assemblies.

Prayer

Dear Lord Jesus, we know that you are like the good shepherd who cares for each one of us. Protect us from any danger today and look after those we love and those who love us. Amen.

Hymn

No 28, 'Loving shepherd of thy sheep', in *Infant Praise* (Oxford University Press).

The Good Shepherd

Psalm 23: 1–6, *Good News Bible*

Teach one of the psalms, i.e. Psalm 23 or Psalm 150 as a choral speaking piece. It can be a very dramatic way of ending 'The Lost Sheep' assembly, if it is done well, paying attention to loud and soft phrasing.

Psalm 23

The Lord is my shepherd;
I have everything I need.
He lets me rest in fields of green grass
and leads me to quiet pools of fresh water.
He gives me new strength.
He guides me in the right paths
as he has promised.
Even if I go through the deepest darkness,
I will not be afraid, Lord,
for you are with me.
Your shepherd's rod and staff protect me.

Pin the Load on the Donkey

Begin by reading Matthew 11: 28, *Good News Bible*: 'Come to me all of you who are tired from carrying heavy loads and I will give you rest.' (Quotation from the *Good News Bible*, published by the Bible Societies/HarperCollins Publishers Ltd, UK and is reproduced with the permission of the publishers).

For this activity you will need:

a large outline of a donkey (with no tail)
a tail
a blindfold
an easel or stand on which to pin the outline of the donkey
a bag that can be pinned onto the donkey's back
several word cards with words such as: 'selfish', 'greedy', 'spiteful', 'unkind', 'lazy'
    and some blank cards and a pen for extra words.

Ask the children if they have ever played 'Pin the tail on the donkey'. Then ask for a volunteer to be blindfolded to try to pin on the donkey's tail. Let several children try. After the fun and laughter, explain the serious message that people take a great deal of trouble about how they look on the outside (i.e. smart looking donkey with his tail), but sometimes they are not very nice inside.

Further explain that the donkey is used to carrying heavy weights, so pin the bag on his back and inform the children that you are going to fill up the bag with all the heavy weights that people carry about with them. Explain that a 'heavy weight' can be anything nasty that we think or do that spoils us and makes us feel unhappy. When we have got rid of all these heavy loads, we will all feel a lot lighter, brighter and happier and look nicer on the outside too.

Using the prepared cards, read out the words clearly to the whole school: 'selfish', 'greedy', 'spiteful', 'unkind', 'lazy'. Then choose a word, e.g. 'selfish'. Tell the children why you have selected this word (or insert others of your own), and then describe an incident illustrating how you have been selfish this week. Put the word into the donkey's bag. Encourage the children to reflect on the prepared words, e.g. 'lazy' – this is, not picking up rubbish, or not picking up their coats off the floor, and ask for volunteers to put these words into the baskets on the donkey's back. Then ask the children if there are any other things weighing them down. (Use the spare cards and explain that anything that makes us unhappy inside can be written down and added to the donkey's load.) Finally, tell the children that Jesus said: 'Come to me, all of you who are tired from carrying heavy loads, and I will give you rest.' Ask the children to try and imagine Jesus sitting on the donkey carrying all our heavy loads so that we can look just as nice inside as we do on the outside.

Prayer

Dear Lord Jesus, we ask you to help us to be kind instead of unkind; generous instead of greedy; loving instead of spiteful; unselfish instead of selfish; hardworking instead of lazy. For your name s sake. Amen.

Hymn

No 38, 'Think, think on these things', in *Someone's Singing Lord* A. and C. Black.

Daniel in the Lion's Den

5–11
Assembly
Judaism (and Christianity)

This wonderful story lends itself to dramatization and not only this story, (Daniel, Chapter 6, verses 1–28 in the Bible) but also the whole book of Daniel makes exciting reading.

You will need the following characters:

Daniel
King Darius
First Prince
Second Prince
Third Prince
120 Princes (10 will do!)
5 Lions
Page Boy
Narrator

Narrator: (*Pointing to each actor in turn, the Narrator introduces the characters to the audience and then says;*) Now we are going to tell you about Daniel, a very brave man, who stood up for his belief in God.

King Darius: Come here, Daniel, I am so pleased with all your work, that I am going to put you in charge of these 120 princes here. Page boy read my proclamation.

(*King puts his arm round Daniel; Page boy reads proclamation*)

Page Boy: Princes, the King has ordered me to tell you that Daniel is to be put in charge of you. You are to go to him and ask his approval before you do anything. Do you understand?

(*10 princes nod, exit King and Page boy*)

First Prince: Can I do this Daniel?

(*Shows piece of paper, Daniel nods*)

Second Prince: Will you sign this Daniel?

(*Daniel signs*)

Third Prince: Can I visit my Aunt?

(*Daniel agrees – exit Daniel*)

Narrator: The King was so pleased with everything that Daniel did for him that he planned to put Daniel in charge of the whole kingdom. But in the meantime, the princes became very jealous that Daniel had found such favour with their King, so they put their heads together to plot against Daniel and to draw up a plan to trick him into disobeying the King.

(*All the princes link arms, heads down in a sort of rugby scrum formation and move to the left*)

Princes: Mutter, mutter, mutter.

(*Heads up, look around, rugby scrum formation again, move to the right*)

Princes: Jabber, jabber, jabber.

(*Heads up, look around, rugby scrum formation again, move to the left*)

Princes: Whine, whine, grumble, whine

First Prince: Right, this is what we'll do. Since we can't find anything wrong with Daniel, the only way to trick him into disobeying the king is to make him go against his precious God. Look, he prays to his God every day, if we make the king sign a proclamation to say that if anyone asks God or man to do anything, during the next thirty days, then we can catch Daniel out, and he will be thrown into the den of lions. Come on let's go to the king and get him to sign this proclamation straight away.

(*Princes go off and find the king*)

Second Prince: King dear, grovel, grovel you are so wise, and so good, and so clever; we, that is my mates and I, think that you should sign a proclamation to say that anyone who asks anything for the next thirty days of any God or man, except you, dear King, should be thrown into the lion's den. What do you say?

Third Prince: (*To the audience*) That will trap beloved Daniel. (*To the King*) Sign here dear King.

King: Well, if you insist, I will sign the paper, but I can't think why.

(*Scratches his head*)

Narrator: The news soon reached Daniel's ears, but Daniel knew that he would still go on praying to God. So he went straight upstairs to his bedroom and opened the windows wide and began to pray.

(*Daniel kneels in prayer*)

The three princes rubbed their hands together in glee. They knew that they had trapped Daniel.

First Prince: We have trapped Daniel. Come on let's go and tell the king, that someone has disobeyed his new rule.

(*They hurry to find the king*)

Second Prince: (*To the King*) Your Majesty, didn't you sign a proclamation saying that anyone, except you, who asked anything of any God for thirty days should be thrown into the lion's den?

King: Yes, that's right, I did.

Third Prince: Well, we know someone who has disobeyed your order. Daniel has disobeyed you. He has been up to his room, praying to his precious God. We heard him, didn't we chaps?

All the Princes: Yes, we heard him, didn't we chaps.

Narrator: When the king heard this news he was terribly upset, he beat his breast and tore his clothes and then walked up and down trying to think of some way of saving Daniel.

  (*King walks up and down, beating his breast and tearing his clothes, then resting his head first on one hand and then on the other*)

Although the king thought and thought all day, he could not think of a way of saving Daniel. The three princes went to see the king again.

Three Princes (in unison): You have made the law, O King, therefore you must carry out the punishment.

  (*They rub their hands in glee*)

King: O, I wish I hadn't made that silly law. I cannot save Daniel now. Send for Daniel and bring him to me.

Page Boy: Here he is, Sir.

King: I'm sorry that I have to do this Daniel, but a law is a law. Perhaps your God will save you?

Narrator: So Daniel was taken and thrown into the lions' den (*lions roar, and try to scratch Daniel with their paws*). The king was so upset that he spent the night without sleeping or eating or drinking. He just paced the floor, backwards and forwards. As soon as it was light, the king rushed to the lion's den.

King: Are you alive Daniel? Did your God save you?

Daniel: Yes I'm alive, your Majesty. God protected me from the lions, see for yourself, I am completely unharmed.

King: Bring Daniel out of the lions' den this instant, and today I will make it known to all the nations that we shall serve Daniel's God, because he is the true and living God.

The Teacher needs to gather the threads together by saying something like, Daniel was very brave to remain true to his God in the face of certain death. I wonder if we would be brave enough to stand up for what we believe in. Daniel was a very courageous man.

Prayer

Father God, we thank you for saving Daniel's life. We thank you for his example of courage and bravery. Protect each one of us. Amen.

Hymn

No 67, 'Hallelu, hallelu, hallelu, hallelujah, praise ye the Lord' in *Junior Praise*, (Marshall Pickering).

Divide the assembled children into two groups. One half sings the 'Hallelu' part, the other half sing 'Praise ye the Lord'. The group that is singing, stands up for their part and then sits down. So there is a continuous standing up and sitting down, at different times, by the two groups. Then the children can swap parts. All children, but particularly Jewish and Christian children who often sing this lively hymn, love it, and it certainly has the effect of waking everyone up!

A very different version of 'Hallelujah' can be found on the CD, *The Real Complete Passover Seder, 35 Celebrated Songs and Blessings of the Haggadah*, performed by David and the High Spirit. It is available from:

Jewish Music Distribution
P O Box 67
Hailsham
East Sussex BN27 4UW,
UK
Tel/Fax: 01323 832863
Email: jmduk@hotmail.com
Website: www.jmi.org.uk/jmd

The Boy Who Saved a Swan

5–7
Assembly
Buddhism

The whole class can mime this story.

You will need the following:

Characters

> Prince Siddhārtha
> Devadatta (the prince's cousin)
> Flock of Swans
> Wounded swan
> Group of Wise Men
> Group of flowers in the garden
> Narrator

Props and Costumes

> Prince's cloak
> Bow and arrow
> Swan costumes
> Red patch for wound
> Simple robes
> Flower masks

Narrator: Prince Siddhārtha was a very kind and caring boy. One day he was playing in the palace gardens.

> (*Prince walks round the exotic flowers. Suitable music can be played. Flowers gently sway in the breeze*)

Suddenly, a beautiful flock of swans flew over the gardens. The Prince stood and watched the beautiful birds.

> (*Swans dance to suitable music*)

Narrator: The Prince's cousin, Devadatta, was also playing in the palace gardens and when he saw the swans, he took his bow and arrow and shot at the birds. One graceful bird was hit and it fell at the Prince's feet.

> (*Swan falls at Prince's feet with an arrow stuck in its wing and a red patch of blood staining the feathers*)

Narrator: The Prince tried to help the bird, but it was so frightened and shocked that it flapped its wings and hissed at the prince. But the bird could not fly. Gradually the young prince calmed the frightened bird by talking softly to it and stroking its head. Eventually, he was able to pull the arrow out. He ripped up a piece of his beautiful cloak and bound it around the bird's damaged wing.

Just then the Prince's cousin came running over. He was shouting that as he had shot the swan, it belonged to him. He tried to pull the swan away from the Prince.

(*There follows a tussle with the bird first pulled one way and then the other*).

Narrator: The Prince put his hand up and said 'Stop, we are only going to harm this beautiful bird, why do you want it anyway?' Devadatta said that he wanted to roast the bird at a huge party that he was having for his friends.

(*He mimes the action*)

The Prince sadly shook his head and said that he only wanted to care for the swan and make it better and strong enough to return it to the flock. The Prince said, 'Let us go to the wise men and ask them to settle our quarrel'.

(*Enter group of wise men, who sit cross-legged on the floor*)

Narrator: The two boys carried the swan to the wise men and asked them who should keep the swan. For a long time, the wise men put their heads together to decide to whom the swan should be given. Then the oldest wise man stood up, and pointing to Prince Siddhārtha, he said that the swan should be given to the Prince, because the Prince had tried to save the swan's life. Whereas the Prince's cousin, Devadatta had tried to take its life away.

The Prince joyfully took the beautiful bird away. He stroked it and fed it and talked to it and eventually the swan was strong enough and well enough to fly back to the flock. Devadatta was left scowling and angry and he stamped his feet in rage.

Prayer

Father God, may we never harm birds, or be cruel to animals. Amen

Hymn

No 42, 'I love God's tiny creatures', in *Someone's Singing Lord* A. & C. Black.

The Donkey in Lion's Clothing

This is the story that Guru Gobind Singh told in order to show his Sikh followers how important it was to have a uniform that was respected. He told the story in 1699 when the brotherhood or Khalsa was first formed.

You will need the following:

Characters	Props/Costumes
Donkey	Donkey ears, tail
Donkey's master	Master's stick
Master's friend	Lion skin and mask
Cockerel	Cockerel mask
Pig	Pig mask
Dog	Dog mask
Cat	Cat mask
6 townspeople	6 robes for townsfolk
Tiger	Tiger mask
Monkeys at waterhole	Monkey masks
Birds	Bird masks
Tree	Tree costume

The whole class can be involved in the mime. The teacher or one of the older children could act as a narrator.

Narrator: Once upon a time there was a donkey with big ears and a long tail.
    (*Donkey comes to the front of the hall and shows his big ears and tail*)
Narrator: He was a very lazy animal and he would much rather eat than work. The Donkey's master had to prod him to get him to move or to carry his baskets to market for him.

   (*Master prods donkey with a stick, the donkey refuses to move; the master prods the donkey again; the donkey brays and moves one step. The action is repeated a few times*)

Narrator: One fine day, the master went to visit his friend. The friend showed the master the head and skin of a lion that had been shot by some poachers. (*Mime the action*) While the two friends were talking, the donkey started to sniff around for a bucket of food, when suddenly the lion's head and skin fell onto the donkey's head.

   (*Donkey ears are exchanged for the lion mask*)

Narrator: The friend and the master were so busy talking that they had not seen what had happened and when they turned round all they saw, or thought they saw, was a lion. They ran away in fright.

   (*Mime the action*)

Narrator: A cockerel was pecking some corn when he looked up and he too, thought he saw a lion, so he flew off squawking and flapping his wings.

(*Mime the action*)

Narrator: A pig was scratching about for food when it backed into the donkey wearing the lion skin. It gave one enormous squeal and rushed out of the yard.

(*Mime the action*)

Narrator: A dog was chewing a bone and had not seen the kefuffle going on until the donkey ambled up to smell the bone, to see if he would like to nibble it. The dog was so frightened that it could not bark and ran off with its tail between its legs.

(*Mime the action*)

Narrator: A cat was sitting in the sun licking its paws and washing behind its ears, when suddenly she saw the lion's shadow in front of her. She gave one long miaow and ran away.

(*Mime the action*)

Narrator: The donkey could not think why everyone was running away from him, but he did not really care, as long as they had left him some food, he would eat it all up.

(*Donkey eats the food*)

Narrator: By and by, the donkey began to get bored in the yard and decided to go off to town to see what food he could find there. He was most surprised when he met a group of townspeople and they all ran off in different directions, screaming.

(*Townsfolk mime the actions*)

Narrator: The donkey wandered back through the jungle, when suddenly he came across a tiger. The donkey was very afraid because he was certain that the tiger would chase him, but to his utmost surprise, the tiger took one look at him and disappeared.

(*Mime the actions*)

Narrator: The donkey made his way to the waterhole, where a group of monkeys were having a drink. They were chittering and chattering and at first they did not notice the donkey, until one monkey pointed and all the other monkeys clutched each other in fright, and made a fearful, terrified racket, before leaping off into the trees.

(*Monkeys mime the action and noise*)

Narrator: Poor old donkey had no idea why everyone was running away from him. As it was near dusk he came across some peaceful birds all roosting and trying to go to sleep. But when they saw the donkey in the lion's skin, they woke up and squawked and flew off in all directions.

(*Birds fly all round the hall in and out of the seated children, squawking, before coming to rest*)

Narrator: The donkey went to sleep and in the morning he decided to go and find his master, as he was very hungry by this time. (*Enter master*) As soon as he saw his master, he started to bray loudly, 'hee-haw, hee-haw' he said. The master was just about to run away when it occurred to him that it was very strange for a lion to bray like his donkey (*Master stands and stares*). In his rush to get to his master, the donkey's headdress and skin got caught up in a thorn tree; it was whisked off the donkey's back and he became a donkey once more. (*Mime the action*). At once, the master recognized the donkey and took out his stick and gave him a prod.

End the drama by explaining that all the time that the donkey was wearing the lion's head and skin, everyone was afraid of him. Guru Gobind Singh told this story to his followers in order to show them that all the time that they wore their uniforms, people would show them respect.

Prayer

Heavenly Father, help each one of us to respect each other, whatever our race or colour or creed. Amen.

Hymn

No 30, 'You'll sing a song and I'll sing a song' in *Tinder-box: 66 Songs for Children*, A. & C. Black.

The Thirsty Dog (An Islamic Tale)

(This story is a liberal adaptation by E.C. Peirce of the story 'A Thirsty Dog' in *Love All Creatures* by M.S. Kayani, published by the Islamic Foundation, Leicester, UK and is reproduced with their permission.)

Many years ago, a man called Hasan felt that it was time for him to make his pilgrimage to Makkah. He lived in a tiny village near Medina. The journey to Makkah would be very long and arduous. Being a poor man, he could not afford the camel transport to Makkah, so he decided to walk. He took with him a white robe, sandals, a skin containing water and enough bread for the first two or three days of the nine-day journey. He thought that he could stop on the way to buy more food and to ask for more water at the Bedouin camps that he would pass on the rest of the journey.

All went well for the first few days. He stopped and chatted to people on his way. He told them that he was making his Hajj or pilgrimage to Makkah and the people always gave him water to drink; once or twice he was invited to share an evening meal with a family on the route. He slept under the stars, only wrapping his cloak tightly around him as the heat of the days turned into cool nights.

Soon he left the towns and villages behind him and he knew that he must cross a huge desert before he reached Makkah. He made sure that he had enough water in his water skin and enough food to make this perilous part of the journey. He had with him his very own astrolabe or compass that had been given to his family many years before, and had been passed down from father to son, over the generations. With this instrument, he could navigate his way by the stars. The astrolabe had been invented by very clever Muslim scientists many centuries earlier.

As the desert was so hot, he thought that it would be better to travel by night and rest during the day. Once again, all went well for the first two or three days and nights, when suddenly, Hasan realized that he was running out of water. He decided to use the water very sparingly, to make sure that it lasted until he reached the next camp. But even so, his throat began to get parched and his lips began to crack and he saw no signs of civilization ahead. Hasan began to feel desperate. He looked this way and that. All he could see was sand; miles and miles of dusty sand, stretching in every direction. Hasan began to feel very weak and tired now. He drained the last drops of water from the skin, and stumbled on, afraid that he would surely die.

Fearing that the end was near, he stumbled against a clump of rocks. As he sank to his knees, Hasan's hand touched something round and hard. This was no ordinary rock, it was something man-made, certainly. The stones had been hewn and placed in a circular pattern. Frantically, Hasan brushed away the sand with his bare hands, and, sure enough, there was a round circle of stones underneath the sand. Over the top of the circle, lay a heavy stone. Heaving this aside, with all the energy that he could muster, Hasan discovered a deep, dark cavern. Could this hold water? And even if it did, how could he get down to it? He looked quickly about him to see if he could find a small pebble that he could drop into the depths, to listen for the 'plopping' sound, that would tell him that the stone was hitting water. To his great relief, he did not have to search for long. There beside the circular stones was a chipping left by the men who had hewn out the rock. Very carefully, and very gingerly, he leant over the edge and dropped the stone. For a few seconds, he heard absolutely nothing; nothing but silence. Then to his great joy, somewhere, deeply below him, within the tubular hole, he heard a tiny splash. WATER. He nearly danced for joy, until he realized with utter dismay, that he had no way of getting the water up. He did not have a rope on which to let down his water skin, or on which he could lower himself down to the water. The life-saving drink was utterly useless to him. He was within reach of water and yet he was going to die of thirst.

He lay back in the sands, too tired to move, too tired to think. Yet as he lay there, he slowly knew what he was going to do. If he was going to die anywhere, why not die trying to reach the water, rather than in this baking sun?

He heaved himself over the side of the well and to his amazement, he found a foothold for his right foot. Letting himself down gently, a bit further, he found another small crevice for his left foot. But he was still hanging on to the circular top with his hands. What on earth was he going to do, when he had to let go of the top? Cautiously, he eased himself down a bit further, and gripped the stones above his head as he went. He managed to hang on to the rough rock above him, while he searched first with one foot for a crevice and then with the other foot. Inch by inch, he eased himself slowly downwards. It was a tiring and exhausting journey and he was not at all sure that he would make it, let alone have the energy to get back up again. Miraculously, after a very long time in the dark, dank tunnel, his toes touched something cold and wet. Gingerly, he poked his toe a little bit further down and found that he had reached the water. Easing himself down still further, he let go with one hand and managed to swing his water skin into the water. Sadly, he could not obtain much water in this way, but he was afraid that if he went down any further into the water, he would slip. Very slowly, he pulled the skin up to his lips and drank the pure, clean water. Precariously balanced as he was, he repeated this action several times, until his thirst was quenched. Finally, he made his ascent, once again, up the perilous rocks.

Slowly, slowly he pulled himself up, until at last his fingertips reached the curved stones and he was able to pull himself out of the well. He lay there on the sand panting with exhaustion and drained the last drop of water from the skin. He knew that he must re-start his journey, now that he had quenched his thirst, and find the nearest camp for food. Just as he pulled himself to his feet, a dog appeared out of nowhere. Hasan could see instantly that the dog was exhausted and as thirsty, and as near to death as he had been. What on earth could he do to help the poor animal? He had drained the last drop of water from his water skin, and he certainly could not make that perilous journey down the well again.

As Hasan looked at the dog, the dog whimpered and licked Hasan, and looked up at him with big, sad, trusting eyes. 'Oh no', thought Hasan, 'don't look at me like that. I really can't help you.' The dog whimpered again and licked Hasan's hand, this time the dog fell over, as he was so weak and lay dying in the sand.

'Hold on', croaked Hasan 'I'll save you if I can.' Without thinking about his own safety, Hasan went down the well a second time. He slipped several times, cutting his fingers and feet in his efforts to cling onto the sides of the well. But in the end he made it back up to the top with a small skin full of the reviving water. Gently he dripped the water on to the dog's parched tongue. Slowly, slowly the dog revived and sat up. But it was now dark. Hasan felt in his pockets for his astrolabe to guide him out of the desert. To his dismay, it had gone. It must have fallen into the water when he had slipped on that perilous second journey. Once again Hasan knew that he was facing death. Without his compass, he would be completely lost, destined to die in the sand.

Puzzled by a tug on his robe, he looked down to see the dog, trying to pull him to a place beyond the rocks. 'Stop it, silly dog', Hasan admonished the animal, 'Aren't we in enough trouble without you ripping my robe by pulling me over these rocks?' But the dog insisted and kept pulling Hasan's robe. Then the dog ran ahead, and only stopped to look behind him to see if Hasan was following him. When Hasan stood in puzzlement the dog ran back and gave Hasan a further tug as though he wanted Hasan to follow.

It was pitch black and Hasan stumbled after the dog for what seemed like hours. Suddenly, as the sun began to rise, Hasan saw beyond him the unmistakable shapes of dwellings and a dog barking for joy.

Prayer

Almighty God, may we always be kind to all animals. Amen

8 INSPIRATIONAL LEADERS

Jesus: Friend of the Friendless

(Based on an idea by J Gattis Smith in *Show Me, Creative Resources Two* published by the Bible Society, 1985. This adaptation was first published by E.C. Peirce in *Assembly File 1*, Folens 1996).

The story of Jesus befriending Zacchaeus shows children that it is never too late to change. If they have been dishonest or they have taken something that does not belong to them, then they can change, mend their ways and try to make reparation. These are very important concepts for young children, that they can say they are sorry, accept forgiveness and attempt to put things right.

Begin in the following way:
I am going to tell you a story about Zacchaeus, but I will need you all to help me do the actions. Zacchaeus was a very dishonest tax collector who took more money from all the people than he was entitled to take.

(*Everyone helps to count the money and echoes, 'One for you; one, two, three, four for me. One for you; one, two, three, four for me.*)

One day, he got out of bed, yawned and stretched.

(*Everyone yawns and stretches*)

He put on his clothes.

(*Everyone puts clothes on; first the trousers, then the long shirt*)

Because he had heard that Jesus was coming to his village that day and he really wanted to see Him, he ran down to the market.

(*Run on the spot*)

But when he got down to the Market Square, he found that a huge crowd had already gathered. He tried to see through the middle of them.

(*Mime trying to part the crowds*)

But he could not see Jesus and being so small, he could not see over their heads.

(*Mime standing on tiptoe*)

So he tried looking to the left of the crowd.

(*Mime leaning to the left with hand shading eyes*)

And he tried looking to the right of the crowd.

(*Mime leaning to the right and shade eyes*)

But he still could not see Jesus. He tried looking through their legs.

(*Crouch down and look through legs*)

But it was no use.

(*Shake head sadly*)

Suddenly, he had a bright idea.

(*Face lights up, holds hands up*)

He would climb that tree over there, so that he could see Jesus over the top of the crowds' heads. He ran to the tree.

(*Run on the spot*)

He began to climb the tree as fast as he could.

(*Mime climbing action*)

When he got to the top, he shaded his eyes.

(*Shade eyes with hands*)

Sure enough, there was Jesus and he was coming this way. Jesus looked right up into the tree and beckoned Zacchaeus.

(*Mime looking up and beckoning*)

'Come down at once, Zacchaeus' said Jesus, 'I am coming to your house for tea.' Zacchaeus climbed down the tree as fast as he could.

(*Climbing down action*)

And he ran all the way home to make tea for Jesus.

(*Running on the spot*)

All the people began to mutter that Jesus was having tea with a sinner.

(*Mutter, mutter, mutter*)

But Zacchaeus stood up and said 'Look Jesus, I'm sorry for what I have done, I am going to try and make amends. I will give half of all that I own to the poor and if I have cheated anybody out of anything, I will pay them back four times the amount.'

(*Counts coins back into imaginary hands; four for you and four for you and four for you*)

Jesus was very happy when Zacchaeus said this and so were all the people.

(*End with big smiles*)

Teacher: Whatever we do wrong, we can always say we are sorry, change our ways and try to put things right.

Prayer:

Jesus, forgive us when we do wrong and help us to put things right. Amen

Hymn:

No 60, 'God forgave my sin in Jesus' name', in *Mission Praise* (Marshall, Morgan and Scott).

Video:

Luke Street published by Scripture Union. Eight different stories (including Zacchaeus) are beautifully retold by Roy Castle. Available from:

Scripture Union
Customer Services
P.O. Box 300
Kingston Broadway
Carlisle
Cumbria CA3 0QS

Abraham's Story

Abraham's story is very important to Jews, Christians and Muslims alike. The story can be read in the Torah, or in the Bible, Genesis, Chapter 12–25, or in the Qu'ran.

To the Jews, Abraham, is seen as the father of the Jewish people – a righteous man, who taught that there was only one God. The Torah tells of the convenant that God made with Abraham and how God would make him the father of a very great nation, and that all his descendants would become God's 'chosen people'. God would give them their own special land, if Abraham obeyed and went where God would lead him.

The story can be told, just as it is, or it can be acted out (see following pages). Emphasize the facts that Abraham (then called Abram) and Sarah (then called Sarai) were very courageous to set out on an unknown path, simply trusting God and leaving a very comfortable life in the City of Ur, to start a new life in an unknown land that God would show them. They had to leave behind them family and friends, and even then, Sarah was quite old and childless.

The class should understand how worried Sarah must have felt when she did not have the promised baby straight away. They should also understand something of the significance of the three visitors to Abraham and Sarah's tent in the land of Canaan and finally, understand the joy when the baby eventually arrived. The baby was called Isaac. One of Abraham's grandchildren was later called Jacob (or Israel) and he, in turn, had twelve sons who became the fathers of the twelve tribes of Israel. Abraham was also the father of Ishma'il. See p. 115. If looking at the story from the Islamic perspective then it must not be dramatised.

The children can act out the story as the teacher reads from the book.

You will need the following characters:

> God
> Moon God
> Abraham
> Sarah
> Crowd
> Servants
> Friends
> 3 Visitors
> Baby

The main elements of the story are these:

1   The people are all worshipping Moon Gods.
    (*Crowd bows down before Moon God*)
2   God speaks to Abraham and promises that if Abraham will go where God leads him, God will make him the father of a very great nation.
    (*Mime the actions*)

3   So Abraham sets off with his servants.
     (*Abraham, Sarah and servants trudge round the hall several times. They can weave in and out of the children, looking for a place to rest. The teacher can ad lib the actions*)
4   Friends laugh at Abraham, for not knowing where he will eventually settle down.
     (*Friends mime the action*)
5   Many years passed, at last they reached the land of Canaan. Abraham and Sarah were getting very old and Sarah was very upset that she still did not have the promised baby.
     (*Sarah mimes her weeping to Abraham*)
6   Then three men appear at Abraham's tent door. Abraham kills the best calf and Sarah bakes some cakes. They give the visitors the food.
     (*Characters mime these actions*)
7   One of the visitors tells Abraham, that by this time next year, Sarah will have a son. Sarah, who is listening at the tent door laughs, because she does not believe him.
     (*The characters mime the actions*)
8   Abraham knows that this is God speaking, so when the visitors depart, Abraham and Sarah hug each other with joy.
     (*Action is mimed*)
9   Finally the baby arrives, they call him Isaac. Sarah and Abraham invite all their friends to a special celebration.
     (*Friends dance and have a party. The baby is shown to all the people*)

Hymn

               'Oz V'Shalom'
               Psalm 29 verse 11 (See tune below)
               Adonai oz l'amo yiteyn
               Adonai oz l'amo yiteyn
               Adonai y'vareh et amo b'shalom
               Adonai y'vareh et amo b'shalom

               The Lord will give strength to his people
               The Lord will bless his people with peace

or

'Adon Olam' in *Sephardic Songs of Praise*, by Abraham Lopes Cardozo published by Tara Publications, Cedarhurst, N.Y.
This can be sung to the tune of Clementine or Waltzing Matilda (see words and music below).

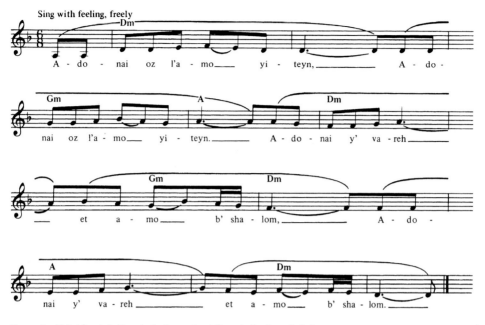

Singers should feel free to hold on to the long notes at the end of each musical phrase.

Adon Olam

Adon Olam is often sung at the end of morning services on Shabbat or a festival. It has a regular, common metre and fits many existing tunes although Jewish composers have written umpteen melodies especially for it. (Angela Wood)

> *Adon olam asher malah b'terem kol y'tzir nivra (Adon olam),*
> *l'eyt na'asah k'hevtzo kol azai meleh sh'mo nikra (Adon olam).*
>
> *V'aharei kihlot hakol, l'va'ado yimloh nora (Adon olam),*
> *V'hu haya v'hu hove, v'hu yiy'yeh b'tifarah (Adon olam).*
>
> *V'hu ehad v'eyn sheyni, l'hamshiylo l'hahbirah (Adon olam),*
> *B'li reshit, b'li tahlit, v'lo haoz v'hamisrah (Adon olam).*
>
> *V'hu eyli v'hai goali, v'tzur hevli b'yom tzarah (Adon olam),*
> *V'hu nisi umanusi, m'nat kosi b'yom ekra (Adon olam).*
>
> *B'yado afkid ruhi, beyt ishan v'a'ira (Adon olam),*
> *V'im ruhi g'viati, adonai li v'lo ira (Adon olam).*

> Eternal Lord who ruled alone
> before creation of all forms,
> when all was made at His desire
> then as the king was He revealed.

And after everything shall end
alone, in wonder, will He reign,
as once He was, so is He now,
the glory that will never change.

He is the One, no other is
to be compared, to stand beside,
neither before, nor following,
His is the strength and His the might.

This is my God, my life He saves,
the rock I grasp in deep despair,
the flag I wave, the place I hide,
He shares my cup the day I call.

Within his hand I lay my soul
both when I sleep and when I wake,
and with my soul my body too,
my Lord is close I shall not fear.

This English translation fits the same metre.

Muhammad ﷺ
('Peace be upon Him')

5–11
Assembly
Islam

It is very important to remember that whenever Muhammad's ﷺ name is mentioned. Muslims pay respect to his name by saying the words 'Peace be upon Him' or by writing the sign for this ﷺ after his name. And because Muslims believe that Muhammad ﷺ was God's messenger, it is inappropriate for children to draw pictures of Muhammad ﷺ or to act out the story of his life. Therefore, this assembly takes the form of a quiet, reflective description of Muhammad's ﷺ birth, life and death.

Muhammad ﷺ was born in AD 570 in the Arabian City of Makkah. His mother's name was Aminah, and his father's name was Abd Allah. Unfortunately, Muhammad's ﷺ father died before he was born and his mother died when he was only six. So he was brought up first by his grandfather, Abd al-Muttalib, until his death two years later, and then by his Uncle, Abu Talib.

Muhammad ﷺ spent the years of his youth tending his uncle's sheep and goats and working with the trading caravans. He became known for his honesty and trustworthiness. He later married Khadijah, his employer, and they had six children.

Muhammad ﷺ was shocked by life in the city of Makkah. He saw the people worshipping stone idols, drinking and fighting. He believed in one God, and so saddened was he by what he saw, that it became his custom to go away alone to the hills and pray to Allah (God).

One night, when he was about 40 years old, alone in a cave on Mount Hira, the Angel Jibra'il appeared to him, with words written on a piece of cloth. The angel told Muhammad ﷺ to repeat the words that he spoke to him, but alas, Muhammad ﷺ could not repeat the words. Three times the angel told Muhammad ﷺ to recite the words, then Jibra'il embraced him and this time he was able to repeat the words. Later these words were written down and they became part of the Qur'an, the Holy Book of the Muslim people. Further revelations continued for the next twenty-three years, and every word was written down.

The name Islam, was given to this new teaching. Allah revealed to Muhammad ﷺ that Allah was the one true God who created the heavens and the earth and everything that lives on the earth. Allah told Muhammad ﷺ that idols were not to be worshipped, and that if people continued to live corrupt lives, they would be punished.

Muhammad ﷺ started to tell the people of Makkah this, but they would not listen to him and plotted to kill him. Muhammad ﷺ managed to escape with the help of his young cousin Ali, who exchanged places with Muhammad ﷺ and lay in his bed. There is a story that a spider and a bird also helped Muhammad ﷺ to escape from his enemies. Muhammad ﷺ was hiding in a cave on Mount Thawr. The spider spun a web and the bird built its nest over the mouth of the cave, so that when the enemies passed by they thought that the cave had not been disturbed for many years and so did not go inside.

Muhammad ﷺ eventually reached the city of al-Madinah. The journey from Makkah to al-Madinah is very important to Muslims, it is called the Hijrah.

It was in al-Madinah, that the first mosque was built. The Muslims prayed five times each day and they learned that they should follow God's law, treat one another with respect and give some of their money to the poor.

After many fierce battles, even the people in Makkah believed the message of Islam. Muhammad ﷺ died when he was sixty-three.

At the end of the story, give the children time to think about some of the things that Muhammad ﷺ taught i.e. that there was only one God, who is the creator of heaven and earth; that the people were not to worship man-made idols, and that all mankind should treat each other with respect.

Mahatma Gandhi

One incident from the life of this great man of peace can be chosen for dramatization. The incident below is the occasion when Gandhi settled land rent disputes first by seeking justice from the Government, and when this failed, through non-violent action. (First published by the author in *Assembly File 1*, Folens 1996).

You will need:

  Gandhi
  Five Farm Workers
  Landlords
  Government Officer
  Two Government Workers
  Narrator

Farmers (Together): Sir, may we speak to you?

Gandhi: Come in and sit down. Now tell me what is the matter?

First Farm Worker: Sir, our landlords have put up the rent for our small fields yet again.

Second Worker: The price is far too high, we cannot afford to pay. We will have to starve our families in order to pay this new price increase.

Third Worker (in despair): Every rupee that I make has to go to pay this huge bill. We just cannot make ends meet.

Fourth Worker: Please help us Sir, you are a very clever lawyer, you will know what to say, we are just simple labourers. We will be put in jail, if we do not pay the bosses.

Fifth Worker: Will you go and see the landlords on our behalf?

Gandhi: Yes, I will help you. I will go to the highest government official in the land and tell him exactly what you have told me. I am sure he will understand. You have got to be able to make a living, you cannot be expected to pay *all* your money to the landlord.

Narrator: So Gandhi set off for the government offices and asked to see the chief officer in charge of land rents. He persisted until he was finally granted an interview with the high-ranking officer. Gandhi knocked politely on the door.

Officer: (*Sitting behind a huge desk shuffling papers*): Come in.

Gandhi: Good morning Sir, I have come to see you on behalf of some farm labourers. They tell me their land rent has been put up yet again and that it is far too high. They cannot possibly pay it.

Officer: Well, I'm sorry to hear that, but if they can't pay, they will be thrown into jail and the land will be given to those who can pay.

Gandhi: But Sir, this is not fair, all they are asking is to pay a fair rent. They must keep some money to feed themselves and their families. They cannot give it all to the landlords.

Officer: I'm sorry there is nothing I can do, the rent has been fixed and they must pay it. I will not listen to you any more. Good day to you, Sir.

Narrator: Gandhi was hustled unceremoniously out of the government buildings by two burly officials. But on the long walk home, he was already forming a plan in his mind; a plan that he hoped would help the farm workers to win their case.

   (*The action is mimed*)

Farm Workers: How did you get on, Sir?

Gandhi: Not very well, the government officer refused to listen to me, but I have a plan that might work.

Farm Workers: Tell us what to do. Shall we fight for our rights?

Gandhi: No, this is my plan. I do not want any fighting of any kind. But I do want you to go on strike.

Farm Workers: Go on strike, what do you mean?

Gandhi: I mean, you and all your fellow workers are not to do any work of any kind, as a protest. This will soon make the government listen to us. But remember, absolutely no fighting, no violence at all. If you are beaten, you are not even to fight back, so that they have no reason to put you in jail. Do you understand?

Narrator: The farm workers agreed to do what Gandhi suggested. Instead of working, they stayed at home in silent protest at their unfair treatment. Some of the landlords took sticks and began to beat the workers, but the workers did not attempt to fight back, they merely tried to fend off the blows. Eventually, the landlords could see that they were getting nowhere and ordered the government to try and persuade Gandhi to call off the strike.

   (*The action is mimed*)

Government Officer: Send for Gandhi. Bring him to me at once.

   (*Gandhi enters*)

All right, I will listen to what you have to say, if you call off the strike and send the labourers back to work.

Narrator: Gandhi agreed and pleaded the case of the farm workers once more. This time, the government listened to him. The government ordered the landlords to repay the high rents back to the workers and to reduce the rents to a fair price. So Gandhi had achieved a good result by peaceful means.

Prayer:

Holy God, this Hindu man of peace set his fellow workers and us a great example to follow. Even in unfair circumstances, he has shown us that rights can be won through peaceful means. Help us to choose this option before anything else.

Hymn:

No 147, 'Make me a channel of your peace' in *Come and Praise 2* (BBC).

Siddhārtha Gautama

Siddhārtha Gautama became the Buddha some six hundred years before the birth of Christ. Buddhists do not believe the Buddha was a God, but they do revere his teaching.

To act out the story of his life, you will need the following characters:

King
Queen
Prince Siddhārtha
2 Wise Men
Yashodharā (Siddhārtha's wife)
Old Man
Sick Man
Dead Man and group of Mourners
First Holy Man
Servant
5 Holy Men
Followers
Narrator

Narrator: One upon a time there lived a King and Queen in northern India. They had a young son called Prince Siddhārtha. He was a lovely boy in every way and the King and Queen loved him very much. One day, when he was still quite young, two wise men came to see the King and Queen.

Wise Men: Your Majesty, let us see your son.

   (*Siddhārtha is brought before the wise men*)

First Wise Man: Your Majesty, we believe that your son will grow up to be a very great leader.

Second Wise Man: We think that he will give up all this wealth and leave the palace forever to teach others how to find peace and happiness.

   (*Exit wise men*)

Narrator: Now the King and Queen were extremely upset when they heard this, and so they decided there and then to protect their son from all unhappiness, so that he would never have to leave home to teach others how to find happiness. They surrounded him with beautiful flowers and gardens and friends in the palace, and they never let him leave the palace walls to see the suffering outside. When he grew up, they found a wife for Siddhārtha, a young cousin called Yashodharā.

   (*Yashodharā puts a wedding veil on and the pair walk around the hall*)

   But one day, Siddhārtha was alone with his servant, and he began to question his servant about the world outside.

Siddhārtha: Please tell me what it is like outside these palace walls?

Servant: I cannot tell you, master, I have been forbidden to talk about the world outside.

Siddhārtha: Then if you will not tell me, show me.

Servant: Oh master, we will get into very serious trouble if I take you outside.

Siddhārtha: Look, I will take all the blame, come on, let's just have a little walk outside these walls.

Narrator: Reluctantly, the servant took the prince outside, but the prince met four people who changed his life forever. The first person he met was an old man.

Old Man: Good day, young Sir.

Siddhārtha: Good day. Tell me sir, why do you hobble and walk with a bent back, and why are you so thin, and your skin is so wrinkled?

Old Man: It is because I am very, very old. Have you never seen an old person before? We must all grow old, you know.

Narrator: Siddhārtha was horrified, he shook his head and held his hands up in horror. Next, the young prince heard someone groaning and saw before him a very sick man.

Siddhārtha: Oh, what is wrong with you? Why are you moaning?

Sick Man: I am very ill, young sir, and I am in dreadful pain. There is no cure for my sickness, oh please help me.

Siddhārtha: I don't know how to help you, how I wish I could. I have never seen a sick person before.

Narrator: No sooner had the prince spoken to the sick man, than he heard a group of people crying. He looked around to see where the noise was coming from and saw a dead man for the very first time.

Siddhārtha: Oh tell me, tell me, why are you all crying.

Mourners: We are crying because our dear friend is dead.

Siddhārtha: What does dead mean?

Mourner: It means that we will not see him any more. He will no longer sit and eat or drink with us. We are crying because we shall miss him very much.

Narrator: The prince shook his head and sadly walked on, he had never seen so much suffering as he had seen that day. The prince met one more person and these four encounters changed his life forever. The fourth person was a Holy man.

Siddhārtha: Oh sir, you look so calm and peaceful, tell me what is the secret of your happiness?

Holy Man: Young man, you must learn this for yourself, by searching out the great truths about living and learn to understand why there is suffering and evil in this world.

Narrator: Without another word, Siddhārtha hurried back to the palace and kissed his sleeping wife and baby goodbye. He took off his princely robes and put on a rough cloak and set off to find the meaning of what he had seen. He found five Holy men who taught him many things. They ate very little and life was very hard.

(*The five Holy men sit in a circle with the prince and mime discussion*)

However, Siddhārtha did not think that they had all the answers. Neither living such a hard life, nor living in such luxury as he had lived in the palace, was the answer to finding happiness. So he left the five Holy men and went away by himself, until he found a large tree. He sat underneath this tree and started to eat a little food and when he felt better, he started to think deeply about the questions that were puzzling him. After thinking for a very long time, Siddhārtha suddenly realized that pain and suffering were a part of life that we all have to accept. It was no use getting angry or upset about it. Old age and death too, are a part of life to which we have to come to terms.

Siddhārtha felt that much unhappiness was caused by people's greed and selfishness. So he set out to tell others about what he had learned, and what he called his Middle Way. It was then that he became known as the Buddha or 'Enlightened One'.

(*The scene ends with the Buddha teaching his followers the things that he had learned*)

A time for quiet reflection is kept.

Hymn

No 102, 'You can't stop rain from falling down', in *Come and Praise 2* (BBC).

Guru Nanak

The birth of Sikhism as a religion begins with the birth of Guru Nanak as a teacher. Guru means teacher or holy man, but Guru Nanak's actual ministry only began when he was about 30 years old.

Some Sikhs object to their Guru being portrayed in drama and so it is proper to check with the local Sikh community before acting the following play. If it proves unacceptable, the part of Nanak should be simply retold by the storyteller.

Guru Nanak's life story is a lovely narrative about a man born to lead his people in a new way. He was, in fact, born into a Hindu family, the son of Mehta Kalu, a rich business man. He was born in Northern India, in the Punjab, which is now part of Pakistan, and was then ruled by the Muslims. Both of these two religions had a great influence on him. But Guru Nanak was to teach that there was neither Hindu nor Muslim and that rituals did not make a person holy but following God was the only way.

The following playlet is a story from his childhood. *You will need the following characters*:

> Nanak
> Mehta Kalu, Nanak's father
> Bala, Nanak's friend
> Villagers
> Holy Men
> Narrator

Mehta Kalu: Nanak my son, come here. I want you to grow up into a fine businessman like me. I am going to give you 20 rupees, so that you can buy as many different things as possible from the nearby villages and then return here to Talwandi and sell the items at a profit. That's how we make our money in business you know.

Nanak: Yes father. I will do as you say, but father, I do not want to become a businessman like you. I am more interested in finding out about God. But of course, I will try to please you.

Mehta Kalu: You must learn my trade my son, or else how are you to become successful like me?

Nanak: I will try father. Can I take my friend Bala along with me?

Mehta Kalu: Yes, of course you can, now off you go. Buy lots of things to bring back and sell.

Narrator: The two boys set off, and went from village to village searching for things to buy, but not seeing anything they particularly wanted, they decided to move on to one of the larger towns.

(The boys mime visiting the villagers, who shake their heads and hold up empty hands)

Suddenly, the boys came across a group of Holy men who were very hungry.

(The Holy men hold out empty begging bowls)

You see, the Holy men had given away all their possessions, in order to give their lives to God, and they depended on the generosity of the people that they met to give them food or money. Without a second's hesitation, Nanak took out his money and gave it all to the Holy men.

Nanak: I can see that you are very hungry. I am sure my father will understand if I give you all our money so that you can buy some food. You seem so hungry. Here you are, please take it. Take it all.

Holy Men: (*In unison*) Thank you, thank you, young man. You will be greatly blessed because of your generosity to us.

Bala: Oh Nanak, how could you give away all the money? Your father will be furious with you. We were supposed to spend the money on buying goods to sell at home. Oh Nanak, whatever shall we do now?

Nanak: We shall go straight home and tell my father exactly what I have done. I am sure my father would have done the same thing in my place. Giving money to starving men is much more important than buying things. Of course he will understand. Come along.

Narrator: So the two boys set off for the long walk home. Nanak's father saw them from a long way off and went out to greet them.

Mehta Kalu: Back so soon, where are the goods you have bought with all my money?

Nanak: Oh father, I know you will understand, I have given all the money away to some starving Holy men, so that they can buy food.

Mehta Kalu: You did what? You wicked boy. Money doesn't grow on trees you know, you will be soundly beaten for your disobedience.

Narrator: Poor Nanak was scolded severely for his kindness, but even as a young boy, he cared more about people than about things. He grew up to love God greatly and when he was about 30 years old, he went away for three days, and on his return he told his friends that he had had a vision of God. He felt that God had told him that being a Hindu or a Muslim was not as important as living holy lives. Guru Nanak travelled the country telling the people to love God and their fellow men. He told the people that all men were equal in God's sight. So that the people would remember his words, Guru Nanak put his message in songs or hymns.

Later these hymns came to be written down and became known as the Mool Mantra or Perfect words, which today are a part of the Sikhs' Holy book, the Guru Granth Sahib.

Prayer

Father God, help us to love you and one another. Help us to live in peace and harmony with all people. Amen.

Hymn

No 146, 'We ask that we live and we labour in peace, in peace', in *Come and Praise 2* (BBC).

Gideon
5–11
Assembly
Judaism (and also Christianity)

This story of an Old Testament hero, an ordinary man who led his people to great victory, is told in Judges, Chapters 6–8. The story could be re-enacted or mimed as it is retold by a storyteller.

You will need the following characters:–

Gideon
Gideon's army   (32,000 soldiers – 32 children would do!)
                (cut-down squeezy bottles for trumpets)
                (small hand-held torches)
The Midianite army + cardboard swords (2 men have speaking parts)
Gideon's servant Purah

Tell the story in the following way. Long ago in the land of Israel there lived a young man called Gideon. There was great trouble at that time in the land where Gideon lived. People called the Midianites used to raid his people's farms and steal their sheep and cattle and all their grain. His people were called Israelites and they were very frightened of the Midianites. So they prayed to God for help.

One day, as Gideon was threshing wheat, an angel appeared to him and told him that God had chosen him to save his country from the Midianites. But Gideon was very surprised and said: 'How can I possibly save Israel? My family is poor and I am the youngest and least important member of my family!' But the angel promised that God would be with him.

When he was alone, Gideon became afraid; he knew that the Midianite army was much larger than the Israelite army and he was not at all sure that God would help him to defeat the Midianites. So he prayed to God to give him a sign that God would help him. Gideon took a sheep's woollen coat, called a 'fleece', and put it outside on the ground that night. Then Gideon asked God to make the fleece wet with dew during the night, but to leave the ground around the fleece dry. If God would do this, Gideon felt that he would know that God had chosen him to be the leader of the Israelite army.

The next day Gideon went outside and found that God had answered his prayer; the fleece was full of water, but the ground around the fleece was quite dry. But still Gideon doubted, and so he prayed to God once more: 'Lord, do not be angry with me. I am still not sure that you want me to be the leader of the people of Israel. Give me one more sign. This time may the fleece be dry and the earth around it wet?'

The next morning when Gideon went to get the fleece it was perfectly dry, although all around the fleece the ground was very wet with dew. This time Gideon was sure that God wanted him to be the leader. Gideon called his army together. He gathered 32,000 soldiers. But God said to Gideon: 'You have too many men. Tell all those who are afraid to go home and not to fight.' This time Gideon did as the Lord commanded, and 22,000 men returned home while 10,000 remained with Gideon. But God said: 'There are still too many men. Take all the men down to the river for a drink. Separate everyone who laps up the water with his tongue like a dog, from those who get down on their knees to drink.' Three hundred men scooped up water in their hands and lapped it like a dog; all the rest got down on their knees to drink. God told Gideon to keep the 300 men who had lapped the water and to send the others home.

Gideon now had a very small army compared with the huge Midianite army. For encouragement, God told Gideon to go down secretly to the enemy camp. Gideon took his servant Purah with him. Outside one of the tents Gideon and Purah overheard two men speaking. One man said, 'Last night I had a strange dream. I dreamed a cake of barley bread tumbled into the camp of Midian. It struck a tent and the tent over-turned. I wonder what it means?' His friend said in a frightened voice, 'It means God is going to help Gideon to defeat us.' This gave Gideon the courage that he needed. He prepared for battle. He divided his 300 men into three groups and gave each man a trumpet and a lamp covered by an earthenware pot to hide the light inside. Gideon said to his men: 'Watch me and do exactly as I do. When we come to the edge of the Midianite camp blow your trumpets on every side and shout: 'The sword for the Lord and for Gideon.'

In the middle of the night Gideon and his men marched towards the enemy camp. Gideon blew his trumpet. All his men did the same and they smashed their pots so that their lamps shone brightly in the darkness. They held their torches in their left hands and their trumpets in their right hands and shouted, 'A sword for the Lord and for Gideon.' The enemy soldiers were so frightened when they heard all the noise and saw all the bright lights that they ran away in fear and even fought each other in their confusion. Gideon and his men chased the Midianite army right out of the land. God had saved the people of Israel by using Gideon and just a few soldiers. Then the people of Israel asked Gideon to be their ruler, but Gideon replied, 'No, the Lord will rule over you.' At last there was peace in the land while Gideon lived there.

Prayer

Father, help us to trust you, just as Gideon trusted you. Guide us in all our plans great or small. Help us to know that you care for each one of us. Amen.

Hymn

No 28, 'The Journey of life', in *Someone's Singing, Lord* A. and C. Black.

Sybil Phoenix Tackles Racism

7–11
Assembly
All

(Based on an account by John Newbury in *Living in Harmony* (Religious and Moral Education Press, 1985). (RMEP is a division of SCM-Canterbury Press Ltd and is used with their kind permission).

Sybil Phoenix's life is an inspiration to everyone, boys and girls, black and white, young and old. This is a story of a black woman who suffered much pain and distress because of her colour, but it is also the story of a woman who achieved greatness through her love and dedication to God and his people.

There follows a description of the main events of her life. She was born Sybil Marshall in British Guiana (now Guyana) in 1927. When she was only 9 her mother died and she went to live with her grandfather. She became a Christian and persuaded her grandfather to allow her to be confirmed. Her grandfather died only two years later and she went to live with her aunt and uncle, who did not really like her and treated her like a servant.

While she was still at school, Sybil helped at her church youth club. When she left school, she did a three-year evening class course to become a social worker. While running the youth club, she met Joe Phoenix, who was to become her husband. In 1956 Sybil and Joe came to England where they were soon married. Life was very hard for them. But Joe found work as a porter for an ice cream company and Sybil went to work in a furniture factory. They found it very hard to find accommodation; to quote John Newbury's book, Sybil once saw a 'To Let' card which read 'No coloureds, no Irish, no dogs.' Today this would be illegal.

In 1962 Sybil and Joe moved to Lewisham with their two children, Lorraine and Trevor. The Methodist minister asked Sybil if she would help to run the church youth club. She readily agreed. Sybil and Joe's third child, Marsha, was born in 1964, and a year later Leticea was born. In 1965 a social worker asked Sybil and Joe if they would become foster-parents. They agreed, and many children found the love and security that they so badly needed in that loving home. John Newbury writes a moving account of their first foster-child, Tracy.

In 1967 another church youth club asked Sybil if she would help to run disco evenings for several hundred black youngsters. She agreed and when the club first opened, it was called the Telegraph Hill Youth Club. Later it was renamed 'Moonshot'. After moving from church hall to church hall, permanent premises were eventually found in Pagnell Street, where Sybil arranged classes in English, typing and accountancy for her black youngsters who often could not find jobs.

In 1972 Sybil was awarded the MBE for all her valuable work in the community. A year later in 1973, when Sybil was driving a group of youngsters back from a beach holiday, she swerved to avoid a motorcyclist who was on the wrong side of the road and in the ensuing crash Marsha, Sybil's daughter, was killed and Sybil herself was badly injured. Sybil's faith in God was severely shaken, but she found the strength to go on believing in Jesus as her friend because of all the love that was shown to her by black and white people alike.

The Pagnell Street Centre began to grow; more classes were arranged; a mothers' project was set up; plans were made for an extension. In 1977 His Royal Highness the Prince of Wales visited the Centre at a time when there was tension between the young people and the police. In December 1977 the Centre was burned to the ground and Sybil was in despair, but not for long. She persuaded the local authority to allow her to use an empty church as a temporary youth club, and she started to raise funds all over again to rebuild the centre. In addition, she raised the money needed to open a hostel for foster-children, which was completed in 1979. She named the hostel the Marsha Phoenix Hostel in memory of her lovely daughter.

In January 1981 tragedy struck again: a house in Deptford was set on fire and thirteen young black people were killed. Sybil immediately went to comfort the grieving parents and offered them her own home. She raised money to help pay for the funerals of the young people. During this time Sybil herself suffered much pain and insults from some people who hated black people and who wanted to stop her work from flourishing. Sybil often found her car tyres slashed, or paint poured over it, and she received many obscene phone calls and threatening letters.

In March 1981 Prince Charles returned to open the new Pagnell Street Centre. In November 1981 Sybil felt it was time to move on, so she resigned as head of the Centre and went to work at a Methodist church in Camberwell. She became director of MELRAW (Methodist Leadership Racism Awareness Workshop). She organized weekend courses and conferences to help people to understand that we all belong to a world-wide family whatever the colour of our skin.

Prayer

Let us close with part of the prayer that Sybil herself wrote in 1984: 'Lord, I know my charge is simple: to love and serve you, to keep faith, to spread your loving kindness. Lord, give me the strength to continue in your service. Amen.'

Song

End the assembly with the song, No 2 'I'd Like to Teach the World to Sing in Perfect Harmony' in *Appuskidu* or a song from *Mango Spice: 44 Caribbean Songs*, A. & C. Black, or No 37, 'Working Together' in *Every Colour Under the Sun*, (Ward Lock Educational).

At the end of his book, *Living in Harmony*, John Newbury gives some excellent practical suggestions for activities such as role play, a West Indian parents' evening, songs, folk tales, music and filmstrips.

Useful addresses

Racial Justice Training Office
Methodist Church House
25, Marlebone Road
London NW1 5JR
Tel: 0207 4675277/8
Fax: 0207 4675238
e-mail: RJTU@methodistchurch.org.uk
Offers training workshops in Racism Awareness, Black Consciousness Raising, etc.

Commission for Racial Equality
Information Department
Elliot House
10–12 Allington Street
London SW1E 5EH
Tel: 0207 8287022
Website: www.cre.gov.uk
Provides information about Racial Discrimination

Resources

A very useful book that raises issues, questions and ways of tackling racism through role play is:

Green, J. (2002) *What do you think about Racism?* Hodder Wayland.

Grace Darling   5–11
Assembly
All

The following topic could form the basis of several assemblies spread over a number of days. Prior to the first assembly, make a visit to the local or regional office of the RNLI, to collect some excellent material for schools in order to set up an exhibition/display.

Give the children some statistics about the number of Royal Lifeboat Stations that there are around our coastal areas, and impress upon them that they are all manned by volunteers who depend upon our support. One of the RNLI films could be shown; or a collection made for RNLI funds; or pencils, badges and flags could be put on sale; or invite someone from RNLI to visit the school and describe their valuable work.

Stress the enormous courage and bravery of crews who brave violent storms and fierce winds and waves to rescue boats in trouble. Perhaps attention could be drawn to a local rescue that has been reported in the newspapers, and a scrapbook could be made up about local heroes.

Finally, tell the story of the young girl, Grace Darling, who rescued several people from drowning after their ship had struck rocks in a terrible storm on the night of 6 September 1838. Grace Darling was born in 1815 in Northumberland in a small place called Bamburgh. Bamburgh was one of the first places to have a lifeboat station. But on this terrible night the storm was so bad that the lifeboat could not put out to sea.

You will need following:

Characters:	*Props*:
Grace Darling	Rocks
Mother	Large steamer
Father	Fishing boat
Fierce waves (with crêpe paper streamers	Mugs
flowing from the children's wrists)	Blankets
Wind	Percussion instruments
Rain	
Captain	
Crew	
52 passengers; 9 survivors	

As the teacher/narrator tells the story, the children begin to mime their parts.

Narrator: Grace Darling lived with her mother and father in the Longstone Lighthouse off the Northumberland coast. Grace's father was the lighthouse keeper. (*Enter father, mother and Grace.*)

Narrator: One night there was a terrible storm. The waves rose up and battered against the rocks in a ferocious way. (*Enter waves to perform a raging, crashing movement, but remain in a 'frozen' pose as the story unfolds and each group acts their part.*)

Narrator: The wind raged and blew the waves and tossed the foam high into the air. (*Enter wind; four children rushing from each corner of the room makes an effective entrance and then 'freeze'.*)

Narrator: The rain poured in torrents to join in a macabre dance of wind, rain and sea. (*Enter wind, rain and waves interact in movement. Percussion instruments and music can be played for this raging dance.*)

Narrator: That very night on 6 September 1838 a steamer called the 'Forfarshire' was on the sea trying to make its way to safety, when suddenly it crashed onto vicious rocks and the ship was broken in half. (*Enter captain and crew who try to steer the ship, passengers cling to each other for safety; then with a crash of cymbals, the ship breaks up and everyone is flung into the water*). Forty-three passengers were drowned and were covered by the waves; nine clung to the wreck. (*The action is mimed.*)

Narrator: Grace woke early that morning, unable to sleep because of the storm, but as she lay listening to the storm, she heard other sounds, desperate cries for help. She leapt out of bed and shouted to her father that there must be a wreck outside. Peering through the mists and gloom, she suddenly caught sight of the wreck and the poor people clinging to it. (*Grace mimes the actions.*)

Narrator: She begged her father to fetch their small fishing boat to rescue the people. But her father sadly shook his head, telling her that it was impossible to reach the people in such a terrible storm. He reminded her that even the Bamburgh lifeboat had not been able to brave those fearful waves. (*Grace and her father mime this conversation.*)

Narrator: But Grace made up her mind to go alone and try to save those poor people. When her father saw that she was determined to go, he relented and agreed to help her. They set out across the raging sea, tossed and turned in every direction, while they rowed with all their strength and might. (*The two row; wind, waves and rain buffet and batter them.*)

Narrator: They struggled desperately until they reached the nine people who were still alive. Somehow they managed to get five of them into their little boat, and they made the gruelling return journey. (*Mime the actions.*)

Narrator: Mrs Darling helped the survivors out of the boat and into the lighthouse, made them hot drinks, warmed them around the fire and gave them blankets to revive their frozen bodies. (*Mime the actions.*)

Narrator: Mr Darling and two of the men that they had saved made the terrifying return journey once more to pick up the remaining four survivors. (*Actions are mimed.*)

Narrator: The news of Grace's courage and bravery soon spread throughout the country, and both she and her father were awarded gold medals for their readiness to risk their own lives in order to save others.

Prayer

Heavenly Father, we ask your blessing on all those brave people who go out to sea to risk their own lives in order that others may live. Amen.

Hymn

No 26, 'When lamps are lighted in the town', in *Infant Praise* (Oxford University Press).

Paul

Read 1 Corinthians Chapter 9, verses 24–25 in the Bible, 'Surely you know that many runners take part in a race, but only one of them wins the prize. Run then in such a way as to win the prize. Every athlete in training submits to strict discipline, in order to be crowned with a wreath that will not last; but we do it for one that will last for ever.' (From the *Good News Bible* published by the Bible Societies/HarperCollins Publishers Ltd., © American Bible Society 1966, 1971, 1976, 1992, 1994. Used with kind permission).

Paul was writing to the Church at Corinth when he compared the Christian endeavour to the strict training of an athlete. Many assemblies could be based on the sayings and life of Paul. This saying has been chosen to demonstrate a simple example.

Find a large picture of an athlete. (*Athletics Weekly* published by Descartes Publishing Ltd., 83, Park Road, Peterborough PE1 2TN could help). Daley Thompson, Gold Medalist Olympic Championships 1984 or Dean Macy, Silver Medalist, World Championships 1999, would be good choices because they were both Decathletes and trained for ten events. Ask ten children to paint the different events and display in a circular fashion around the athletes:

100 Metre Sprint
Long Jump
Shot-put
High Jump
400 Metre Run
High Hurdles
Throwing the Discus
Pole Vault
Throwing the Javelin
1500 Metre Run

On large pieces of card, in large letters, write down some of the following words: Self-discipline, Perseverance, Patience, Kindness to Others, Joy, etc. Explain the meaning of each word or ask the children how they think the words could be applied to each athlete or event. For instance:

Self-discipline is shown by regularly training hard
Perseverance is shown by trying again after failure
Patience is shown by gradually improving performance or waiting turns
Kindness is shown by helping one another to improve, giving advice
Joy is shown when an athlete succeeds, or gives joy to others by his efforts

Let some of the children place the words under each event where they think appropriate and then let the assembled children think of other adjectives that could be applied to athletes in training. For instance:

Inspiration to others
Strength
Agility
Stickability, etc.
Speed
Control
Talent
Flexibility
Getting on with others, even rivals

Draw the assembly to a close by reminding the children of Paul's words at the beginning and explain that every child may not become a gold medallist or world champion for competing in ten events, but at least every child can strive for excellence in one personal or academic area of the curriculum, e.g. kindness to others or trying one's best at sport or scientific studies. Explain that Paul was trying to demonstrate that achieving the prize that he was talking about was not necessarily based on what could be seen by others, but the self-discipline that comes from trying one's best for God.

Prayer

Father God, help us to do our best in everything we do. Amen

Hymn

No 48, 'Do Your Best' in *Every Colour Under The Sun*, (Ward Lock Educational).

Elijah's Story

5–11
Assembly
Judaism (and Christianity)

This Old Testament story about worship, based on I Kings Chapters 17 and 18, can be rehearsed briefly before the assembly or can be read aloud (giving directions as necessary), without any rehearsal at all. It has been found to work as well with top juniors as with infants, as the humour appeals to all ages, alike.

The story can be read from Rock, L. (2001) *The Lion Bible Everlasting Stories*, Lion Publishing PLC. It can be dramatized with a great deal of humour.

The characters can be chosen from the assembled school:

King Ahab
Queen Jezebel
Elijah
4 Ravens
450 Priests of Baal (10 children will actually do!)
4 jar carriers

The outline of the story is as follows: Queen Jezebel persuades King Ahab to build a temple to a new God made of stone (*both bow down and pray*). Elijah warns the pair that if they go on praying to the stone God, Baal, his true God would hold back the rain for three years, and everything would die.

(*Enter Elijah, who wags a forefinger in warning.*)

God keeps his promise and everything dies. However, he shows Elijah a natural spring, where he can get plenty of water, and he sends four ravens to feed him every day.

(*Four ravens flap around the hall looking for food and return to feed Elijah.*)

Elijah returns to King Ahab and challenges him to put the King's new God, Baal, to a test of power with his own true God. The King agrees and all the people are summoned to Mount Carmel, together with 450 priests of Baal.

(*The priests of Baal line up and are given their marching orders by a leader – they march around the hall.*) Elijah commands the 450 priests of Baal to collect sacks of wood and build a high altar. He challenges the priests to ask Baal to consume the wooden altar with fire.

(*The priests collect wood and build the altar; the teacher can enter into the fun by telling the children to work harder and find more imaginary wood.*)

Then the priests perform their prayer-dance.

(*They dance and they hop all round the altar until they drop, but nothing happens.*) Elijah stands up and says that it is his turn, but that wood is too easy for his God to burn, so he fetches twelve big stones.

(*The rest of the children can help Elijah by counting to twelve, as Elijah picks up the imaginary stones.*) Then Elijah digs a deep trench around the stones.

(*The teacher can tell Elijah to put a bit more effort into the digging.*)

Elijah commands four men to fill four large jars of water to throw over the wood and thoroughly drench it. He tells them to do it again, three times. Finally, Elijah kneels and prays that God will burn up the altar to show that He is the one true God.

The teacher needs to quieten the hall as she explains that a great flame roared out of the sky and burned the wood and stones and even the water. The people and priests fall silent and then kneel on the ground and promise to worship the one true God.

Allow a time for quiet reflection.

Hymn

No 61, 'Praise to the Lord, the Almighty, the King of Creation', in New Life (Galliard).

Saint Margaret

This story can be mimed by a class of children. Special days and Saints' days can be remembered throughout the year. A simple assembly can be drawn from the life of a Saint such as St Margaret, who was a real princess. You will need the following characters:

Princess called Margaret
brother, Prince Edgar
sister, Princess Christina
oarsmen
King Malcolm
church builders
eight children
school children
mothers
poor people
sick and needy people

Simple costumes can be worn. Crowns for the King and Queen and ragged clothes for the poor, etc.

One child reads the following story, while the other children mime the actions. A princess called Margaret sailed from England to Scotland with her brother Prince Edgar and sister Princess Christina. (*The princess, brother and sister mime getting into a boat; the oarsmen begin to row.*) King Malcolm of Scotland welcomed the family and he fell in love with Princess Margaret. Later he married Margaret, and she became his Queen. (*A crown is placed on her head.*)

They built a church in Dunfermline to thank God for their happiness. (*Six or eight church builders mime sawing, hammering, building, etc.*) They had eight children. (*Eight children enter and sit at the King and Queen's feet.*) Queen Margaret used to read stories to the children. (*She mimes reading a story.*)

Every day Margaret prayed to God to ask Him how she could help her new people, the people of Scotland. (*Margaret quietly kneels and shuts her eyes to pray.*) She began to open schools where children could learn to read and write. (*Enter children to sit crossed-legged and pretend to write.*) She taught mothers how to make clothes for their children. (*Enter some mothers with material; Margaret makes large sewing movements; the mothers copy.*) Every day the castle doors were opened to the poor, the sick and the needy. (*Mime doors being opened, beggars enter limping, with bandages around their heads, arms, etc. Margaret gives each a bowl of food to eat.*)

The people of Scotland loved Queen Margaret very much because she was so good and kind to everyone. She did all these things because she loved God so much.

Prayer

Thank you God for the lives of ordinary men and women, boys and girls, who, inspired by their great love for you, are enabled to achieve great things for others. Amen.

Hymn

No 63, 'Sing Hosanna', in *New Life* (Galliard).

The Unknown Boy Hero

7–11
Assembly

Adapted for BBC Schools' Radio in 1987 by Elizabeth Peirce from the story 'People aren't always what they seem', in R.H. Lloyd, *Assemblies for School and Children's Church*, RMEP (Chansitor), 1974. This adaptation is used with the kind permission of the Revd Canon R.H. Lloyd.

This story is about a very brave boy who, although he was in great pain, always thought of others before himself. There was once a boy who was very ill indeed. He was taken to hospital and admitted to a very tiny ward with only two beds in it. His bed was placed next to the window and there was an empty bed placed next to the wall. He was known as 'Smiley', because he was always cheerful, even though he was so ill.

One night another young boy called Kevin was brought into the hospital and he was placed in the empty bed beside the wall. As both boys were very ill, all they could do was talk to each other. So day by day the boy Smiley, who was placed next to the window, would describe to Kevin everything that he could see from his window. He described the birds, the flowers, the trees and the shops; and often he would make Kevin laugh by describing the people and the antics of a dog chasing a cat and so on.

Although Kevin loved hearing about what was going on outside, secretly he was very jealous of Smiley being by the window. He envied Smiley's view, and he wished that he too could look out and see all that was going on. So he asked the nurse several times if he could swap beds with his friend, but somehow nothing was ever done about it. As the months went by Smiley continued to amuse Kevin by describing the world outside. He tried to take the other boy's mind off his pain and suffering.

One night Smiley was removed to another hospital for more intensive treatment. So when Kevin saw the empty bed by the window, he asked the nurse again to move him next to the window. This time his request was granted. With great excitement he looked out of the window. But all he could see was a blank wall and two dustbins. Suddenly, he realized that the other boy had imagined all that he saw for his benefit, to try and cheer him up and keep him happy and to take his mind off the pain.

The boy by the window had great courage, didn't he? How easy it would have been for him to grumble about being in hospital, or to moan about his illness. But what did he do? He didn't think about himself at all, or his own problems. He turned all his attention and his imagination to cheering up the other boy. He made up funny stories about different characters just to help to take the other boy's mind off his pain and to make him laugh. Now that takes real bravery. Could you be that brave if you were ill?

Prayer

Father, help us to be like the boy in the story, always ready to cheer up someone else and to think of others rather than ourselves. Amen.

Hymn

No 43, 'Stick on a smile', in *Every Colour under the Sun* (Ward Lock Educational) or No 10, 'Poor child', in *Tinderbox: 66 Songs for Children* A. & C. Black.

9 BACKGROUND INFORMATION FOR TEACHERS

Buddhism

Background Information

The Buddha or 'Enlightened One'

The Buddha was born in the fifth or sixth century BCE. According to tradition, he was known as Siddhārtha Gautama, the son of a north Indian King. He married Yashodharā and lived a life of luxury, protected from the outside world. One day, he went outside the palace and saw four people who changed his life. He saw a sick man, an old man, a dead man and a Holy man. He left home in search of the meaning of suffering. For six years he stayed with five Holy Men, fasting and enduring great hardship almost to the point of death. Then one day, in deep meditation, sitting under a tree, his enlightenment came. From this time onwards, he was known as the Buddha, or 'Enlightened One' and he began his teaching. See the Four Noble Truths and the Eightfold Path below.

The Four Noble Truths

The Buddha taught that:

1   All life involves suffering.
2   Suffering is due to selfishness.
3   If selfishness is subjugated, suffering will stop.
4   The way to end suffering is to follow the Eightfold Path.

The Eightfold Path

1   Right Understanding ⎫ wisdom
2   Right Thought ⎭
3   Right speech ⎫
4   Right action ⎬ morality
5   Right livelihood ⎭
6   Right mental effort ⎫
7   Right mindfulness ⎬ meditation
8   Right concentration ⎭

(From: *Founders, Prophets and Sacred Books* by J.R. Bailey)

Several Types of Buddhism Today

According to tradition, the Buddha lived for eighty years. Attempts to clarify and systematize his teaching in the centuries after his death led eventually to two broad interpretations of what Buddhism is finally all about. The first approach is represented in modern Buddhism by the Theravāda tradition, the Doctrine of the Elders, found particularly in Sri Lanka and South East Asia. This form of Buddhism, claims to represent faithfully the pure original teachings of the Buddha and places particular emphasis on a monastic tradition which leads eventually to individual and personal enlightenment for those who follow the Buddha's path. The other approach, called itself 'Mahāyāna Buddhism', the 'Great Vehicle', and is found nowadays particularly in China, Japan and the other countries of East Asia, and Tibet. Here, although the form of Buddhism represented by Theravāda is not denied, the emphasis is on attaining the very same enlightenment as the Buddha, in order to be able to better benefit all sentient beings. Thus in Mahāyāna Buddhism, kindness to others becomes a particularly prominent theme. (Williams)

Sūtra

Sūtra is the sanskrit of the Pali 'Sutta'. It is the name given to the collection of the Buddha's discourses.

Vinaya

These are the rules for monastic life.

Jātaka (birth) Tales

Jātaka tales are stories relating to the Buddha's previous lives on the path to enlightenment.

Buddhist Family Life

Birth Rites

Often there is no special ceremony to become a Buddhist, (although, for those who are older, there is a ceremony of 'Taking Refuge' in Tibetan Buddhism). Sometimes, a family will invite a Buddhist monk to the house to bless the child, but basically a person becomes a Buddhist by following the Eightfold Path.

A Duty

Buddhist parents feel that they have a duty to give their children a good education, teaching them to be kind to all living creatures; to arrange their marriage; to give money and food to Buddhist monks.

The Buddha Statues

Buddhists will often have a statue of the Buddha in their own home. They show respect by bowing before their statue and will often place flowers in front of their statue. Candles and incense are burnt as a symbol of the light that the Buddha shed with his teaching.

Temple or Vihāra

Buddhists do not have a set time or day to go to the temple, although they will often visit the temple on full moon days and special festival days.

Monks (Bhikkhus) and Nuns (Bhikkhunis) in the Theravāda Tradition

Monks and Nuns learn to have few possessions, such as a simple robe and an alms bowl. They have no money of their own and are given all their food. They also shave their heads. Monks must beg for all their food. The rules which the monks live by are called the Basic Precepts:

1   Not to destroy or harm life
2   Not to steal
3   The rule of chastity, which is not to have sexual relations or marry.
4   Not to tell lies
5   Not to take intoxicating drinks
6   Not to eat other than at meal times
7   Not to go to entertainments like shows, with dancing or music
8   Not to wear perfumes or scents or wear ornaments and decoration
9   Not to sleep on comfortable raised beds
10   Not to accept or handle gold or silver
(From: *Buddhists and Buddhism* by M. Patrick published by Wayland, 1982, page 33.)

In general, all Buddhist people aspire to observe the first five of these rules. Rule 3 is adapted to mean irresponsible sexual relations. A further three rules are observed by families on special Buddhist Holy days.

Meditation

Many Buddhists meditate or think deeply in their own homes. The aim of meditation is to clear the mind of feelings of greed, hatred or laziness and to fill the mind with love and kind thoughts towards others, also to understand better the way things are.

Nirvāna

Is the highest state of happiness which all Buddhists aim to achieve.

Food

Some Buddhists are vegetarians and will not eat any meat or fish or eggs. Others do eat meat.

Clothes

Buddhists usually wear the national dress from their country of origin. For instance, if a Buddhist comes from India, a sari is worn by the women. Men in England will usually wear western clothes. On full moon days, simple white clothes are sometimes worn. (A Theravāda tradition).

Buddhist Festivals

Find out all about Buddhist Festivals. In general, they are held at the time of full moon, and vary from country to country. Some of the following are observed in Sri Lanka.

Vesākha

This is the most important full moon festival held in April or May. It is a celebration of the Buddha's birth, his Enlightenment and his death. It is also the Buddhist New Year. (See p. 13).

Jetthamāsa

The month of June celebrates the spread of Buddhism from India to other countries.

Asālha

In the month of July, there is a celebration in memory of the Buddha leaving home and preaching his first sermon.

Kathina

The month of November, is remembered as the month when the Buddha sent his first 60 disciples to spread his message around India. It also commemorates the making of a new robe on a frame called a Kathina with the Buddha. (See p. 110).

Phussa

This takes place in January. It is a first celebration of the Buddha's first visit to Sri Lanka.

Resources

Books

(P) = Pupils
(T) = Teachers

Bailey, J.R. (1995) *Founders, Prophets and Sacred Books*, Schofield and Sims. (T)
Adiccabandhu and Padmasri (1998) *The Monkey King*, Windhorse Publications. (P)
Adiccabandhu and Padmasri (1998) *The Lion and the Jackal*, Windhorse Publications. (P)
Bancroft, A. (1992) *The Buddhist World*, Simon & Schuster (P&T).
Cole, W.O. (Ed.) (1983) *Religion in the Multi-faith School*, Nelson Thornes (T).
Erricker, C. and J. (1996) *Celebrate: Buddhist Festivals*, Heinemann (P).
Ganeri, A. (1996) *Buddhist Beliefs and Cultures*, Franklin Watts (P).
Ganeri, A. (2000) *Keystones: Buddhist Vihara*, A & C Black (P).
Gibb, C. (2002) *The Dalai Lama, Peacemaker from Tibet*, Hodder Wayland (P).
Goonewardene, A. (1994) *Buddhist Scriptures*, Heinemann (T).
Kohn, S.C. and Kohn, A. (1999) *The Barefoot Book of Buddhist Tales*, Barefoot Paperbacks (P&T).

Marchant, M. (2002) *The Buddha and Buddhism*, Hodder Wayland (P & T).

Morgan, P. (1989) *Being a Buddhist*, Batsford (T).

Morgan, P. (1985) *Buddhism in the Twentieth Century*, Hulton (T).

Morgan, P. *Buddhist Stories*, (P&T)   Available from: Mansfield College
            Buddhist Iconography, (T) Oxford OX1 3TF
                                         Tel: 01865 270999; Fax 01865 270970
                                         Website: www.mansfield.ox.ac.uk

Pant, P. (2000) *Buddhism*, Silverdale Books (T).

Patrick, M. (1982) *Buddhists and Buddhism*, Hodder Wayland (P&T).

Penney, S. (2000) *Discovering Religions: Buddhism*, Heinemann (P&T).

Penney, S. (2002) *Religions of the World: Buddhism*, Heinemann (P).

Penney, S. (2001) *World Beliefs and Cultures: Buddhism*, Heinemann (P).

Samarasekara, D. (2001) *I am a Buddhist*, Franklin Watts (P).

Singh, K. (2000) *My Buddhist Faith*, (Big Book) Rainbows Red Series, Evans Brothers (P).

Snelling, J. (1986) *Buddhism*, Hodder Wayland (P&T).

Snelling, J. (1985) *Buddhist Festivals*, Hodder Wayland (P&T).

Snelling, J. (1986) *Buddhist Stories*, Hodder Wayland (P&T).

Snelling, J. (1987) *The Life of the Buddha*, Hodder Wayland (P).

Snelling, J. (2001) *Thorsons Way of Buddhism*, HarperCollins (T).

Thompson, J. (2000) *The Buddhist Experience: Seeking Religion Series*, Hodder & Stoughton (P&T).

Wangu, M.B. (2002) *Buddhism: World Religions Series*, Facts on File Inc. (T).

Williams, P. (1989) *Mahāyāna Buddhism. The Doctrinal Foundations*, Routledge (For advanced study). (T)

Willson, A. (2000) *Places of Worship: Buddhist Temples*, Heinemann (P).

Wood, J. (1995) *Our Culture: Buddhist*, Franklin Watts (P).

Wright, C. (1997) *Buddhism for Today: Religion for Today Series*, OUP, (P&T).

Yoko, S. (1998) *The Cat that Lived a Million Times*, University of Hawaii Press (P).

Useful Address:
The Buddhist Society
58, Eccleston Square
London SW1V 1PH

Tel: 0207 8345858
Website: www.thebuddhistsociety.org.uk

Videos

Videos for children aged 7+ and 11+ entitled *Buddha's Life and Teaching* and *Buddhist Way of Life* are available from SCM-Canterbury Press, address below. Aspects of Buddhism are included on Video 2, of *The Believe It or Not* videos (Revised Series) for 11+ children, also from SCM-Canterbury Press:

SCM-Canterbury Press Limited
St Mary's Works
St Mary's Plain
Norwich
Norfolk
NR3 3BH

Tel: 0160 3612914
Email: admin@scm-canterburypress.co.uk
Website: www.canterburypress.co.uk

The REaSE Project Video for children aged 7+ and 11+ (Secondary Schools) *Speaking For Ourselves* is available from SCM-Canterbury Press, above. The faiths represented on the video are Buddhism, Christianity, Hinduism, Islam, Judaism and Sikhism.

A good supplier of artefacts, pictures, cassettes and videos is:

Articles of Faith Ltd.
Resource House,
Kay Street,
Bury BL9 6BU

Tel: 0161 7636232
Email: ArticlesFaith@cs.com
Website: www.articlesoffaith.co.uk

Pronunciation Guide to Buddhist Words

A/sāl/ha	'A' as in 'fah'; 'sāl' rhymes with 'Carl'; 'ha' as in 'hah'
Bhik/khun/is	'Bhik' as in 'bick'; 'khun' rhymes with 'soon'; 'is' as in 'ease'
Bhik/khus	'Bhik' as in 'bick'; 'khus' as 'queues'
Bud/dha	'Bud' as in 'pud'; 'dha' as in 'duh'
Dev/ad/atta	'Dev' as it is pronounced phonetically; 'ad' as in 'hard'; 'atta' as in 'utter'
Jāt/a/ka	'Jāt' rhymes with 'part'; 'a' as in 'A'; 'ka' as in 'kuh'
Jett/ha/mā/sa	'Jett' as in 'jet'; 'ha' as in 'hut'; 'mā' as in 'far'; 'sa' as in 'suh'
Kat/hin/a	'Kat' as in 'cat'; 'hin' rhymes with 'been'; 'a' as in 'uh'
Ma/hā/yāna	'Ma' plus 'hā' as in 'car'; 'yāna' rhymes with 'farmer'
Man/tras	'Man' as in 'man'; 'tras' rhymes with 'daz'
Nir/vāna	'Nir' as in 'near'; 'vāna' rhymes with 'farmer'
Pāl/i	'Pā' as in 'car'; 'li' rhymes with 'tree'
Phu/ssa	'Phu' rhymes with 'do' (silent 'h'); 'ssa' as in 'suh'
Sam/sā/ra	'Sam' as in 'sang'; 'sā' rhymes with 'car'; 'ra' as in 'ruh'
San/skrit	'San' rhymes with 'fan'; 'skrit' rhymes with 'writ'
Sidd/hārth/a	'Sidd' as in the name; 'hārth' as in 'heart'; 'a' as in 'uh'
Gaut/a/ma	'Gaut' as in 'gout'; 'a' as in 'far'; 'ma' as in 'muh'
Sūt/ra	'Sūt' as in 'suit'; 'ra' as in 'rah'
Sut/ta	'Sut' as in 'put'; 'ta' as in 'tah'
Thera/vāda	'Thera' as in 'terror' (silent 'h'); 'vāda' rhymes with 'larder'
Ve/sāk/ha	'Ve' rhymes with 'bay'; 'sāk' as in 'ark'; 'ha' as in 'huh'
Vi/hā/ra	'Vi' as in 'vih'; 'hā' as in 'hah', 'ra' as in 'rut'
Vin/ay/a	'Vin' rhymes with 'bin'; 'ay' as in 'eye'; 'a' as in 'hah'
Yash/o/dha/rā	'Yash' rhymes with 'mass'; 'o' as in 'toe'; 'dha' as in 'far'; 'rā' as in 'car'

Christianity

Background Information

Christians

There are many branches of Christianity today: Roman Catholics, Anglicans, Methodists, Salvation Army, Baptists, Congregationalists, Church of Scotland, United Reformists, Pentecostals, Orthodox, Quakers, etc. All have the same fundamental belief that Jesus Christ is the Son of God. They differ to some extent in their particular beliefs and styles of worship, although there are more similarities than differences. (See pp. 216–19 for more detailed description.)

Jesus Christ

All Christians believe that Jesus Christ is God's Son. He was born in Bethlehem 2000 years ago. Jesus means 'God Saves'. Christ means 'The Anointed One'. Mary his mother, was a virgin. Joseph his 'father', was a carpenter. Christians believe that Mary was chosen by God to bear His son as the fulfilment of the promise that He made to the Jews in the Old Testament. Jesus grew up in Nazareth and started his ministry when he was 30 years old. His birth, life and death are recorded in the Gospels in the New Testament of the Bible.

Symbol of the Cross

Christians believe in only one God. He is known and worshipped as three persons, God the Father, God the Son and God the Holy Spirit. The cross has become the symbol of Christianity as a reminder that God sent his son Jesus Christ to be crucified on a cross, to be the perfect sacrifice for the sins of the world, as foretold in the old Testament of the Bible. After Jesus' death, He sent His Holy Spirit to empower all disciples.

Holy Bible

Christians believe this Holy Book was inspired by God. It is divided into two parts, the Old and New Testaments. The first part records the history of the Jewish people and the promise of the Messiah, The Anointed One. It also contains the Wisdom Writings, such as the Psalms and Job and the Prophets such as Isaiah. The second part describes Jesus, His life, teachings, miracles and parables. It also contains the letters that Jesus' followers wrote to each other after His death.

Worship

Christians worship God in many different ways through singing, praising, praying, going to church and dedicating their lives, like monks, nuns and missionaries. They try to obey God's commandments in the Old Testament and follow the teaching of

Christ in the New Testament. Christians usually attend church every Sunday and believe that Christianity is a way of life and that they belong to the world-wide family of God. Therefore, worship is not confined to Sundays only, but Christians pray each day, read their Bibles, attend prayer meetings and Bible study groups during the week, as well as caring for others and giving to charity work.

Christian Family Life

Baptism

In the Roman Catholic, Anglican and Orthodox Churches, babies are baptized or christened. In the Pentecostal, Baptist and Free Churches, baptism only occurs when people are old enough to profess their own faith in Jesus Christ as their Saviour. (See pp. 216–19)

Confirmation

Each Christian denomination varies in the age when their children/adults are confirmed. (See pp. 216–19). Traditionally in the Roman Catholic and Anglican churches, confirmation occurs around the age of thirteen years. A young person must attend confirmation classes and accept the Christian beliefs for him or herself. He or she is confirmed by the Bishop and is able to receive Holy Communion. This is the regular service of sharing bread and wine in remembrance of Christ's body and blood that was shed for the forgiveness of sins. Roman Catholic children will have been able to share in this service long before confirmation as they generally make their First Communion around the age of seven. However, they will be confirmed later as teenagers, when they can fully understand the promises that they are making. In addition, in the Church of England today, there is a move to invite *all* children to take part in Holy Communion where the child has demonstrated and understands, what he or she is participating in, without formal confirmation.

Sunday

As God commanded in the Old Testament, many Christians try to keep this as a special family day. That is, they attend church, treat the day as a day of rest and leisure and do not work (except for those who have to work in the essential services, like doctors, nurses, the fire brigade, police force, rescue services, hospitals, old people's homes and children's homes, etc.)

Junior Church

Many children attend Sunday School or special classes for young people. Often they will join the adults at a family service and may even present the worship themselves.

Choir/Band

Many churches have impressive bands today to enhance the Sunday worship. All kinds of instruments are used: trumpets, horns, drums, violins, tambourines, guitars, recorders, flutes, hand-bells, etc. The band is a particular feature in Salvation Army worship, although today there is likely to be a band for worship in many of the other denominations, except Quakers, where there is no music.

Ministers

In different churches the spiritual leader of the church has different names such as Priest, Father (Roman Catholic, Orthodox, some Anglican); Vicar, Rector (Anglican); Pastor (Pentecostal, Baptist, Free Churches) etc. The Minister can be a man or a woman, although some parts of the Roman Catholic and Anglican Church resist the ordination of women. In some cases the Minister will wear special clothing as a sign of his or her calling and responsibility. They conduct services, preach or teach the people in their congregations about the Bible and the Sacraments (i.e. the use of bread and wine at Holy Communion; the use of water at Baptism; the laying on of hands by the Bishop at Confirmation; Confession and Forgiveness; Holy Orders; Marriage; Healing. The Salvation Army and the Quakers do not celebrate all these Sacraments. Other duties include officiating at weddings and funerals; visiting the sick or elderly; running children's/youth groups; attending meetings to do with church finance, buildings, policy, etc.

Christian Festivals

There follows a brief description of the major Christian Festivals:

Easter

This festival takes place in the spring. It is the most important Christian festival. Jesus Christ's death and resurrection to new life are commemorated. (See Easter Sunday below).

Good Friday

Christians remember how Jesus was tried, mocked, tortured and crucified on this day. Some churches hold services lasting three hours, in remembrance of the final three hours that Jesus hung upon the cross and the sky turned black from twelve o'clock until he died at three o'clock. (See Luke, Chapter 23).

Easter Sunday

On this day Jesus rose from the dead to new life. It is a joyful day for Christians everywhere. (Read Luke, Chapter 24). The churches are decorated with many flowers. Special hymns of thanks and praise are sung. Many churches build a miniature garden tomb with the stone rolled away, as a reminder of the empty tomb in Jerusalem where Jesus was buried. Easter Eggs (a symbol of new life) are given as gifts.

Lent

This is the forty days before Easter. Christians remember this as the time when Jesus fasted in the desert and was tempted by the devil before he started his ministry. In remembrance of this, Christians often try to fast or to give up something that they particularly like during Lent. The money thus saved is then given to charity. *Ash Wednesday* is the first day of Lent. In some churches, Christians are marked on their foreheads with ash, as a sign of remorse for their sins and as a symbol of the death that they deserve. *Pancake Day* or *Shrove Tuesday* precedes Ash Wednesday, as a day when traditionally all the fat supplies and rich, sweet food would be eaten up before the Lenten fast.

Palm Sunday

This was the time of the Jewish Passover when Jesus rode into Jerusalem and was hailed as King. It is commemorated today on the Sunday before Easter. Some churches give crosses made out of palm leaves to their congregation, as a reminder of this and as a reminder of the death that Jesus was about to suffer on the cross.

Advent

The four weeks before Christmas are called Advent or 'The Coming'. Christians reflect on the passages from the Bible which foretell God's promise of the coming of a Saviour, Jesus Christ, His own Son.

Christmas

The celebration of the birth of Jesus Christ in Bethlehem. Many churches and schools re-enact the scene at the time as described in Luke, Chapter 2. That is, the angels appearing to the shepherds to announce the birth of Christ; the scene in the stable with Mary and Joseph, ox and asses; the Wise Men following a bright star to Bethlehem, bringing costly gifts in homage, etc. Gifts are exchanged in memory of this. Special festive food is enjoyed as everyone celebrates the birth of the promised Saviour.

Whitsun

The festival is sometimes called *Pentecost* (the Greek word meaning fiftieth), because it was the festival celebrated by the Jews called *Shavout*, fifty days after the Passover meal. Today Christians everywhere remember this day, as the day when God sent His Holy Spirit to his disciples, fifty days after his resurrection. The disciples were gathered together in a room when suddenly there was a rush of wind and they saw 'tongues of flaming fire' above each other's heads, they were filled with the Holy Spirit and began to speak in other languages. (See Acts, Chapter 2, verses 2–4).

Saints Days

There are many days in the Christian calendar when particular saints, men and women, are remembered for the special contribution that they made to the faith. Roman Catholics and Orthodox churches particularly remember more Saints than other denominations, but other branches of the world-wide church do keep some special saints' days.

A Brief Description of some Christian Denominations

Roman Catholics

The first disciples did as Jesus commanded them and began to spread the message of Christianity throughout the world. Peter (one of Jesus' disciples) was chosen as the first Bishop of Rome and became known as 'Papa' or Father, i.e. the first Pope. As head of the Roman Catholic Church, the Pope today resides in the Vatican in Rome, Italy. He has special authority in the world-wide Catholic church, its laws and rules.

Roman Catholics believe in one God in three persons: Father, Son, and Holy Spirit. Mary, the mother of God's son, Jesus, is given special honour in the faith. Roman Catholics attend their parish church each Sunday where Mass or a reminder of the Last Supper is celebrated. They believe that the special bread, called the Host, and the wine become the actual body and blood of Jesus at their communion service.

After careful study and preparation classes, children of about 6 or 7 years old are allowed to make their First Communion. They wear special clothes for this event and sometimes have a party afterwards. Later, as teenagers, they will come to be confirmed by the Bishop.

The rosary is a set of beads, used as an aid to prayer. The Lord's Prayer is said, and special prayers to Mary, Jesus' mother, are made.

Eastern Orthodox Christians

The early Christian leaders in different countries were called 'Bishops'. They met to discuss various matters relating to church life and the Christian faith. However, in 1054, the Bishop of Rome and the Bishop of Constantinople became involved in a fearful struggle for power, which led to a split in the early church. The followers of the Bishop of Rome became known as Roman Catholics and the followers of the Bishop of Constantinople became known as Orthodox Christians. 'Orthodox' means 'right belief'.

Many Orthodox Christians live and worship in Greece, Cyprus, Russia, Yugoslavia, America and Britain today. Like all Christians, Orthodox Christians believe in one God, in three persons and that Jesus Christ is His Son; Mary, Jesus' mother, also has a very special place in their worship.

Icons, or religious pictures in the church are kissed by the worshippers before the Sunday service. The sign of the cross is made on entering the church, and each member of the congregation lights a candle. Incense is burnt, as a symbol of the prayers rising to God. Like the Roman Catholics, Orthodox Christians believe that the bread and wine become Christ's body and blood at Holy Communion.

Every Orthodox baby is usually given the name of one of the saints, or Christ Himself, or Mary, the mother of Jesus, at a special baptismal service. The baby is put into water mixed with oil, three times, in the name of the Father, the Son and the Holy Spirit. Confirmation is administered immediately after baptism. Name days are very important in the Orthodox Church, and everyone makes a special effort to attend the church on their particular day.

The Protestant Reformation

The early church was to split again many times. It began in the early sixteenth century with a German priest called Martin Luther. He complained to the Pope that all the rules and regulations that had grown up around worship often prevented ordinary men and women from coming close to God.

This was the beginning of the Protestant movement. The Lutheran Church became important in Germany, Scandinavia and later America. The Anglican Church (or Church of England) is a Protestant Church and spread throughout the world. The Calvinist Church (named after John Calvin) 'laid the foundations of the Church of Scotland and other Presbyterian Churches' (Ward, 1973, p. 15). Basically, this early Protestant movement attempted to return to the teachings of the early church as revealed in the Bible. The reformers abolished many holy days to give more importance to Christmas, Easter, Pentecost and Sunday worship. They emphasized the importance of baptism and Holy Communion.

Congregational Church

Although the Church of England had separated from Rome, many people in England still felt that the reforms had not gone far enough and that the established church was very corrupt. The Separatist Movement began as early as 1550 and gained momentum under the leadership of Robert Browne. Their central belief was that the local congregation formed the body of the church, with Jesus Christ as the head. They believed (as do all Christian believers) that where two or three are gathered together in His name, Christ is among them.

Each local congregation today chooses its own minister. No special dress is worn by the minister, although a black gown is usual for Sunday worship. Deacons are appointed from among the church members to run the church and to help with all matters financial and spiritual.

Baptist Church

Like the Congregationalists, the group calling themselves Baptists (in the early seventeenth century) were persecuted in England and fled to Holland. They differed from the Congregationalists in that they believed strictly in adult baptism, as depicted in the New Testament. Just as Jesus was baptized at the beginning of his ministry, Baptists believe that a person can only be baptized when he or she is ready to make his or her own promises to God. Baptists are completely submerged under water at the special baptismal service, as a sign of dying to sin and rising to a new way of life.

John Smyth, one of the exiles, was the first leader of this new movement in Holland in 1609. Many of his followers returned to London in approximately 1612 to set up Baptist churches and soon the movement grew all over the world.

Communion today in the Baptist Church is open to all who 'love the Lord Jesus Christ', and not just those who have been baptized. 'The Churches are gathered in local unions which belong in turn to the Baptist Union, meeting in annual assembly under an elected president' (Ward, 1973, p. 38).

Methodists

John Wesley was an Anglican clergyman who did not set out to break with the Anglican Church. But, disillusioned by what he saw in the established churches, in the early eighteenth century he set about bringing 'the church' to the ordinary people by preaching in the open air. His message was the need for a personal faith and for conversion to a new way of life or 'method' for living, i.e. disciplined prayer life, reading the Bible and practising Christianity.

However, the break came about gradually, with John Wesley conducting the ordination of deacons and priests to preach in America; 'in 1784 the people called Methodists were recognized by Law (Ward, 1973, p. 41). After his death in 1791 the Methodists broke away from the Church of England, and Methodism soon spread throughout the world through the appointment of overseas missionaries.

The message today is much the same as for other Christians; namely, a recognition of personal sin, a desire to be saved, a personal faith in Jesus Christ and evidence of a reformed way of life. Methodist services are more free than Anglican services today. There is more emphasis on hymn singing and extemporaneous prayer.

The Salvation Army

William Booth, himself a Methodist minister, was the founder of the Salvation Army in 1865. He found Methodism too constricting, so founded a new movement, first called the East London Christian Mission but changed to the Salvation Army in 1878. William Booth decided to organize his volunteers along military lines to fight against evil and poverty. He appointed himself as the general, his fellow ministers became officers and the congregation became the soldiers, all wearing a uniform as a 'sign that they belonged to God's Army' (Blackwell, 1984, p. 5).

The brass band is an important feature of Salvation Army worship. The lively band music helps to spread the Gospel message both at open air meetings and inside the Salvation Army citadels or halls.

The services are lead by a commanding officer or major who has been specially trained; many are women. The 'holiness meeting' or service does not follow a regular pattern. Sometimes the officers invite members of the congregation to give their testimony about following Jesus Christ, there is always a sermon, a Bible reading, joyful singing and a time of quiet reflective prayer. Other meetings are held such as the 'praise meeting' or the 'salvation meeting', and Salvation Army members hold music festivals and worship God through the use of drama.

Just like their founder, today's Salvation Army members are at the forefront of the caring services, helping people who are the victims of poverty, earthquakes, wars and disasters.

Pentecostals

The Pentecostal movement began in the United States in the early twentieth century, drawing support primarily from African-American people.

Pentecostal conduct and style of worship are very much Bible-based, attempting to reflect the life-style of the early church and the teaching of Jesus. At Whitsun or Pentecost (fifty days after the resurrection of Jesus) Jesus' disciples were gathered together in one place for the Jewish festival of Shavout, when suddenly they heard a great noise like a rushing wind and saw 'little tongues of fire' above each other's heads. This was the coming of the Holy Spirit which enabled the disciples to speak in foreign languages, so that people from different countries could understand what they were saying (see Acts 2). Pentecostals today pray for God's spirit to come upon them in the same way. They call this 'Baptism in the Spirit', which means being filled with the Holy Spirit and speaking in 'tongues', speech which has to be understood through an interpreter (Pettenuzzo, 1993, p. 30).

There are many Pentecostal churches all over the world today and their number is still growing. It is a particularly popular form of worship in the West Indies, Africa, America and Britain.

No one can be 'born' a Pentecostal. Each church member has to confess his or her sins and agree that Jesus Christ is Lord and Saviour and that they intend to live a 'new' life. Usually this takes place at an adult baptismal service, but children can be baptized too, so long as they are mature enough to understand the promises they are making. Baptism is by complete immersion in water, following the pattern of Jesus' own baptism in the River Jordan.

Music plays a very important part in Pentecostal worship. Singing, hand-clapping, instrument playing (especially the tambourine), rhythmic movement are all associated with Pentecostal worship. The congregation is often led by impressive choirs.

The leaders of the churches are called 'Pastors', who can be men or women and who are ordained ministers of the Pentecostal church. They are often assisted by Deacons or Elders. Evangelists or Lay Preachers also assist the Pastor at services on Sundays, such as the 'Divine Worship Service', the Lord's Supper, or at a 'Healing Service'. Afterwards, just as Jesus took a towel after the last supper with his disciples and began washing their feet, so too, Pentecostals wash one another's feet after the Lord's Supper.

Resources

Books

(P) = Pupils
(T) = Teachers

Amery, H. (2002) *The Easter Story*, Usborne Publishing (P).
Bates, J. (1986) *Visiting a Methodist Church*, The Lutterworth Press (P & T).
Bailey, J.R. (1995) *Founders, Prophets and Sacred Books*, Schofield and Sims (T).
Bailey, J.R. (1995) *Religious Buildings and Festivals*, Schofield and Sims (T).
Bailey, J.R. (1995) *Religious Leaders and Places of Pilgrimage Today*, Schofield and Sims (T).
Bennet, O. (1986) *Festivals*, Bell and Hyman (P).
Bennet, O. (1985) *People*, Bell and Hyman (P).
Bennet, O. (1984) *Worship*, Bell and Hyman (P).
Blackwell, M. (1984) *Visiting a Salvation Army Citadel*, The Lutterworth Press (P & T).
Brown, A. (2002) *Jesus and Christianity, Great Religious Leaders Series*, Hodder Wayland (P).
Brown, A. (2001) *Religions of the World: Christian World*, Hodder Wayland (P & T).

Brown, A. and Seaman, A. (2000) *Keystones: Christian Church*, A and C Black (P).

Brown, A. and Seaman, A. (2000) *Rainbows, Red, My Christian Faith*, Evans Brothers Ltd (P).

Caldwell, J.C. (1983) *Let's Visit the West Indies*, Burke (P).

Campbell, K. (1983) *The Caribbean*, Macdonald Educational (P).

Collins, M. and Price, M.A. (1999) *The Story of Christianity*, Dorling Kindersley (T).

Collinson, C. and Miller, C. (1985) *Celebrations: Festivals in a Multi-faith Community*, Hodder and Stoughton (T).

Currie, N. (1999) *2000 Years. The Christian Faith in Britain*, Lion Publishing (P & T).

de Paola, Tomie (1990) *Book of Bible Stories*, Hodder and Stoughton (P).

Doney, M. (1997) *Jesus, the Man who Changed History*, Lion Publishing (P).

Ganeri, A. (2002) *Celebrations Christmas*, Heinemann (P).

Ganeri, A. (2002) *Celebrations Easter*, Heinemann (P).

Geldart, A. (2000) *Christianity*, Heinemann (T).

Hackel, S. (1993) *The Orthodox Church*, St Stephen's Press (P & T).

Hall, S. (2003) *Who is Jesus*, Lion Publishing (P).

Harrison, S.W. and Shepherd, D. (1991) *A Christian Family in Britain*, RMEP (Chansitor) (P & T).

Hirst, M. (2002) *Celebrate: Easter*, Hodder Wayland (P).

Hoffman, M. (2000) *Parables: Stories Jesus Told*, Frances Lincoln (P).

Killingray, M. (1993) *I am an Anglican*, Franklin Watts (P).

Logan, J. (1995) *World Religions, Christianity*, Hodder Wayland (P).

Long, R. (1994) *The Lutheran Church*, RMEP (Chansitor) (There are many more books in this Christian Denomination series) (P & T).

Lye, K. (1988) *Let's Go to Jamaica*, Franklin Watts (P) (There are many more books in this series).

Mayled, J. (1986) *Pilgrimage*, Hodder Wayland (P).

Mayled, J. (1987) *Religious Dress*, Hodder Wayland (P).

Owen, G and Seaman, A. (1998) *Looking at Christianity: Jesus and Mary*, Hodder Wayland (P).

Owen, G and Seaman, A. (1998) *Looking at Christianity: Special Occasions*, Hodder Wayland (P).

Penney, S. (1999) *Christianity, Discovering Religions Series*, Heinemann (P & T).

Penney, S. (2001) *Christianity, World Belief and Culture Series*, Heinemann (P & T).

Penney, S. (2002) *Religions of the World: Christianity*, Heinemann (P).

Pettenuzzo, B. (1993) *I am a Pentecostal*, Franklin Watts (P).

Pettenuzzo, B. (2001) *I am a Roman Catholic*, Franklin Watts (P).

Powers, M. (1985) *Follow the Year. A Family Celebration of Christian Holidays*, Hodder and Stoughton (P & T).

Robson, G. (1999) *Places of Worship: Orthodox Churches*, Heinemann (P).

Richards, C. (1999) *Places of Worship: Catholic Churches*, Heinemann (P).

Roussou, M. (1993) *I am a Greek Orthodox*, Franklin Watts (P).

Rye, J. (1986) *The Story of the Christians*, Cambridge University Press (P & T).

Self, D. (1998) *Stories from The Christian World*, Hodder Wayland (P & T) (The 1987 version had more stories than this later version, but it is still good).

The Good News Bible (1994) Bible Societies/HarperCollins (P & T).

The Lion Illustrated Encyclopedia of the Bible (2001) Lion Publishing (2001) (P & T).

Thomas, R. and Stutchbury, J. (1986) *The Pope and the Vatican*, Macdonald (P).

Thompson, J. (1996) *Celebrate Christian Festivals*, Heinemann (P).

Thorley, S. (1993; 2003) *Christianity in Words and Pictures*, RMEP (Chansitor) (P & T).

Ward, M. (1973) *Protestant Christian Churches*, Ward Lock Educational.

Watson, C. (1997) *Christian Beliefs and Cultures*, Franklin Watts (P).

Watson, C. (2001) *What Do We Know About: Christianity?* Hodder Wayland (P).

Wildsmith, B. (1995) *The Easter Story*, Oxford University Press (P).

Wood, A. (1998) *Where We Worship: The Christian Church*, Franklin Watts (P) (Also in the series: *Buddhist Temple, Muslim Mosque, Hindu Mandir, Jewish Synagogue*. All published in 1998).

Audio-visual Aids

Posters on Christian Festivals (Christmas, Easter, Whitsun, Harvest), Places of Worship, Religious Belief (with a CD-ROM), My Neighbours Religion, etc. Available from Pictorial Charts Educational Trust, 27 Kirchen Road, London W13 0UD.
Tel: 0208 567 9206
Fax: 0208 566 5120
Website: www.pcet.co.uk

General, Inspirational, Funny Posters available from: The Festival Shop, 56 Poplar Road, King's Heath, Birmingham B14 7AG
Tel: 0121 444 0444
Fax: 0121 441 5404
Email: info@festivalshop.co.uk

Posters on Jesus Worldwide, Christmas, Easter, etc., by African and Asian artists and a CD-ROM telling the story of Christianity in Britain (suitable for upper Juniors) available from: Resources, Christian Education Movement, Royal Buildings, Victoria Street, Derby, DE1 1GW
Tel: 01332 296 655
Fax: 01332 343 253
Website: www.retoday.org.uk

Posters, slides, videos, CD-ROMS on Christian themes available from: St Paul Multimedia Productions, Middle Green, Slough SL3 6BS
Tel: 01753 577 629
Fax: 01753 511 809
Email: productions@stpaulmultimedia.co.uk

Luke Street Video (eight occasions when Jesus meets different people described in Luke's Gospel, beautifully retold by Roy Castle, suitable for infants) and *The Champion* Video (telling the Easter story with lovely music by Garth Hewitt, suitable for upper juniors), plus many other resources available from: *Scripture Union*, 207–209 Queensway, Bletchley, Milton Keynes MK2 2EB
Tel: 01908 856 000
Fax: 01908 856 111

Judaism

Background Information

Tenakh

The collected 24 books of the Jewish Bible, comprising three sections. Torah, Nevi'im and Ketuvim.

Torah

Contains the Law and teaching. The Five Books of Moses. 'Jews believe that the five books of the Torah contain the words that God spoke to Moses on the Mount Sinai about 3400 years ago'. (Sarah Thorley)

Nevi'im

Contains the Prophets. This is the second section of the Tenakh.

Ketuvim

Contains the Writings. This is the third section of the Tenakh.

Talmud

The Talmud provides a detailed explanation of the Torah. It contains the Mishnah, the first written documentation of the Oral Tradition. An authoritative work, which was codified about 200 CE. And the Gemara, which is a commentary on the Mishnah.

Abraham

He lived approximately 4000 years ago. He taught the people that there was only one God. Before that, the people had worshipped many gods.

The Covenant

The Torah tells how God made a covenant with Abraham. God promised that Abraham and his descendants would be God's 'Chosen people', but this would place a responsibility on them to work for Him. He would lead them to a new land and He would be their God. Abraham's descendants became the twelve tribes of Israel, the Israelites.

Moses

About 400 years after the death of Abraham, the Israelites were made slaves in Egypt. Moses lead the Israelites out of Egypt. Read the exciting story of the parting of the Red Sea in the Torah or in Exodus, Chapter 14. Later, God gave Moses the Ten Commandments and other Laws about how the Israelites should live their lives. This is also in the Torah or Exodus, Chapter 20. More rules for living can be read in the book of Leviticus.

Hebrew

This was the language that was spoken by the early Jews and is spoken in Israel today and all over the world.

Aron Hakodesh, the Holy Ark

The Torah scrolls are kept in the Ark, usually in the east end of every synagogue, facing towards Jerusalem. (N.B. it is in the east end only in western societies!)

Menorah

This is the seven-branched candlestick. Reference to the candlestick can be found in Exodus, Chapter 25, verses 31–7. This is the official emblem of the state of Israel.

Jewish Family Life

Naming Ceremony

Boys and girls are sometimes given a secular name as well as a Hebrew name and a blessing at the synagogue on the Shabbat (or Sabbath) after his or her birth. There is a special circumcision ceremony for a boy eight days after he is born. (Read Genesis, Chapter 17, verses 10–14 for the special covenant made between God and Abraham regarding this ceremony.)

Bar/Bat Mitzvah

There is a special Bar Mitzvah ceremony for boys at about the age of thirteen. Girls become Bat Mitzvah at twelve years of age. Bar Mitzvah means 'Son of the Commandment', Bat Mitzvah means 'Daughter of the Commandment'. The child becomes responsible for himself or herself and for observing the Jewish Law. He or she passes from childhood to adulthood. Until Bar or Bat Mitzvah, the child's parents would be responsible for the child's deeds. Now the child is considered old enough to judge right from wrong. Before Bar or Bat Mitzvah the child will have studied hard under the guidance of a Rabbi or teacher. Now he or she will be called to read the Torah in front of everyone at the synagogue. (See Assembly on p. 121).

Shabbat or Sabbath

Shabbat is observed from sunset on Friday night to sunset on Saturday night. No work is done during this time. Three special meals are prepared, and the Sabbath candles are lit on the Friday night by the mother of the family, who says the Shabbat prayer over the candles.

Kiddush

The father recites a blessing or Kiddush over the wine at these special meals.

Hallot

These are two special twisted loaves of bread. There are two, as a reminder of the double portion of manna that God gave to the Jews each Sabbath when they were wandering in the wilderness.

Hannukiyah

Nine-branched candlestick used in synagogues and Jewish homes during the festival of Hannukah.

Shalom

A greeting of peace, each member of the family greets each other and friends with this distinctive word.

Synagogue

This is the Jewish place for study, meeting and prayer. The main service is held on Saturday. The Ark is opened and a Torah scroll is taken out and read.

Rabbi

The teacher or spiritual leader of the Synagogue. Sometimes he conducts the services (although lay people do so as well), and he acts as the judge in the Jewish courts and as the teacher. He would have studied for many years and would be a man of great learning.

Mitzvot

This is the name given to the good works. It means praying, studying the Torah, giving to charities, keeping the Ten Commandments, etc.

Tefillin

A small leather box containing writings from the Torah. The Orthodox Jew fastens one on to his head, to show that he thinks about God, and another onto his left arm to show that he loves God. (N.B. *should not be touched, as they are the Holy Scriptures.*)

Tallit

This is the prayer shawl worn by men when they pray.

Yamulkah

This is the small skullcap. Some Jews wear it all the time, others wear it with the prayer shawl when praying.

Kosher Food

Jews have very strict rules regarding food. Certain foods must not be eaten, such as pork, rabbit or shell-fish. (Read Leviticus, Chapter 11.) Meat must be koshered. (i.e. the animal is killed with a knife, and the blood is drained away.) Meat and dairy products should not be eaten at the same meal. There should always be separate plates, pans and cutlery for milk and meat dishes in a Kosher kitchen.

Havdallah

Marks the end of Shabbat. The traditional plaited Havdallah candle is lit, and a box of sweet smelling spices is passed around for everyone to smell, to remind each other to take the sweet smell of Shabbat into the week with them.

Jewish Festivals

Rosh Hashana

The Jewish New Year. It begins in the Hebrew month of Tishri. (That is, September or October). (See p. 9.)

Yom Kippur

The day of Atonement. A special day of fast when Jews ask God for the forgiveness of their sins. (See p. 9.)

Sukkot

The week-long harvest festival that takes place in October. (See p. 75.)

Simhat Torah

Celebrating the Torah. Over the year, the Torah is read in the synagogue, from beginning to end. On this day, the end of the reading and the beginning of the re-reading is celebrated.

Hannukah

The Festival of Lights, held in December, celebrating the winning back of the Temple of Jerusalem. (See p. 100.)

Purim

The Festival of Purim or the Feast of Lots is celebrated in the Jewish month of Adar around February/March time. The teacher will find the account in the Bible (The Book of Esther). It is called the Feast of Lots, because Haman cast lots to 'choose the best day on which to kill the Jews'. (See p. 105.)

Pesah

Passover. A special meal and the service known as Seder marks the beginning of this seven or eight-day celebration in the Spring. Find out about the special and symbolic representation of the food that is eaten at the Seder meal. (See picture p. 227; and see also p. 91)

Shavout

This is held seven weeks later. It is a celebration of the giving of the Law at Mount Sinai. Why not make your own scrolls using two dowling rods with a piece of paper attached. (See illustration on p. 28.)

Resources

Books

(T) = Teachers
(P) = Pupils

Aylett, L. and O'Donnell, K. (2000) *The Jewish Experience*, Seeking Religion Series, Hodder and Stoughton (P & T).

Bailey, J.R. (1995) *Founders, Prophets and Sacred Books*, Schofield and Sims (T).

Bailey, J.R. (1995) *Religious Buildings and Festivals*, Schofield and Sims (T).

Barnett, V. (1991) *A Jewish Family in Britain*, RMEP (Chansitor) Canterbury Press (P & T).

Barron, S. (1998) *Festivals*, Looking at Judaism Series, Hodder Wayland (P).

Barron, S. (1998) *Special Occasions*, Looking at Judaism Series, Hodder Wayland (P).

Bastyra, J. (1996) *Hanukkah Fun*, Kingfisher (P).

Broadbent, L. and Logan, J. (2000) *Let my People Go: A Story for Passover*, RMEP (Chansitor) (P).

Charing, D. (2001) *Religions of the World: Jewish World*, Hodder Wayland (P & T).

Charing, D. (1993) *The Torah*, Heinemann (P & T).

Charing, D. (1984) *Visiting a Synagogue*, Lutterworth Educational (P & T).

Clarke, A. and Rose, D. (1999) *My Jewish Life*, Everyday Religion Series, Hodder Wayland (P).

Cole, W.O. and Morgan, P. (2000) *Six Religions in the Twenty-first Century*, Nelson Thornes (T).

Cooper, J. (1989) *Jewish Festivals, Celebrations*, Hodder Wayland (P).

Domnitz, M. (1986) *Judaism*, Religions of the World Series, Hodder Wayland (P).

Fay, D. (1997) *Festivals of the World, Israel*, Heinemann (P).

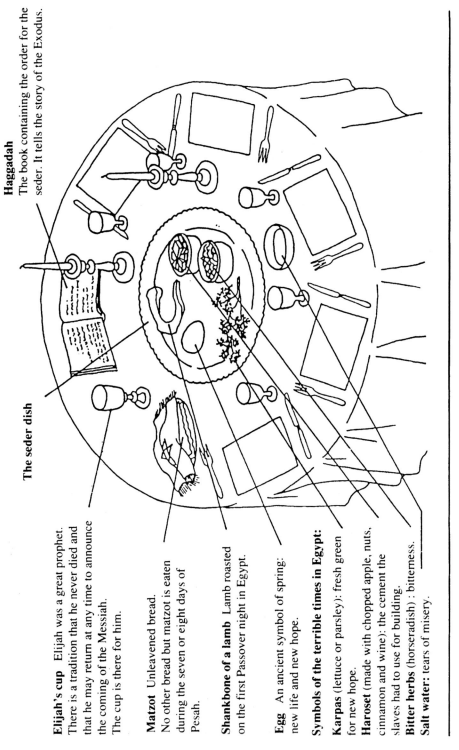

The seder dish

Haggadah
The book containing the order for the seder. It tells the story of the Exodus.

Elijah's cup Elijah was a great prophet. There is a tradition that he never died and that he may return at any time to announce the coming of the Messiah. The cup is there for him.

Matzot Unleavened bread. No other bread but matzot is eaten during the seven or eight days of Pesah.

Shankbone of a lamb Lamb roasted on the first Passover night in Egypt.

Egg An ancient symbol of spring: new life and new hope.

Symbols of the terrible times in Egypt:

Karpas (lettuce or parsley): fresh green for new hope.
Haroset (made with chopped apple, nuts, cinnamon and wine): the cement the slaves had to use for building.
Bitter herbs (horseradish) : bitterness.
Salt water: tears of misery.

Source: Judaism in Words and Pictures, by S. Thorley, RMEP (Chansitor) Canterbury Press Ltd., 1997. Reproduced by kind permission of SCM-Canterbury Press Ltd. RMEP is a division of SCM-Canterbury Press, Ltd.)

Fine, D. (1999) *What Do We Know About Judaism?* Macdonald Young Books (P & T).
Frank, P. (1986) *Queen Esther Saves Her People*, Lion Publishing (P).
Ganeri, A. (2001) *Jewish Stories*, Evans Brothers Limited (P & T).
Geldart, A. (2001) *Judaism*, Exploring Religions Series, Heinemann (Older P & T).
Geras, A. (Compiled by) (1996) *A Treasury of Jewish Stories*, Kingfisher (P).
Goldin, B. (1990) *Just Enough is Plenty. A Chanukah Tale*, Heinemann (P).
Grimmit, M. (et al) (1995) *A Gift to the Child*, Nelson Thornes (P & T).
Hannigan, L. (1994) *Sam's Passover*, A and C Black (P).
Hirst, M. (2002) *Celebrate Series, Passover*, Hodder Wayland (P).
Holm, J. (1991) *Growing up in Judaism*, Longman (P & T).
Innocenti, R. (1996) *Rose Blanche*, Harcourt Brace International (P).
Jungman, A. (2002) *Waiting for Elijah*, Celebration Stories, Hodder Childrens' Books (P).
Kadish, S. (1999) *Synagogues*, Places of Worship Series, Heinemann (P).
Kalman, B. (1988) *We Celebrate Hanukkah*, Crabtree Publishing Company (P).
Koralek, J. (1992) *Hanukkah*, Walker Books (P).
Lawton, C. (1993) *I am a Jew*, Franklin Watts (P).
Lawton, C. (1984) *Matza and Bitter Herbs*, Hamish Hamilton (P).
Morrison, M. and Brown, S.F. (1991) *Judaism*, Facts on File (T).
Neuberger, J. (1986) *The Story of the Jews*, Cambridge University Press (P & T).
O'Brien, J. and Palmer, M. (2002) *Festivals of the World*, Hodder Wayland (P).
Oberman, S. (1995) *Always Adam*, Gollancz Childrens' Books (P).
Parlat, L. (1986) *Jewish Tales, The Eight Lights of the Hanukkiya*, Beehive Books (P & T).
Patterson, J. (1987) *A Happy New Year*, Hamish Hamilton (P).
Patterson, J. (1988) *Mazal-Tov, A Jewish Wedding*, Hamish Hamilton (P).
Penney, S. (2001) *Judaism*, World Beliefs and Culture Series, Heinemann (P & T).
Penney, S. (2002) *Religions of the World: Judaism*, Heinemann (P). (Also in the series: *Christianity, Islam, Buddhism, Sikhism, Hinduism*)
Pirotta, S. (2000) *Jewish Festivals*, Hodder Wayland (P).
Rose, D. and G. (2000) *Passover*, A World of Festivals Series, Evans Brothers Limited (P).
Rosenberg, L. (2000) *Jewish Synagogue*, Keystones Series, A and C Black (P).
Ross, M. (2002) *Celebrations: Hanukkah*, Heinemann (P).
Scholefield, L. (1991) *Passover*, The Living Festival Series, RMEP (Chansitor) (P).
Schotter, R. (2000) *Hanukkah*, Little, Brown and Company (P).
Senker, C. (2000) *Ann Frank*, Hodder Wayland (P).
Sheridan, S. (1998) *Stories from the Jewish World*, Hodder Wayland, 1998 (P).
Stoppleman, M. (1996) *Jewish: Beliefs and Culture Series*, Watts Books (P).
Thorley, S. (1997) *Judaism in Words and Pictures*, RMEP (Chansitor) Canterbury Press (P & T).
University of Warwick (1994) *The Seventh Day is Shabbat*, Heinemann (P).
Unterman, A. (1997) *Dictionary of Jewish Lore and Legend*, Thames and Hudson (T).
Wood, A. (2000) *Festivals: Passover*, Hodder Wayland (P).
Wood, A. (1996) *Celebrate Jewish Festivals*, Heinemann (P).
Wood, A. (1998) *Jewish Synagogue*, Where we Worship Series, Franklin Watts (P).
Wood, A. (1997) *Judaism for Today*, Oxford University Press (P & T).
Wood, A. (1999) *Judaism*, World Religion Series, Franklin Watts (P).

Posters

Jewish Festivals: Rosh Hashanah, Yom Kippur, Pesach, Hanukah, Purim, Sukkot, available from:
Pictorial Charts Educational Trust
27 Kirchen Road
London W13 0UD

Tel: 02085 679 206
Fax: 02085 665 120
Website: www.pcet.co.uk

Useful Addresses

The Jewish Museum, Camden Town
Raymond Burton House
129–131 Albert Street
London NW1 7NB
Tel: 02072 841 997
Fax: 02072 679 008
Email: admin@jmus.org.uk
Website: www.jewishmuseum.org.uk

The Jewish Museum, Finchley
The Sternberg Centre
80 East End Road
London N3 2SY
Tel: 02083 491 143
Fax: 02083 432 162
Email: enquiries@jewishmuseum.org.uk

Songbooks, CDs cassettes, videos
Jewish Music Distribution, UK
PO Box 67
Hailsham
East Sussex BN27 4UW
Tel/Fax: 01323 832 863
Email: jmduk@hotmail.com
Website: jmi.org.uk/jmd

Pronunciation Guide to Jewish Words

a	'a' as in 'fah'
ai	'ai' as in 'sigh'
ad/on/ai	'ad' as in 'bud'; 'on' as in 'on'; 'ai as in 'sigh'
ad/on/o/lam	'ad' as in 'bud'; 'on' as in 'on'; 'o' as in 'no'; 'lam' as in 'dramb'
akh/shav	'akh' rhymes with 'Bach'; 'sh' as in 'shut'; 'av' as in 'halve'
a/ley/nu	'a' as in 'fah'; 'ley' as in 'lay'; 'nu' rhymes with 'shoe'
all/e	'all' as in 'pal'; 'e' as in 'led'

am/o	'am' as in 'lamb'; 'o' as in 'toe'
ar/on hak/o/desh	'ar' as in 'are'; 'on' as in 'on'; 'hak' as in 'back'; 'o' as in 'toe'; 'desh' rhymes with 'flesh'
ash/er	'ash' as in 'dash'; 'er' as in 'air'
az	'az' pronounced 'as'
az/ai	'az' as in 'as'; 'ai' as in 'sigh'
ba	'ba' as in 'bah'
bash/an/ah	'bash' rhymes with 'dash'; 'an' as in 'van'; 'ah' as in 'fah'
bim/ro/mav	'bim' rhymes with 'Tim'; 'ro' rhymes with 'toe'; 'mav' rhymes with 'halve'
bit/fill/a	'bit' rhymes with 'fit'; 'fill' as in 'feel'; 'a' as in 'fah'
be-rosh hashan/a	'be' as in the phonetic sound 'b'; 'rosh' rhymes with 'gosh'; 'ha' as in 'h'; 'sh' as in 'shut'; 'ana' as in Anna
b'terem	'b' as in 'bat'; 'tere' rhymes with 'care'; 'em' as in the phonetic sound 'm'
ch	as in Bach
der	pronounced as phonetic sound 'd'
die	pronounced 'dee'
dov/en	'dov' pronounced phonetically; then add 'n'
dovt	'dov' pronounced phonetically; then add 't'
e	as in led
ē	as in they
Esther	pronounced Ester; silent 'h'
et	as in get
etz/li	'etz' rhymes with 'gets'; 'li' rhymes with 'tree'
gin/na	'g' as in 'give'; 'i' as 'see'; 'na' rhymes with 'fah'
go/ali	'go' as in 'go'; 'ali' rhymes with 'valley'
g'viati	'g' as in 'get'; 'v' as letter name 'V'; 'ati' rhymes with 'batty'
ha	as in 'fah'
ha/kol	'ha' as in 'fah'; 'kol' as in 'collar'
hall/el	'hall' rhymes with 'pal'; 'el' as in 'ale'
ha/lo	'ha' as in 'fah'; 'lo' as in 'low'
Haman	'Ha' as in 'hay'; 'man' rhymes with 'van'
Hann/u/kah	'Han' rhymes with 'ban'; 'u' as in 'you'; 'kah' as in 'kah'
h/as/do	guttural 'h'; 'as' as in 'has'; 'do' rhymes with 'toe'
h/as/i/dim	guttural 'h'; 'as' as in 'has'; 'i' as in 'me'; 'dim' as in 'dim'
hash/vi/i	'hash' rhymes with 'dash'; 'vi' rhymes with 'tea'; 'i' rhymes with 'tea'
Hat/hach	'Hat' rhymes with 'hut'; 'hach' rhymes with 'Bach'
hatz/av	'hatz' as in 'hats'; 'av' as in 'halve'
hav/a na/gi/la	'have' as in 'halve'; 'a' rhymes with 'fah'; 'na' as in 'far'; 'gi' rhymes with 'tea'; 'la' as in 'fah'
ho/du l'ad/on/ai	'ho' rhymes with 'hoe'; 'du' as in 'you'; 'l'ad' as in 'lad'; 'on' as in 'on'; 'ai' as in 'sigh'
kitov	'ki' rhymes with 'tea'; 'tov' as it sounds phonetically
hof	silent 'h'
i	as in 'me'
ken/er	'ken' rhymes with 'ten'; 'er' as in 'a'

k'/h/evtz/o	'k' as in 'Kate'; guttural 'h'; 'evtz' rhymes with 'bets'; 'o' as in 'toe'
k/ihl/ot	'k' as in 'Kate'; 'ihl' rhymes with 'heel'; 'ot' as in 'lot'
klep/pen	'klep' as it sounds phonetically; 'pen' rhymes with 'den'
klept	as it sounds phonetically; then add a 't'
kol	like collar
ko/sher	'ko' rhymes with 'toe'; 'sher' rhymes with 'fur'
l'eyt	pronounced 'late'
l'hit/a/re/ah	'l' as in 'lah'; 'hit' as in 'heat'; 'a' as in 'fah'; 're' as in 'ray'; 'ah' as in 'fah'
libb/e/nu	'libb' as in Lee(b); 'e' as in 'say'; 'nu' as in 'you'
mal/ah	'mal' rhymes with 'mall'; 'ah' as in 'fah'
mat/hil/a	'mat' rhymes with 'cat'; 'hil' as in 'heel'; 'a' as in 'fah'
mel/e/h	'mel' rhymes with 'bell'; 'e' as in 'get'; guttural 'h'
men/or/ah	'men' rhymes with 'mun'; 'or' as in 'or'; 'ah' as in 'fah'
m'/hu/bad	'm' sounded phonetically; guttural 'h'; 'u' rhymes with 'do'; 'bad' as in 'sad'
mi/kkol	'mi' rhymes with 'tea'; 'kkol' as in 'collar'
m'/lah/te/ha	'm' sounded phonetically; 'lah' pronounced 'l'; guttural 'h'; 'te' rhymes with 'say'; 'ha' as in 'fah'
Mor/dec/ai	'Mor' rhymes with 'saw'; 'd' as in the phonetic sound 'd'; guttural 'c'; 'ai' rhymes with 'sigh'
na'a/sah	'na'a' rhymes 'bah'; 'sah' rhymes with 'fah'
nik/ra	'nik' rhymes with 'tick'; 'ra' rhymes with 'fah'
niv/ra	'niv' rhymes with 'give'; 'ra' rhymes with 'fah'
no/ra	'no' as in 'gnaw'; 'ra' as in 'rah'
nosh/an/a	'nosh' rhymes with 'gosh'; 'an' rhymes with 'fan'; 'a' as in 'fah'
o	as in 'boat'
o/gena	'o' as in 'toe'; 'g' as in 'give'; 'en' rhymes with 'fen'; 'a' as in 'fah'
o/la/mim	'o' as in 'toe'; 'la' as in 'fah'; 'mim' rhymes with 'meem'
o/seh	'o' as in 'toe'; 'sey' as in 'say'
oz v'shalom	'oz' as in Wizard of Oz'; 'v' as in the letter name 'V'; 'shal' as in 'shall'; 'lom' rhymes with 'mom'
pa/am	'pa' as in 'pah'; 'am' rhymes with 'Sam'
par/ha	'par' rhymes with 'far'; guttural 'h'; 'ha' rhymes with 'cah'
pe/sah	'pe' as in 'pay'; 'sah' as in 'a', guttural 'h'
pi/tom	'pi' rhymes with 'tea'; 'tom' as in 'Tom'
pu/rim	'pu' as in 'pooh'; 'rim' as in 'rim'
Reb/be	'Reb' rhymes with 'deb'; 'be' as in the letter name 'b'
Rab/bi	'Rab' rhymes with 'dab'; 'bi' rhymes with 'sigh'
rak	'ra' rhymes with 'fah'; silent 'k'
rosh hash/an/a	'rosh' rhymes with 'gosh'; 'hash' rhymes with 'dash'; 'an' as in 'fan'; 'a' as in 'fah'
sam/e/ah	'sam' rhymes with 'dram'; 'e' rhymes with 'say'; 'ah' as in 'fah'; guttural 'h'
setav	pronounced saav; long 'aa' sound

shabat	'sh' as in 'shut'; 'a' as in 'halve'; 'ba' as in 'fah'; 't' is pronounced
shal/om	'shal' rhymes with 'shall'; 'om' rhymes with 'mom'
shav/u/ot	'sh' as in 'shut'; 'av' as in 'have'; 'u' as in 'oo'; 't' as in 'top'
she/shet	'she' as in 'sheh'; 'shet' rhymes with 'get'
shluf/en	'shluf' pronounced phonetically and then add 'n'
shluf/t	'shluf' pronounced phonetically and add the 't'
sh'/mo	'sh' as in 'shut'; 'mo' rhymes with 'toe'
sho/far	'sho' rhymes with 'toe'; 'far' as in 'far'
sho/shan/a	'sho' rhymes with 'show'; 'shan' as it sounds phonetically; 'a' as in 'fah'
sh/ve/gen	'sh' as in 'shut'; 've' rhymes with 'day'; 'g' as in 'get'; 'en' like the letter name 'N'
shveygt	'shvetygt' rhymes with 'fate'
su/kkot	'su' as in 'Sue'; 'kkot' as in 'cot'
ta/a/seh	'ta' as in 'ta'; 'a' as in 'ah'; 'sey' as in 'say'
ta/llit	'ta' as in 'fah'; 'llit' as in 'feet'
tash/lich	'tash' rhymes with 'dash'; 'lich' as in 'leek'; guttural final 'h'
te/fill/in	'te' pronounced as phonetic 't'; 'fill' as in 'fill'; 'in' rhymes with 'bin'
te/he	'te' as in 'say'; 'he' as in 'hay'
to/rah	'to' rhymes with 'door'; 'rah' rhymes with 'fah'
tzur	pronounced 'tz' plus 'oor'
um'/va/de/ah	'um' as in 'locum'; 'va' as in 'fah'; 'de' as in 'day'; 'ah' as in 'fah'
u'/ru/a/him	'u' as in 'oo'; 'ru' as in 'rue'; 'a' as in 'fah'; guttural 'h'; 'him' rhymes with 'Tim'
v'/ah/a/rei	'v' as in 'van'; 'ah' as in 'a'; guttural 'h'; 'a' as in 'up'; 'rei' rhymes with 'day'
va/sh/ti	'va' as in 'vah'; 'sh' as in 'shut', 'ti' rhymes with 'tea'
ve/shon/a	've' as in the phonetic sound 'v'; 'shon' as in 'shown'; 'a' as in 'ah'
vey/nen	'vey' rhymes with 'day'; 'nen' as in the phonetic sound 'n'
veynt	rhymes with faint
v'/im/ru	'v' as in 'van'; 'im' as in 'Tim'; 'ru' rhymes with 'shoe'
v'/nis/'m/hah	'v' rhymes with 'day'; 'nis' rhymes with 'niece'; 'm' as sounded phonetically; 'hah' as in 'fah'
vo	rhymes with 'toe'
v'yom	'v' as in 'van'; 'yom' rhymes with 'mom'
ya'/a/seh	'ya' as in 'yah'; 'a' as in 'ah'; 'sey' rhymes with 'say'
yad	as in yah'd
ya/fa	'ya' as in 'yah'; 'fa' as in 'fah'
ya/min	'ya' as in 'yah'; 'min' rhymes with 'been'
ya/mul/kah	'ya' as in 'yah'; 'mul' as in 'mool'; kah' as in 'fah'
Yis/r/ael	Yis' as it sounds; 'r' as in 'ray'; 'ael' as in 'ale'
yi/teyn	'y' as in 'yellow'; 'i' rhymes with 'see'; 'teyn' rhymes with 'ten'
yom kip/pur	'yom' rhymes with 'mom'; 'kip' rhymes with 'keep'; 'pur' rhymes with 'poor'

yom/ru	'yom' rhymes with 'mom'; 'ru' as in 'you'
yom zeh m'/hu/bad	'yom' rhymes with 'mom'; 'zeh' rhymes with 'day'; 'm' as phonetic sound; guttural 'h'; 'hu' rhymes with 'do'; 'bad' as in 'bah'd'
y't zir	'y't' as in 'fit'; 'zir' rhymes with 'dear'
y'/va/reh	'y' as in phonetic sound 'y'; 'va' as in 'fah'; 're' as in 'red'; guttural 'h'
ze	rhymes with 'zeh'
zingen	like 'singin' but with a 'z'

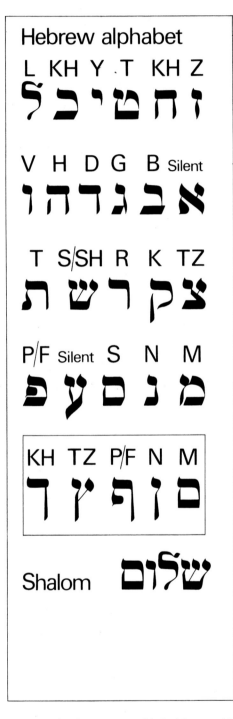

Source: My Belief: I am a Jew, by C. Lawton published by Franklin Watts, 1993. Artwork by Tony Payne. Reproduced with the kind permission of the publishers, The Watts Publishing Group Ltd.

Hinduism

Background Information

There is no one founder, central figure or sacred book. Hinduism developed over many centuries and takes its name from the River Indus in North-west India. (For more detailed information, see the book list at the end of this section.) A brief description of the place of the gods and goddesses is given below.

One god or thirty-three million gods

Both statements would be true. Many Hindus believe in Brahman or World Soul, but they also believe in many gods and goddesses, who are aspects of World Soul. Worshippers seem to fall into three main groups; those who see Lord Vishnu (or one of his incarnations) as their main god; those who see Shiva as their main god; and those who see the mother goddess as more powerful, than all the other gods.

Lord Vishnu

Lord Vishnu is believed to have existed before the world was created. He is often worshipped in the form of one of his many avatars or incarnations, such as the gods, Ram or Krishna. Lord Vishnu is depicted with four hands, in which he holds a conch shell, a lotus, a mace and a discus. He takes on one of his many different forms when evil threatens the world.

Lord Shiva

Shiva is sometimes called Lord of the Dance; his energy keeps the world turning throughout eternity, but eventually his energy will bring about the destruction of the world, before it is recreated again and again through his dance. He is often depicted as a holy man, wearing prayer beads and carrying a snake, a three-pronged spear and an axe. In the middle of his forehead he has a third eye.

The mother goddess or devi

For some Hindus, the goddess is the central deity (Bahree, p. 14, *The Hindu World*, Macdonald). She is thought to protect mothers and children, and once again, she is worshipped in many forms. She is often depicted as the beautiful kind mother goddess. She is *Parvati* the wife of Shiva. Sometimes, she takes the form of the all-powerful warrior goddess *Durga*, with her ten arms, who rides on the back of a lion, to slay the evil demon king. (see p. 114.) At yet other times, she is depicted as the goddess *Kali* who brings storms and floods, earthquakes and illnesses. As *Lakshmi*, she is the wife of Vishnu and the goddess of good fortune, wealth and beauty. She is worshipped at the festival of Diwali. She is often depicted standing or sitting on a lotus blossom, holding the conch shell and lotus, similar to the ones that her husband holds.

Other Deities

Brahma

He is regarded as equal with Lord Vishnu and Lord Shiva. He is usually depicted with four faces riding on a swan. In his hands, he carries a book, a sceptre and an alms bowl.

Saraswati

She is the beautiful wife of Brahma and she is also depicted riding on a swan, carrying a musical instrument and a book, as she is the goddess of music, literature and art.

Hanuman

He is the monkey god, who helped Ram rescue his wife Sita, from the demon king. (See p. 102 for this story.)

Ganesh

He is the elephant-headed god, son of the goddess Parvati. He is often depicted riding on a rat. He is the remover of obstacles; often worshippers will pray to Lord Ganesh, before starting a new job.

Surya

He is the sun god, who is often depicted driving his sun chariot across the sky during the day.

Chandra

He is the moon god, who travels the sky by night.

Agni

He is the god of fire, and he is present wherever there is a fire.

Prasad

Is the food offered to the gods and then eaten by the worshippers.

Hindu Literature

Vedas is the name given to some of the most ancient Hindu literature. It consists of four collections of hymns known as Rig, Sama, Yajur and Atharvan. Other Hindu literature includes the Brahmanas (priestly writings), Aranyakas (forest stories) and Upanishads (the discussions with Gurus and Holy men). The Bhagavad Gita, part of the famous epic called Mahabharata, is Krishna's sermon on duty.

Sanskrit

This is the ancient written language which is still used today for ritual purposes.

Mandir

This is the name given to the Hindu temple, and domestic shrines. Many Hindus worship images or pictures of Gods in their own homes. Everybody must take off their shoes outside the temple as a mark of respect.

Hindu Family Life

Naming Ceremony

In Hindu culture, there are many different naming ceremonies, according to the caste or region where the child is born. However, most name-giving ceremonies are determined by the child's own horoscope. The ceremony takes place after the child's birth and before his first birthday, when the family priest works out the baby's exact horoscope. Using this information, he will select the initial letter for the child's name. Hindu names, usually have a special meaning i.e. if the letter is 'R', for instance, then the child may be named Ram, after one of the gods (see Assembly on p. 102).

Mundan

This is the ceremony when a boy's head is shaved. Before this, his hair has not been cut at all. In the mundan, families feel that the last traces of his previous life are removed. There are many different customs regarding the mundan. In the Punjab region, for instance, Hindus believe the ceremony should take place during the first year of life before the child's first birthday or certainly before his third or fifth birthday, providing that no relative has died during the previous year. (Celebrations are delayed to the third or fifth year of life if there has been a death in the family, because no celebration can take place for a full year after a death). A barber attends and shaves the child's head. Then the child is washed and dressed in new clothes, usually bought by the child's maternal uncle. The child receives gifts of money from all who attend the ceremony.

Hindu Family and Caste System

Families vary greatly according to caste, sect, linguistic group, and whether they are westernized, urban or rural. Brahmins are the highest caste; the priestly caste. Kshatriyas are the military caste. Vaishyas are the caste that works mainly in trade or farming. Shudras are the servants of the other castes. The lowest caste is known as the Untouchables.

Very occasionally, there are inter-caste marriages, and some members of lower castes have highly paid jobs. But some of the older generation find it difficult to break with tradition and some Hindus would feel it was unthinkable even to eat with a member of a different caste.

Sari

This is the name given to the beautiful dress worn by many Hindu women and girls. It is made from one piece of material which is approximately 130 centimetres wide and 6 metres long. The cloth is wound around the waist, pleated and then tucked into an underskirt, allowing the remaining part of the material to be draped across the shoulder in different styles. In Britain today, both men and women, boys and girls often wear western clothes, although some women wear their sari daily and others wear it only for special occasions.

Food

Some Hindus are vegetarians as they believe it is wrong to kill any living creature. However, many Hindus do eat meat, although they may not eat beef as the cow is a sacred animal. The reason for this is that the cow is often described as a mother, because she gives us milk to drink. Vegetables are cooked with all kinds of spices. As food was traditionally eaten with the hands, that is, without knives and forks, there are very strict rules about washing hands before and after each meal.

Hindu Festivals

Find out about Hindu Festivals. Include some of the ones listed below. There are some very useful books to help you in the resources section.

Navratri

This means nine nights. The festival takes place following the new moon in September/ October. At this time Hindus worship the goddess. In one of her many forms she is called Durga (with her ten arms).

In a sense, this festival is similar to Harvest Festival in Britain as the farming community in India await harvest after the hard work on the land during the summer and the monsoon rains (see p. 114).

Dussehra

This is the tenth day of the above festival. In some parts of India young children are taught the alphabet on this day. In other parts the story of Ram and Sita is acted out. Huge models of Ravan, the demon King, are made and then ceremoniously burnt. Why not try to write some Hindi script or make a huge effigy of Ravan (see p. 240 for an example of Hindi script).

Diwali

The festival of lights (late October). In some parts of India, this festival is regarded as a celebration of the renewal of life; in other parts it is regarded as the festival for protection against King Bali, the King of the underworld. King Bali could only rule where there was no light, so everyone makes sure that many lamps keep him away. In yet other parts of India, the festival is a celebration of the return of Ram, when everyone lit lamps to guide him home after his exile, and Ram and Sita were crowned King and Queen. (see pp. 102–4).

Lakshmi, the Goddess of Wealth, is also worshipped at this time, and many Hindus light candles to welcome her into their homes. Why not make a special candle for this occasion, known as diva/diwa. (Traditionally, a small clay saucer, with a cotton wool wick soaked in clarified butter, would be used. Diwali takes its name from these little candles or diva). Or re-enact the play of Ram and Sita in your school assembly (see pp. 102–4). Perhaps you could make masks for Ram, Sita, Ravan (with ten heads) and Hanuman, the monkey god who helped Ram.

Some families send Diwali cards to each other, or paint rangoli patterns of welcome on their doorsteps. Others paint Mehndi patterns on their hands. Find out about these traditions and make your own cards and patterns.

Holi

Celebrates the coming of Spring. Revellers squirt coloured water at each other. Agni the God of Fire is worshipped by lighting huge bonfires and dancing around the fires. The story of Prince Prahlad and Princess Holika is retold. Find out about this exciting story by reading *Celebrations* by C. Collinson and C. Miller, or read, *Holi, Festival of Spring*, by O. Bennett. (See Assembly on pp. 86–7.)

Janmashtami

The birthday of Lord Krishna is celebrated in August by waiting up until midnight, the time that it is thought that Lord Krishna was born. Special sweets are given to one another and stories about Lord Krishna are told.

The Hindi Script

A	Á	I	Í	U
अ	आ	इ	ई	उ

Ū	RI	RÍ	LRI	
ऊ	ऋ	ॠ	लृ	

É	AI	O	AU	(M)
ए	ऐ	ओ	औ	अं

H	K	KH	G	GH
अः	क	ख	ग	घ

N	C	CH	J	JH
ङ	च	छ	ज	झ

Ṅ	Ṭ	ṬH	Ḍ	ḌH
ञ	ट	ठ	ड	ढ

Ṇ	T	TH	D	DH
ण	त	थ	द	ध

N	P	PH	B	BH
न	प	फ	ब	भ

M	Y	R	L	V(W)
म	य	र	ल	व

SH	Ṣ	S	H	KSH
श	ष	स	ह	क्ष

TR	JÑ(GÑ)			
त्र	ज्ञ			

Source: My Belief: I am a Hindu by M. Aggarwal Franklin Watts, 1993. Artwork by Tony Payne. Reproduced with the kind permission of the publishers, The Watts Publishing Group Ltd.

Resources

Books

(P) = Pupils
(T) = Teachers

Aggarwal, M. (1993) *I am a Hindu*, Franklin Watts (P).
Bahree, P. (1992) *The Hindu World*, Simon and Schuster (P & T).
Bailey, J.R. (1995) *Founders, Prophets and Sacred Books*, Schofield and Sims (T).
Bailey, J.R. (1995) *Religious Buildings and Festivals*, Schofield and Simms (T).
Bennett, O. (1986) *Festival! Diwali*, Thomas Nelson (P & T).
Bennett, O. (1992) *Holi Hindu Festival of Spring, The Story of Prahlad and Holika*, Evans Brothers Limited (P).
Bond, R. (1990) *The Adventures of Rama and Sita*, Walker Books Limited (P).
Claybourne, A. (2002) *Famous Lives: Gandhi – The Peaceful Revolutionary*, Hodder Wayland (P).
Cole, O. and Loundes, J. (1995) *The Story of Prahlad*, Heinemann (P).
Cole, W.O. (Ed) (1983) *Religion in a Multi-faith School*, Nelson Thornes (T).
Cole, W.O. and Morgan, P. (2000) *Six Religions in the Twenty-first Century*, Nelson Thornes (T).
Collinson, C. and Miller, C. (1985) *Celebrations: Festivals in a Multi-faith Community*, Hodder and Stoughton (P & T).
Cooper, J. (1989) *Hindu Festivals, Celebrations Series*, Hodder Wayland (P).
Das, R. (1999) *Places of Worship: Hindu Temples*, Heinemann (P).
Das, R. (2001) *My Life, My Religion: Hindu Priest*, Franklin Watts (P).
Deshpande, C. (1994) *Diwali*, A and C Black (P).
Ganeri, A. (1995) *Beliefs and Cultures: Hindu*, Franklin Watts (P & T).
Ganeri, A. (2002) *Celebrations, Divali*, Heinemann (P).
Ganeri, A. (2000) *Hindu Mandir*, Key Stones Series, A and C Black (P).
Ganeri, A. (2001) *Hindu Stories*, Evans Brothers Limited (P).
Ganeri, A. (1999) *My Hindu Faith*, Evans Brothers Limited (P).
Ganeri, A. (1993) *Varanasi, Holy City Series*, Evans Brothers Limited (P & T).
Ganeri, A. (1999) *What Do We Know About Hinduism?* Hodder Wayland (P).
Gavin, J. (2002) *Out of India*, Hodder Childrens' Books (P).
Gavin, J. (1986) *Stories from the Hindu World*, Macdonald (P).
Gilmore, R. (1994) *Lights for Gita* (In Bengali/English) (More Stories in this series) Mantra Publishing Limited (P).
Godden, R. (1996) *Premlata and the Festival of Lights*, Macmillan Childrens' Books (P & T).
Grimmit, M. (et al) (1995) *A Gift to the Child*, Nelson Thornes (P & T).
Heaslip, P.C. (1987) *Chapatis Not Chips*, Methuen Childrens' Books (P).
Hirst, J. and Pandey, G. (1991) *Growing Up in Hinduism*, Longman (P & T).
Jackson, R. and Killingley, D. (1988) *Approaches to Hinduism*, John Murray (T).
Jackson, R. and Nesbitt, E. (1990) *Listening to Hindus*, Unwin Hyman (P & T).
Jaffrey, M. (1985) *Seasons of Splendour*, Pavilion Books Limited (P & T).
Kadodwala, D. (1999) *Diwali*, A World of Festivals Series, Evans Brothers Limited (P).
Kadodwala, D. (1996) *Hindu Festivals*, Celebrate Series, Heinemann (P).

Kadodwala, D. (2000) *Holi*, A World of Festivals Series, Evans Brothers Limited (P).
Kadodwala, D. and Chhapi, S. (1996) *My Hindu Life*, Hodder Wayland (P).
Kadodwala, D. and Prior, K. (1999) *Hinduism*, Franklin Watts (P & T).
Kanitkar, V.P. (1994) *Discovering Sacred Texts: Hindu Scriptures*, Heinemann (T).
Kanitkar, V.P. (1985) *Hinduism*, Hodder Wayland (P & T).
Kanitkar, V.P. (1986) *Hindu Stories*, Hodder Wayland (P & T).
Killingley, D. (1984) *A Handbook of Hinduism*, Grevatt & Grevatt (T).
Marchant, K. (2001) *Ceremonies and Celebrations: Feasts and Fasting*, Hodder Wayland (P).
Marchant, K. (1999) *Diwali*, Hodder Wayland (P).
Marchant, K. (2002) *Great Religious Leaders: Krishna and Hinduism*, Hodder Wayland (P & T).
Marchant, K. (2001) *Festivals Cookbook: Hindu*, Hodder Wayland (P & T).
Marchant, K. (2001) *Hindu Festivals*, Hodder Wayland (P & T).
Marchant, K. (2000) *Hindu Tales*, Hodder Wayland (P).
Marsh, H. (1994) *The Living Festival Series: Divali*, RMEP (Chansitor) Canterbury Press (T).
Mayled, J. (1991) *Hindu Festivals*, RMEP (Chansitor) Canterbury Press (T).
Penney, S. (1997) *Hinduism*, Heinemann (P).
Ray, S. (1991) *A Hindu Family in Britain*, RMEP (Chansitor), Canterbury Press (P & T).
Singh, R. (1984) *The Indian Story Book*, Heinemann (P).
Soloman, J. (1984) *Sweet-tooth Sunil*, Hamish Hamilton (P).
Thompson, R. (1986) *My Class at Diwali*, Franklin Watts (P).
Wangu, M.B. (1991) *Hinduism*, Facts on File Limited (T).
Wood, J. (1995) *Our Culture Hindu*, Watts Books (P).

Posters

Hindu Festivals: Maha-Shivratri, Navaratri, Janmastami, Divali available from:

Pictorial Charts Educational Trust,
27, Kirchen Road
London W13 0UD

Tel: 02085 679 206
Fax: 02085 665 120
Website: www.pcet.co.uk

Useful Addresses

Hindu Centre
39 Grafton Terrace
Kentish Town
London NW5 4JA

Tel: 0207 485 200

Commonwealth Resource Centre
Commonwealth Institute
Kensington High Street
London W8 6NQ

Tel: 02076 034 535 Extension: 210
Email: crc@commonwealth.org.uk
Website: www.commonwealth.org.uk

Oxfam Education Department
274 Banbury Road
Oxford OX2 7DZ

Tel: 01865 313 600
Email: oxfam@oxfam.org.uk
Website: www.oxfam.org.uk

Resources

Video of a Hindu Wedding is covered in *Aspects of Hinduism*. Other aspects of Hinduism for 11+ children are covered in the *Believe It or Not* videos (Revised Series) and are both available from:

SCM-Canterbury Press Limited
St Mary's Works
St Mary's Plain
Norwich
Norfolk NR3 3BH

Tel: 01603 612 914
Email: admin@scm-canterburypress.co.uk
Website: www.scm-canterburypress.co.uk

The REaSE Project Video for children aged 11+ (secondary schools) *Speaking For Ourselves* is also available from SCM-Canterbury Press. The faiths represented on the video are Buddhism, Christianity, Hinduism, Islam, Judaism and Sikhism.

Suppliers of artefacts and pictures are:

Suresh Shah
Shah's Pan House
523 Foleshill Road
Coventry

Tel: 02476 665 277
Fax: 02476 664 277

Articles of Faith Ltd.,
Resource House,
Kay Street,
Bury BL9 6BU

Tel: 01617 636 232
Email: ArticlesFaith@cs.com
Website: www.articlesoffaith.co.uk

Pronunciation Guide to Hindu Words

An/na Prash/an	'An' rhymes with 'un' as in 'undo'; 'na' rhymes with 'far'; 'Prash' as in 'rush'; 'an' as in 'un'.
Bha/rat	'Bha' as in 'but'; 'rat' as in 'rut'.
Diw/a/li	'Diw' rhymes with 'give'; 'a' as in 'far', 'li' rhymes with 'see'.
Duss/eh/ra	'Duss' rhymes with 'thus'; 'e' as in 'let'; 'ra' as in 'far'.
Gan/esha	'Gan' is pronounced 'gun'; 'esh' rhymes with 'aish' as in 'facial'; silent 'a'.
Han/u/man	'Han' rhymes with 'Hun'; 'u' as in 'moo'; 'man' rhymes with 'calm'.
Ho/li	Pronounced 'holy'.
Ho/lik/a	'Ho' as in 'hoe'; 'lik' as in 'tick'; 'a' as in 'calm'.
Jan/mash/ta/mi	'Jan' as in 'gun'; 'mash' as in 'marsh'; 'ta' as in 'far'; 'mi' rhymes with 'see'.
Ka/li	'Ka' as in 'car'; 'li' rhymes with 'see'.
Krish/na	'Krish' rhymes with 'dish'; 'na' rhymes with 'far'.
Laksh/mi	'Laksh' is pronounced 'Lucksh'; 'mi' rhymes with 'see'.
Lank/a	'Lank' is pronounced 'Lunk'; 'a' as in 'calm'.
Laxsh/man	'Laxsh' is pronounced 'Lucksh'; 'man' rhymes with 'mun'.
Man/dir	'Man' rhymes with 'mun'; 'dir' rhymes with 'deer'.
Nav/ra/tri	'Nav' is pronounced 'Nuv'; 'ra' as in 'far'; 'tri' rhymes with 'see'.
Par/vat/i	'Par' rhymes with 'far'; 'vat' as in 'rut'; 'i' rhymes with 'see'.
Prah/lad	'Prah' as in 'uh'; 'lad' as in 'calm'.
Pra/sad	'Pra' as in 'uh'; 'sad' as in 'guard'.
Rama	'Ram' rhymes with 'calm'. Silent 'a'.
Ra/vana	'Ra' as in 'far'; 'van' as in 'fun'. Silent 'a'.
Shiv/a	'Shiv' rhymes with 'live'; 'a' as in 'cat'.
Si/ta	'Si' rhymes with 'see'; 'ta' as in 'far'.
Vish/nu	'Vish' rhymes with 'fish', 'nu' rhymes with 'moo'.

Islam

Background Information

Muslim Family Life

Birth Rites

A Muslim child is a member of the faith from birth. These words are spoken in the ears of the child at birth:

'La illah illa Allah Muhammad 鬱 Abduhu wa rassoulu hu'. 'There is no God but Allah and Muhammad 鬱 is his servant and Prophet'.
The boy child is circumcised soon after birth. About seven days later, in Muslim countries, there is a naming ceremony called 'Aqiqa'. The child's head is shaved, and a sacrifice of two sheep (or goats) is made for a boy child. A sacrifice of one sheep is made for a girl and the meat is given to poor people. (Hoad, A. *Islam*, published by Wayland, 1986.)

Muhammad 鬱

Respect is paid to Muhammad 鬱, by saying the words 'Peace be upon him', whenever his name is mentioned, or writing the sign 鬱 after his name, which means the same. He was born in Arabia, in the City of Makkah, (Mecca) in 570 A.D. The people worshipped many Gods, at that time, but when Muhammad 鬱 was about forty years old, he was told by the Angel Jibra'il that he was to become Allah's messenger and that he should teach the people that there is only one God.

Al-Qur'an

This is the Holy book of the Muslim people. As Muhammad 鬱 could not read or write, he had to learn by heart and recite all the messages from Allah. These were later written down and became known as the Qur'an (Koran).

The Hadith

The other important books for Muslims are called the Hadith. These are the books containing the accounts of Muhammad's 鬱 doings and sayings.

Islam

This is an Arabic word. It is the name given to the Muslim religion and means submission to God.

The Five Pillars of Islam

Every Muslim must carry out these five duties.

1   A Muslim must say, and act accordingly, that: 'There is only one God and Muhammad 醬 is his prophet' (or messenger). (Thorley, S. *Islam in Words and Pictures*, RMEP, 1982).
2   A Muslim must pray five times each day. *Fajr* is the prayer said at dawn. *Zuhr* is the midday prayer. *Asr* is said in the afternoon. *Maghrib* is the prayer to be said at sunset. *I'sha* is said approximately an hour and a half later.
    Hands, mouth, nose, face, arms, head, ears, neck, and feet must be washed before each prayer.
    The Muezzin calls people to prayer from the top of the minaret of the mosque.
3   *Zakat* Every Muslim must give alms to the poor. Approximately 2½ per cent of their savings is given every year.
4   Fasting or *Sawm* During the month of Ramadan each year a Muslim must fast between dawn and sunset.
5   *Hajj* It is the duty of every Muslim to make a pilgrimage to Makkah at least once during his lifetime, if he can afford it.

Mosque

This is the Muslim place of worship. Shoes must be removed as a mark of respect for God. (It also keeps the floors clean, as foreheads touch the ground in prayer). Prayer mats are used. These must face Makkah. The Mihrab is an alcove which shows the direction of Makkah. There are no chairs, statues or pictures of living creatures in the Mosque, so that the people cannot be distracted from worshipping God. Women pray in a different part of the Mosque. Sometimes prayer beads are used. There are usually 33 beads, to remind Muslims of the 99 names of God in the Qur'an. For example, God the Merciful, etc.

Imam

This is the man who leads the prayers.

Al-Wudhu

This is the name given to the washing ritual before praying.

Food

Muslims have very strict rules regarding food. Pork is forbidden and alcohol is forbidden. Only meat from animals that have been killed by cutting the throat and letting the blood drain away, '*halal*', is permitted. Special prayers are said before and after each meal and the hand and mouth must be washed, before and after each meal.

Clothes

The Qur'an makes it clear that dress for both men and women should be modest. Today, dress for Muslims varies in different countries. Strictly speaking, Muslim women should cover their bodies, almost completely, in public. However, this does depend on the country and the convictions of the particular Muslim. It is usual to see Muslim girls in Britain wearing shalwar (loose trousers), a kameez (a long loose top) and a veil for the head and shoulders.

Madressa (school)

Muslim children in Britain attend Qur'an classes after the normal school day.

Muslim Festivals

Find out about the Muslim religious festivals. A few are mentioned below. The dates of the festivals vary from year to year, because the Muslim calendar is counted from the year that Muhammad 鸞 went from Makkah to Medina; and they are not on the same day each year, because the Muslim months are shorter than the Christian months. Copies of the annual Calendar of Religious Festivals may be obtained from:

The Festival Shop
56 Poplar Road
Kings Heath
Birmingham B14 7AG

Tel: 01214 440 444
Email: info@festivalshop.co.uk

Ramadan and the Festival of Eid-ul-Fitr

Ramadan, or the month of fasting, is the ninth Islamic month. It is a very important month in the Islamic calendar. Eid-ul-Fitr takes place at the end of Ramadan. Money is given to poorer people. Special food is prepared for the feast. New clothes are bought and presents are given to each other. Special Eid cards are sent to friends (see p. 74 and see calendar for dates.)

Eid-ul-Adha

This is the festival that takes place at the end of Hajj or pilgrimage. If they can, each family will sacrifice a sheep or a cow, giving part of it away to families who cannot afford to make the sacrifice. This is done in remembrance of Ibrahim's willingness to sacrifice his son. (Muslims believe Ibrahim was a great prophet. You can read about this story in the Qur'an, Chapter 2, verses 126–8 or in the *Bible*, Genesis, Chapter 22, verses 1–19. If the story is read in the Bible, remember that it is Isaac who is sacrificed and not Ishma'ail as stated in the Qur'an).

Muharram

This is the first month in the Muslim calendar. It is the Muslim New Year. (See calendar for date.)

Melad-ul-Nabi

This is the birthday of Muhammad 鑫 ; the twelfth day of the third Islamic month.

Lailat-ul-Qadr

This is known as the 'Night of Power', when Muhammad 鑫 received the revelations from the Angel Jibra'il. It is celebrated on the twenty-sixth night of Ramadan.

Lailat-ul-Bara'at

This is known as the 'Night of Forgiveness'. It takes place in the middle of the month *before* Ramadan in preparation for the holy month of Ramadan.

Lailat-ul-Mi'raj

This is known as the 'Night of Ascension'. It is celebrated on the twenty-sixth night of the Islamic month known as Rajab.

Resources

Books

(P) = Pupils
(T) = Teachers

Aggarwal, M. (1984) *I am a Muslim*, Franklin Watts (P).
Ahsan, M.M. (1985) *Muslim Festivals*, Hodder Wayland (P).
Al-Saleh, K. (1985) *Fabled Cities, Princes and Jinn from Arab Myths and Legends*, Peter Lowe, (P & T).
Bailey, J.R. (1995) *Founders, Prophets and Sacred Books*, Schofield and Sims (T).
Bailey, J.R. (1995) *Religious Buildings and Festivals*, Schofield and Sims (T).
Bailey, J.R. (1995) *Religious Leaders and Places of Pilgrimage Today*, Schofield and Sims (T).
Bladon, E.H. (1999) *Mosques, Places of Worship Series*, Heinemann (P).
Cole, W.O. (Ed) (1983) *Religion in the Multi-Faith School*, Hulton (T).
Cole, W.O. and Morgan, P. (2000) *Six Religions in the Twenty-first Century*, Nelson Thornes (T).
Cooper, J. (1989) *Celebrations, Muslim Festivals*, Hodder Wayland (P).
Dorling Kindersley Eyewitness Guides (2002) *Islam*, Dorling Kindersley (P & T).
Droubie, R.E. (1990) *Islam, Living Religions Series*, Wark Lock Educational (P & T).
Droubie, R.E. (1999) *My Muslim Life, Everyday Religion Series*, Hodder Wayland (P).
Ganeri, A. (2001) *Islamic Stories*, Evans Brothers Limited (P & T).
Gordon, M. (1991) *Islam, World Religions*, Facts on File Ltd. (T).
Hannaford, J. (1991) *Ramadan and Id-ul-Fitr*, Living Festival Series, RMEP (Chansitor) (P & T).
Harrison, S.W. and Shepherd, D. (1983) *A Muslim Family in Britain*, RMEP (Chansitor) (P & T).
Hegedus, U. (2000) *Muslim Mosque*, Key Stone Series, A and C Black (P).

Hirst, M. (2002) *Celebrate: Id-ul-Fitr*, Hodder Wayland (P).

Husain, S. (1997) *Holy Cities: Mecca*, Evans Brothers Limited (P & T).

Husain, S. (1999) *What do we know about Islam?*, Hodder Wayland (P & T).

Jones, J. (1987) *Going to Mosque School*, Blackie and Son Limited (P).

Kerven, R. (1997) *Ramadan and Id-ul-Fitr*, Evans Brothers Limited (P).

Khattab, H. (1996) *Stories from The Muslim World*, Ta-Ha Publishers (P & T).

Knight, K. (1996) *Islamic Festivals, Celebrate Series*, Heinemann (P).

Knight, K. (2000) *My Muslim Faith, Rainbows Red Series*, Evans Brothers Limited (P).

Larson, H. (1988) *Wedding Time*, Hamish Hamilton (P).

Lawton, C.A. (1995) *Celebrating Islam*, Young Library Limited (P & T).

Macdonald, F. *A 16th Century Mosque*, Hodder Wayland, 1996 (P & T).

Maqsood, R.W. (1993) *The Qur'an, Discovering Sacred Texts Series*, Heinemann (P & T).

Marchant, K. (2001) *Festival Tales: Muslim Festivals*, (Stories, Poems, Plays) Hodder Wayland (P).

Marchant, K. (2000) *Festival Tales: Muslim Tales*, Hodder Wayland (P).

Marchant, K. (1999) *Festivals: Id-ul-Fitr*, Hodder Wayland (P).

Marchant, K. (2002) *A Present for Salima. A Story About Id*, Hodder Wayland (P).

Penney, S. (1999) *Islam: Discovering Religions Series*, Heinemann (P & T).

Penney, S. (2001) *Islam: World Belief and Culture Series*, Heinemann (P & T).

Protheroe, R. (1984) *Visiting a Mosque*, Lutterworth Education (P).

Ross, M. (2002) *Celebrations: Ramadan and Id*, Heinemann (P).

Stone, S. (1994) *Eid-ul-Fitr*, A. and C. Black (P).

Tames, R. (1999) *Islam, World Religions Series*, Franklin Watts (P).

Tames, R. (1994) *The Muslim World*, Simon and Schuster Young Books (P & T).

The University of Warwick (1994) *Something to Share, Bridges to Religions*, The Warwick R.E. Project, Heinemann (P).

Thompson, J. (2002) *Islam, A New Approach*, Hodder and Stoughton (T).

Thorley, S. (1993) *Islam in Words and Pictures*, RMEP (Chansitor) (P & T).

Wood, A. (1996) *Festivals: Eid-ul-Fitr*, Hodder Wayland (P).

Wood, A. (1998) *Muslim Mosque, Where We Worship Series*, Franklin Watts (P).

Useful Addresses:

The Islamic Cultural Centre
146 Park Road
London NW8 7RG
Tel: 02077 243 363
Website: www.islamicculturalcentre.co.uk

Muslim Educational Trust
130 Stroud Green Road
London N4 3RZ
Tel: 02072 728 502
Email: info@muslim-ed-trust.org.uk

Pronunciation Guide to Islamic Words

Abd al-Mutt/a/lib	'Abd' as it sounds phonetically; 'al' rhymes with 'pal'; 'Mutt' as in 'moot'; long 'a'; 'lib' rhymes with 'beeb'
Ab/u Ta/lib	'Ab' as it sounds phonetically; 'u' as in oo'; 'Ta' as in 'tar'; 'lib' rhymes with 'beeb'
Ad/han	'Ad' as in 'add'; 'han' rhymes with 'fun'
Ag/ar/bat/tis	'Ag' as it sounds phonetically; 'ar' as in 'far'; 'bat' as in 'bart'; 'tis' rhymes with 'kiss'
A/lai/kum	'A' as in 'uh'; 'lai' as in 'lie'; 'kum' rhymes with 'tomb'
A/llah	'A' as in 'uh'; 'llah' long 'a' sound
A/lla/hu Ak/bar	'A' as in 'uh'; 'lla' long 'a' sound; 'hu' rhymes with 'shoe'; 'Ak' as in 'suck'; 'bar' rhymes with 'car'
Al-Mad/in/ah	'Al' rhymes with 'pal'; 'Mad' rhymes with 'sad'; 'in' as in 'been'; 'ah' as in 'car'
Al-Tash/a/hud	'Al' rhymes with 'pal'; 'Tash' as it sounds phonetically; long 'a' sound; 'hud' as in 'hood'
A/min/ah	'A' as in 'are'; 'min' rhymes with 'been'; 'ah' as in 'car'
A/qiq/a	'A' as in 'are'; 'qiq' as in 'kick'; 'a' as in 'car'
Ash had/u	'Ash' rhymes with 'dash'; 'had' as in 'hard'; 'u' as in 'shoe'
Ass/a/la/mu	'Ass' as in 'ass'; long 'a' sound; 'la' as in 'lah'; 'mu' rhymes with 'shoe'
A/than	'A' as in 'are'; 'than' rhymes with 'van'
Eid-ul-Ad/ha	'Eid' pronounced 'id'; 'ul' as in 'pull'; 'Ad' as in 'add'; 'ha' as in 'huh'
Eid-ul/Fit/r	'Eid' pronounced 'id'; 'ul' as in 'pull'; 'Fit' as in 'fit'; 'r' as in 'here'
Faj/r	'Faj' long 'a' sound; 'r' as in 'here'
Fat/i/ha	'Fat' as in 'fut'; 'i' as in 'ee'; 'ha' as in 'huh'
Hajj	'Hajj' rhymes with 'badge'
Hay/ya al/al fal/ah	'Hay' as in 'hi'; 'ya' as in 'yah'; 'al' as in 'ul'; 'fal' rhymes with 'pal'; 'ah' long 'a' sound
Hay/ya al/as sal/ah	'Hayya' as above; 'al' as in 'ul'; 'las' rhymes with 'grass'; 'sal' rhymes with 'pal'; 'ah' long 'a' sound
Hi/ra	'Hi' as in 'here'; 'ra' long 'a' sound
I/bra/him	'I' as in 'ee'; 'bra' long 'a' sound; 'him' as in 'him'
Ill/a/llah	'Ill' as in 'eel'; long 'a' sound; 'llah' long 'a' sound
I/mam	'I' as in 'ee'; 'mam' long 'a' sound
I/qua/mat	'I' as in 'ee'; 'qua' long 'a' sound; 'mat' rhymes with 'cat'
I'/sha	'I' as in 'ee'; 'sha' long 'a' sound
Jib/ra/'il	'Jib' rhymes with 'bib'; 'ra' long 'a' sound; 'il' as' in 'eel'
Kha/di/jah	'Kha' as in 'car'; 'di' rhymes with 'tea'; 'jah' as in 'jar'
Lai/lat ul Bar/a/'at	'Lai' as in 'lie'; 'lat' rhymes with 'cat'; 'ul' as in 'pull'; 'Bar' as in 'bar'; long 'a' sound; 'at' as in 'sat'
Lai/lat ul Mi'/raj	'Lai' as in 'lie'; 'lat' rhymes with 'cat'; 'ul' as in 'pull'; 'Mi' as in 'me'; 'raj' long 'a' sound
Lai/lat ul Qad/r	'Lailat ul' as above; 'Qad' as in 'quad'; 'r' as in 'here'
Mak/kah	'Mak' as in 'mack'; 'kah' as in 'car'

Me/lad-ul-Na/bi	'Me' as in 'May'; 'lad' as in 'lud'; 'ul' as in 'pull'; 'Na' long 'a' sound; 'bi' as in 'bee'
Mih/rab	'Mih' rhymes with 'here'; 'rab' long 'a' sound
Min/ar/et	'Min' rhymes with 'been'; 'ar' as in 'car'; 'et' rhymes with 'get'
Min/bar	'Min' rhymes with 'been'; 'bar' as in 'bar'
Mu/ez/zin	'Mu' rhymes with 'shoe'; 'ez' rhymes with 'fez'; 'zin' rhymes with 'bin'
Mu/har/ram	'Mu' rhymes with 'shoe'; 'har' as in 'fur'; 'ram' as in 'rum'
Qib/la	'Qib' rhymes with 'bib'; 'la' rhymes with 'car'
Qur/'an	'Qur' rhymes with 'pure'; 'an' rhymes with 'barn'
Rah/mat/u/llah	'Rah' rhymes with 'car'; 'mat' as in 'mut'; 'u' rhymes with 'shoe'; 'llah' rhymes with 'car'
Ra/ma/dan	'Ra' rhymes with 'car'; 'ma' as in 'uh'; 'dan' rhymes with 'darn'
Ras/u/llu/llah	'Ras' rhymes with 'grass'; 'u' as in 'shoe'; 'llu' as in 'shoe'; 'llah' rhymes with 'car'
Sawm	'Sawm' rhymes with 'born'
Ta/war/rok	'Ta' as in 'tar'; 'war' as in 'were'; 'rok' as in 'rock'
Wa	'Wa' rhymes with 'car'
Wud/hu	'Wud' as in 'wood'; 'hu' rhymes with 'shoe'
Zak/at	'Zak' as in 'back'; 'at' as in 'cat'
Zu/hr	'Zu' as in 'zoo'; 'hr' as in 'here'

Sikhism

Background information

Guru Nanak

Guru Nanak was the founder of Sikhism. He was born in 1469 and died in 1539. Born into a Hindu family in a Muslim village in the Punjab, Guru Nanak spent the years after his thirtieth birthday teaching that Hindus and Muslims were one. It was when he was 30, that he had a vision of God, and so he began to teach the people that there was one true God, and that followers should worship Him. The words Guru Nanak spoke became known as the *Mool Mantra* or the basic Credal statement.

The Guru Granth Sahib

This is the Sikhs' Holy book. It contains the writings of the Sikh Gurus. It was Guru Gobind Singh who told the Sikhs that there would not be another human Guru, but they should follow the sacred words of all the Gurus that had been written down, and which then became known as the Guru Granth Sahib. It was written in the Gurmurki script, and this book was, and is, treated as a living Guru.

The Ten Gurus

Listed below are the names and dates of the Ten Gurus, some of whose writings make up the Guru Granth Sahib.

Guru Nanak	1469–1539	
Guru Angad	1539–1552	
Guru Amar Das	1552–1574	
Guru Ram Das	1574–1581	
Guru Arjan	1581–1606	
Guru Hargobind	1606–1644	
Guru Har Rai	1644–1661	They did not compose any hymns
Guru Har K'ishan	1661–1664	
Guru Teg Bahadur	1664–1675	
Guru Gobind Singh	1675–1708	His compositions are in a separate collection called the Dasam Granth.

Guru Ram Das began building the famous city of Amritsar. It was Guru Arjan who built the Golden Temple and who called it the 'House of God' or 'Har Mandir Sahib', or 'Darbar Sahib'.

Worship

This takes place in a Gurdwara (or building) which houses the Guru Granth Sahib. The Guru Granth Sahib is usually placed on the Manji Sahib (or stool) which is situated on a raised platform called the Takht. There are no priests or ministers, the reader is called the Granthi. Sikhs will put their hands together and bow towards the Guru Granth Sahib, as a mark of respect, when entering or leaving the Gurdwara, where the Holy book is read and hymns from the Guru Granth Sahib are sung. The congregation sit crosslegged on the floor. All Sikhs, whether or not they have been initiated into the Khalsa (or brotherhood), may read from the scriptures. (see below).

Sikh Family Life

Naming Ceremony

Soon after the birth of a Sikh baby, 'the words of the Mool Mantra are whispered into the baby's ear and a drop of honey is placed on his or her tongue'. (Bailey: *Worship, Ceremonial and Rites of Passage*.)

The baby is then taken to the Gurdwara to be given a name. This is chosen by randomly opening the Guru Granth Sahib, and on whichever page the book opens, the first letter of the first hymn is taken to be the first letter of the child's name.

Prayers are recited and after the ceremony, friends and relatives join together for a celebratory meal.

The Khalsa (or Brotherhood) Initiation Ceremony

Sikhs believe that men and women are born equal and so at about the age of fourteen or fifteen, when a young Sikh is capable of being responsible for his or her own actions, he can become a full member of the Sikh Faith (or Khalsa) by taking part in the initiation ceremony called, Amrit Sanskar.

First, a young Sikh must possess the five K's of Sikhism:

  Kesh   – uncut hair and beard
  Kangha – comb
  Kaccha – shorts
  Kara   – steel bracelet, to be worn on the right wrist
  Kirpan – sword

Then the young person must promise to obey certain rules such as not cutting their hair or beards; not eating meat that has been prepared by a Muslim (Halal); not to commit adultery. They must promise too, to respect the words of the Guru Granth Sahib, to be honest and to give money to the poor. The young person will have learnt the words of the Mool Mantra by heart, and so will repeat these words at the ceremony. Each male Sikh is given the name Singh (meaning lion) and every girl is given the name Kaur (meaning princess).

After the ceremony Karah Prasad (food made from flour, butter, sugar, etc.) is shared and eaten.

The Granthi

The Granthi or reader is trained to read from the Holy book, and he officiates at weddings and funerals. Sometimes, the Granthi also teaches the Sikh children about the Guru Granth Sahib and about the lives of the different Gurus. He may also teach the children the Gurmurki script.

Prayers and Worship

In the morning before praying, Sikhs wash themselves and then spend time in prayer and meditation. They will have learned the first section of the Guru Granth Sahib called the *Japji*, by heart. This can then be recited or hymns from the Gutka (also part of the Guru Granth Sahib) can be read. The prayer known as the *Rehraas* is said in the evening, and the prayer known as the *Sohila* is said before going to bed.

Weddings

The parents choose the bride or groom for their respective son or daughter. This is called an 'arranged' marriage. The wedding usually takes place in the Gurdwara with the Guru Granth Sahib. It is a very colourful affair, because the bride wears red shalwar (trousers) and kameez (tunic) and a red chunni (scarf). The father places a garland of flowers over the Guru Granth Sahib and the couple walk round the Holy book four times during the service. (See Assembly on p. 125.)

Sikh Festivals

Baisakhi

This is the first month of the New Year in the Sikh calendar (April). Since 1699, it has become a special celebration to mark the beginning of the Khalsa or brotherhood. This is because the tenth Guru, Guru Gobind Singh, asked his followers to prove their allegiance to their Guru, by offering to die for him. Five volunteers were called for, and although the congregation heard the swish of the sword and saw blood appear outside the tent where the volunteers were, not one was killed. They emerged, wearing new uniforms and the new brotherhood was formed.

The Birthday of Guru Nanak

The anniversary of any of the Gurus' births or deaths is an occasion to hold a special celebration called a Gurpurb. Guru Nanak's birthday is celebrated in this way. There is usually a procession and the whole of the Guru Granth Sahib is read, in turn, by different readers in the Gurdwara. Afterwards there is a special feast. We know that Guru Nanak was born in 1469, and the Festival usually takes place in October/November time, although according to some scholars his actual birthday was in April.

Hola Mohalla

This Festival takes place in the Spring (March). It is very similar to the Hindu Festival, in that bonfires are lit, and coloured water is squirted at one another, but the reason behind the Festival has a slightly different emphasis for Sikhs. It was the tenth Guru, Guru Gobind Singh, who first introduced displays of 'swordsmanship, horsemanship, archery and wrestling competitions' (J.G. Walshe, *Celebrations Across the Cultures*.)

Diwali

This winter Festival of Light (November) has special meaning for Sikhs everywhere. The sixth Guru, Guru Hargobind had been imprisoned by the Moghal Emperor, but on his release in 1620, Guru Hargobind returned to Amritsar. The Golden Temple was lit with hundreds of candles and lamps for joy at his return. Today the Festival is still celebrated and Sikhs light candles in their homes and attend the Gurdwara for worship and festive meals. (See assembly on p. 111).

Resources

Books

(P) = Pupils
(T) = Teachers

Aggarwal, M. (2001) *I am a Sikh*, Franklin Watts (P).

Arora, R. (1987) *Guru Nanak and the Sikh Gurus*, Religious Stories Series, Hodder Wayland (P). (Also in this series: *Buddhist Stories, Chinese Stories, Hindu stories*, etc.)

Bailey, J.R. (1995) *Founders, Prophets and Sacred Books*, Schofield and Sims (T).

Bailey, J.R. (1995) *Religious Beliefs and Moral Codes*, Schofield and Sims (T).

Bailey, J.R. (1995) *Religious Buildings and Festivals*, Schofield and Sims (T).

Bailey, J.R. (1995) *Religious Leaders and Places of Pilgrimages Today*, Schofield and Sims (T).

Bailey, J.R. (1995) *Worship, Ceremonial and Rites of Passage*, Schofield and Sims (T).

Bennett, O. (1985) *A Sikh Wedding*, Hamish Hamilton (P).

Bennett, O. (1984) *Kikar's Drum*, Hamish Hamilton (P).

Chambers, C. (1995) *Sikh, Beliefs and Culture Series*, An Information and Activity Book, Franklin Watts (P) (Also in this series: *Buddhist, Christian, Hindu, Jewish, Muslim*).

Clutterbuck, A. (1991) *Growing up in Sikhism*, Longman (P & T).

Cole, W.O. and Sambhi, P. Singh (1991) *Baisakhi*, RMEP(Chansitor), Canterbury Press (P & T).

Cole, W.O. and Sambhi, P. Singh (1997) *A Popular Dictionary of Sikhism*, Curzon Press Ltd., Revised Edition (T).

Cole, W.O. and Sambhi, P. Singh (1991) *A Sikh Family in Britain*, RMEP (Chansitor), Canterbury Press, (P & T).

Cole, W.O. and Sambhi, P. Singh (1995) *The Sikhs; Their Religious Beliefs and Practices*, 2nd Edition, Sussex Academic Press (T).

Collinson, C. and Miller, C. (1985) *Celebrations: Festival in a Multi-faith Community*, Edward Arnold.

Coutts, J. (1996) *Celebrate Sikh Festivals*, Heinemann (P). (Also in this series: *Christian Festivals, Jewish Festivals, Islamic Festivals, Buddhist Festivals, Hindu Festivals*).

Davidson, M. (1991) *Guru Nanak's Birthday*, RMEP (Chansitor), Canterbury Press (P).

Dhanjal, B. (1994) *Amritsar*, Holy City Series, Evans Brothers Limited (P). (Also in this series: *Rome, Jerusalem, Varanasi, Mecca*, etc.)

Dhanjal, B. (1987) *Sikhism*, Batsford (T).

Dhanjal, B. (2001) *What do we Know about Sikhism?*, Hodder Wayland (P).

Ganeri, A. (2001) *Sikh Stories*, Evans Brothers Limited (P). (Also in this series: *Buddhist Stories, Christian Stories, Hindu Stories, Islamic Stories, etc.*)

Grimmit, M. (et al.) (1995) *A Gift to the Child*, Nelson Thornes (P & T).

Kapoor, S.S. (1985) *Sikh Festivals*, Hodder Wayland (P & T).

Kaur, G. (2000) *Sikh Gurdwaras*, Places of Worship Series, Heinemann (P). (Also in the series: *Buddhist Temples, Mosques, Synagogues, Catholic Churches, Orthodox Churches, Hindu Temples, Protestant Churches*)

Kaur-Singh, K. (1999) *My Sikh Life*, Everyday Religion Series, Hodder Wayland (P).

Kaur-Singh, K. (2001) *Sikh Granthi, My Life*, My Religion Series, Franklin Watts (P). (Also in the series: *Anglican Curate, Catholic Priest, Hindu Priest, Jewish Rabbi, Muslim Imam*)

Kaur-Singh, K. (1998) *Sikh Gurdwara*, Where We Worship Series, Franklin Watts (P). (Also in the series: *Hindu Mandir, Christian Church, Jewish Synagogue, Buddhist Temple, Muslim Mosque*)

Lyle, S. (1977) *Pavan is a Sikh*, A and C Black (P).

Ross, M. (2002) *Baisakhi*, Celebration Series, Heinemann (P). (Also in the series: *Divali, Ramadan and Id-ul-Fitr, Wesak*, etc.)

Sambhi, P. Singh (1989) *Sikhism*, Stanley Thomas (T).

Sambhi, P. Singh (1994) *The Guru Granth Sahib*, Heinemann (T).

Singh, D. and Smith, A. (1992) *The Sikh World*, Hodder Wayland (P & T).

Singh, K. (2000) *My Sikh Faith*, Rainbow Red Series, Evans Brothers Limited (P). (Also in the series: *My Buddhist Faith, My Christian Faith, My Jewish Faith, My Hindu Faith, My Muslim Faith*)

Singh, Nikky-Guninder Kaur (1993) *Sikhism*, Facts on File Limited (T).

Singh, R. and J. (1985) *Stories from the Sikh World*, Macdonald (P).

Wood, J. (1995) *Our Culture: Sikh*, Franklin Watts (P).

Videos

The video entitled *Aspects of Sikhism* (All ages) featuring worship in a Gurdwara, worship at home, a birth and naming ceremony and religious dress is available from SCM-Canterbury Press, address below. Other aspects of Sikhism are included on *Video 2*, of *The Believe It or Not* videos (Revised Series) for 11+ children, also available from SCM-Canterbury Press; and the REaSE Project Video for children aged 11+ (Secondary Schools) *Speaking For Ourselves* is also available from SCM-Canterbury Press:

SCM-Canterbury Press Limited
St Mary's Works
St Mary's Plain
Norwich
Norfolk NR3 3BH

Tel: 01603 612 914
Email: admin@scm-canterburypress.co.uk
Website: www.canterburypress.co.uk

A good supplier of artefacts, posters and videos is:

Articles of Faith Ltd.,
Resource House,
Kay Street,
Bury BL9 6BU

Tel: 01617 636 232
Email: ArticlesFaith@cs.com
Website: www.articlesoffaith.co.uk

and books, posters and calendars from:

The Festival Shop Ltd.,
56 Poplar Road
Kings Heath
Birmingham B14 7AG

Tel: 01214 440 444
Fax: 01214 415 404
Email: info@festivalshop.co.uk

Pronunciation Guide to Sikh Words

Ak/hand Path	'Ak' as in 'back'; 'hand' as in 'hand'; 'Path' as in 'path'
Am/rit Sans/kar	'Am' as in 'am'; 'rit' rhymes with 'fit'; 'Sans' as in 'sands'; 'kar' as in 'car'
Am/rits/ar	'Am' as in 'am'; 'rits' rhymes with 'bits'; 'ar' as in 'far'
An/and/pur	'An' as in 'an'; 'and' as in 'and'; 'pur' as in 'poor'
Bai/sak/hi	'Bai' as in 'bye'; 'sak' rhymes with 'lark'; 'hi' as in 'he'
Bal/a	'Bal' as in 'pal'; 'a' as 'ah'
Chack/ra	'Chack' rhymes with 'Jack'; 'ra' as in 'ruh'
Dar/bar Sa/hib	'Dar' rhymes with 'far'; 'bar' rhymes with 'far'; 'sa' as in 'car'; 'hib' pronounced 'heeb'
Das/am Granth	'Das' as in 'has'; 'am' as in 'am'; 'Granth' as it sounds phonetically
Da/ya Ram	'Da' as in 'die'; 'ya' as in 'yuh'; 'Ram' as in 'ram'
Dhar/am Das	'Dhar' as in 'far'; 'am' as in 'um'; 'Das' as in 'pass'
Diw/a/li	'Diw' as it sounds phonetically; 'a' as in 'far'; 'li' rhymes with 'tea'
Du/patt/a	'Du' as in 'do'; 'patt' as in 'pat'; 'a' as in 'far'
Granth/i	'Granth' as it sounds phonetically; 'i' as in 'ee'
Gurd/war/a	'Gurd' rhymes with 'curd'; 'war' as in 'were'; 'a' as in 'ah'
Gur/mukhi	'Gur' rhymes with 'purr'; 'mukhi' as in 'mucky'
Gur/purb	'Gur' rhymes with 'purr'; 'purb' rhymes with 'curb'
Gu/ru Am/ar Das	'Gu' rhymes with 'do'; 'ru' rhymes with 'do'; 'Am' as in 'am'; 'ar' as in 'far'; 'Das' as in 'pass'
Gu/ru An/gad	Guru as above; 'An' as in 'fan'; 'gad' rhymes with 'fad'
Gu/ru Ar/jan	Guru as above; 'Ar' as in 'far'; 'jan' rhymes with 'fan'

Gu/ru Go/bind Rai	Guru as above; 'Go' as in 'go'; 'bind' as in 'bin' plus a 'd'; 'Rai' as in 'rye'
Gu/ru Go/bind Singh	Guru Gobind as above; 'Singh' as in 'sing'
Gu/ru Granth Sa/hib	Guru as above; Granth as it sounds phonetically; 'sa' as in 'car'; 'hib' as in 'heeb'
Gu/ru Har/go/bind	Guru as above; 'Har' as in 'car'; 'go' as in 'go'; 'bind' as in 'bin' plus a 'd'
Gu/ru Han K'ish/an	Guru as above; 'Har' as in 'car'; 'K'ish' rhymes with 'dish'; 'an' as in 'can'
Gu/ru Har Rai	Guru as above; 'Har' as in 'car'; 'Rai' as in 'rye'
Gu/ru Nan/ak	Guru as above; 'Nan' as in 'nan'; 'ak' as in 'back'
Gu/ru Teg Ba/had/ur	Guru as above; 'Teg' rhymes with 'leg'; 'Ba' as in 'bah'; 'had' as in 'had'; 'ur' as in 'poor'
Gut/ka	'Gut' rhymes with 'foot'; 'ka' as in car
Gwal/i/or	'Gwal' rhymes with 'pal'; 'i' as in 'me'; 'or' rhymes with 'poor'
Har Man/dir Sa/hib	'Har' as in 'car'; 'Man' as in 'mun'; 'dir' as in 'deer'; 'sa' rhymes with 'far'; 'hib' pronounced 'heeb'
Him/mat Rai	'Him' as in 'him'; 'mat' as in 'mat'; 'Rai' as in 'rye'
Ho/la Mo/hal/la	'Ho' rhymes with 'toe'; 'la' as in 'lah'; 'Mo' as in 'mow'; 'hal' rhymes with 'pal'; 'la' as in 'far'
Jap/ji	'Jap' rhymes with 'cap'; 'ji' as in 'jeep'
Kacch/a	'Kacch' as in 'catch'; 'a' as in 'far'
Kam/eez	'Kam' rhymes with 'lamb'; 'eez' as in 'breeze'
Kang/a	'Kang' as it sounds phonetically; 'a' as in 'far'
Kar/a	'Kar' as in 'car'; 'a' as in 'uh'
Kar/a Pra/sad	'Kar' as in 'car'; 'a' as in 'uh'; 'Pra' as in 'far'; 'sad' as in 'sud'
Kaur	'Kaur' rhymes with 'pour'
Kesh	'Kesh' rhymes with 'race'
Khal/sa	'Khal' rhymes with 'pal'; 'sa' as in 'far'
Khan/da	'Khand' rhymes with 'hand'; 'da' as in 'far'
Kir/pan	'Kir' rhymes with 'purr'; 'pan' as in 'pan'
Man/ji Sa/hib	'Man as in 'man'; 'ji' as in 'jeep'; 'Sa' as in 'car'; 'hib' pronounced 'heeb'
Meht/a Ka/lu	'Meht' as in 'met'; 'a' as in 'uh'; 'Ka' as in 'car'; 'lu' rhymes with 'shoe'
Mool Man/tra	'Mool' rhymes with 'pool'; 'man' as in 'man'; 'tra' rhymes with 'far'
Muk/ham Chand	'Muk' as in 'muck'; 'ham' as in 'hum'; 'Chand' rhymes with 'hand'
Nis/an Sa/hib	'Nis' rhymes with 'kiss'; 'han' as in 'hun'; 'Sa' as in 'car'; 'hib' pronounced 'heeb'
Pal/ki	'Pal' as in 'pal'; 'ki' as in 'key'
Reh/raas	'Reh' rhymes with 'tea'; 'raas' rhymes with 'grass'
Sa/hib Chand	'Sa' as in 'car'; 'hib' pronounced 'heeb'; 'Chand' rhymes with 'hand'
Shab/ads	'Shab' rhymes with 'drab'; 'ads' as in 'adds'
So/hil/a	'So' as in 'so'; 'hil' as in 'heel'; 'a' as in 'uh'